Microsoft Dynamics GP 2010 Reporting

Create and manage business reports with
Dynamics GP

David Duncan

Christopher Liley

BIRMINGHAM - MUMBAI

Microsoft Dynamics GP 2010 Reporting

First published: April 2011

Production Reference: 1180411

Published by Packt Publishing Ltd.
32 Lincoln Road
Olton
Birmingham, B27 6PA, UK.

ISBN 978-1-849682-18-3

www.packtpub.com

Cover Image by David Guettirrez (bilbaorocker@yahoo.co.uk)

Credits

Authors

David James Duncan

Christopher Liley

Reviewers

Amy Walsh

Christina M. Belding

Acquisition Editor

Kerry George

Development Editor

Maitreya Bhakal

Technical Editor

Ajay Shanker

Project Coordinator

Leena Purkait

Proofreader

Aaron Nash

Indexers

Hemangini Bari

Rekha Nair

Graphics

Geetanjali Sawant

Production Coordinator

Arvindkumar Gupta

Cover Work

Arvindkumar Gupta

Foreword

As the business management solution tool of choice for over 42,000 customers, Microsoft Dynamics GP continues to drive better business processes and improve organizational performance. As a comprehensive enterprise resource planning solution, Dynamics GP offers a wide-range of functionality that can be tailored for organizations in a variety of industries. With a Dynamics GP solution in place, end users can enter and track the details of day-to-day business processes. As soon as this data is recorded in Dynamics GP, organizations possess a unique advantage over others in their industry: raw data.

But this data is useless if some level of insight cannot be gained from it. By using built-in reporting tools for Dynamics GP, as well as other familiar products, the Dynamics GP organization can turn this raw data into a more meaningful picture of trends and key performance metrics. This, in turn, allows for better decision-making, the opportunity to improve current business processes, and the opportunity to proactively lead competitors into new markets. To facilitate this process, reporting tools for Dynamics GP are designed with the end user in mind. Rather than waste time learning a clunky reporting tool, the native reporting tools for Dynamics GP are intuitive and can be put to effective use immediately. Additionally, the Dynamics GP solution offers over 200+ built-in Microsoft Excel reports that can further jump-start the end user's ability to analyze and make sense of their Dynamics GP data.

While many of these tools are intuitive enough to use, training is still a vital component to learning how to gain the most from the reporting tools employed by your organization. Resources such as the book you now hold in your hand are critical to taking the extra step in uncovering the trends locked deep within your data. Not only will this book offer insight into the many reporting tools currently available for GP, it will also offer a unique perspective on how each reporting tool can be used to meet specific challenges faced by your organization. For example, if you've ever wondered what the most effective reporting tool is for an environment that contains multiple data sources, or how to identify the GP reporting tool with the best board-room quality formatting and presentation functionality, then this book has the answer for you!

As you read through this book, remember that reporting for Dynamics GP is increasingly about taking the onus of creating and developing reports out of the traditional IT department's hands and placing it into the hands that matter most: the end user. In fact, this concept is evident with the latest Roadmap for Dynamics GP. This roadmap shows future versions of Dynamics GP adding new functionality in the area of role tailored and contextual business intelligence and reporting tools. This is seen in GP 2010 R2, the latest release for Dynamics GP 2010, which will feature new reporting tools and updates to existing reporting tools such as:

- Performance improvements to the existing Report List functionality
- The ability to generate Word Templates for any standard report in GP
- A Report Builder Integration tool that offers the ability to view SSRS reports from within Dynamics GP
- Additional out-of-the-box SSRS reports that can be deployed for instant visibility into your organization's data
- And much, much more!

Happy Reporting!

Errol Schoenfish

Errol Schoenfish has been a member of the Dynamics community for over 24 years.

About the Authors

David Duncan is a Microsoft Dynamics GP certified consultant with I.B.I.S., Inc., a Microsoft Gold Certified Partner based in Norcross, GA. In addition to experience with implementing Dynamics GP, David has extensive experience in designing and providing business intelligence and reporting tools for clients who use Dynamics GP. David has also served as a content provider for the GP portion of the Sure Step 2010 Methodology.

David has developed custom SSAS cubes for several GP modules such as Project Accounting and Fixed Assets that seamlessly integrate with Microsoft's Analysis Cubes for Excel product. David has also assisted numerous clients in analyzing their strategic business plans by designing business intelligence solutions that allow them to incorporate data from multiple applications into a single reporting environment. David also has a degree from Clemson University.

When not on-site with a client, David resides in Decatur, GA with his wife, Mary Kathleen.

Acknowledgement

First and foremost, my thanks go to my colleague and co-author, Chris Liley. Without him, this book would not have been possible.

I have had the special privilege to work and learn under Andy Vabulas, Dwight Specht, and Clinton Weldon while at I.B.I.S., Inc. All three of them have mentored me and provided me many of the opportunities that enabled the creation of this book.

I am especially grateful for my colleagues at I.B.I.S., Inc., including Tan Le, Mark Polino, Abby Moore, and others. All have left an indelible impression on me.

Along with being exceptional colleagues at I.B.I.S., our technical reviewers Christina Belding and Amy Walsh deserve the highest praise for stepping forward to help Chris and I complete this project.

Special thanks is reserved for Kerry George, Maitreya Bhakal, Leena Purkait, and the rest of the Packt Publishing team for guiding us every step of the way in producing our first publication.

And last, but certainly not least, this book would not be possible without the loving support and patience of my wife, Mary Kathleen, whose encouragement helped me through many late night sessions with the more challenging chapters of this book!

Chris Liley is a Principal Consultant with I.B.I.S., Inc.; a Microsoft Gold Certified Partner based in Norcross, GA, and is a Microsoft Certified Information Technology Professional for Dynamics GP. He is a graduate of Georgia State University with a B.B.A in Accounting and has worked with the Dynamics GP product since 2001. Chris has also previously participated in the Dynamics Partner Advisory Board.

Chris' experience ranges from financial analysis, software implementation, data conversions and integrations to designing and developing customizations in both the functional and technical area of consulting for Dynamics GP.

In addition, Chris has extensive experience in designing Business Intelligence solutions and has assisted numerous clients in analyzing their business plans with these solutions.

Acknowledgement

First and foremost, my thanks and appreciation go to my colleague and co-author, David Duncan. We spent many nights in hotel lobbies working on this book and without this dedication; this book would not have been possible.

I would also like to thank our incredible management team at I.B.I.S., Inc. for allowing us the opportunity and support in writing this book.

I am especially grateful for my colleagues at I.B.I.S., Inc. It is truly a privilege to work with them each and every day. All have left an indelible impression on me as consummate professionals.

No book is the sole work of just the author and along with being exceptional colleagues at I.B.I.S., our technical reviewers Christina Belding and Amy Walsh deserve the highest praise for stepping forward to help David and I complete this project. We truly appreciate their candid comments and the professionalism it takes to critique your fellow colleagues.

Special thanks is reserved for Kerry George, Maitreya Bhakal, Leena Purkait, and the rest of the Packt Publishing team for guiding us every step of the way in producing our first publication. We could not have done this without you.

And finally I want to thank my boss and my friend Clinton Weldon. It is because of his mentorship over the past 10 years that I have been able to learn so much about ERP products and bring that knowledge to every customer that I visit.

About the Reviewers

Amy Walsh is a consultant with I.B.I.S., Inc. and Microsoft Certified Business Management Solutions Professional. She is a graduate of Georgia Military College and Mercer University with a concentration in Accounting and Finance. She has over 15 years of experience working with domestic and international enterprises ranging from start-up to established global B2B companies. Her goal is to help businesses succeed in their endeavors through process streamlining, education, and finding the right ERP solution.

Christina is a Project Management Professional (PMP), Certified Information Systems Auditor (CISA), and Microsoft Certified Business Management Solutions Professional (MCP) with over 20 years of industry experience, many of those spent implementing and managing large ERP engagements.

Christina has spent a large portion of her career focusing on ERP implementations and management, but also has a detailed background in training and development—creating custom curriculums that focus on new business initiative deployments and enterprise wide process improvement and audit.

Before concentrating predominately with Microsoft systems in 2007, she previously worked for Automatic Data Processing (ADP), and her own practice Belding Associates, LLC. (a small professional services organization).

Christina has served as a subject matter expert (SME) and content editor on several other publications. She resides in Alpharetta, GA with her husband Dan and daughters Rachael and Jenn.

www.PacktPub.com

Support files, eBooks, discount offers and more

You might want to visit www.PacktPub.com for support files and downloads related to your book.

Did you know that Packt offers eBook versions of every book published, with PDF and ePub files available? You can upgrade to the eBook version at www.PacktPub.com and as a print book customer, you are entitled to a discount on the eBook copy. Get in touch with us at service@packtpub.com for more details.

At www.PacktPub.com, you can also read a collection of free technical articles, sign up for a range of free newsletters and receive exclusive discounts and offers on Packt books and eBooks.

http://PacktLib.PacktPub.com

Do you need instant solutions to your IT questions? PacktLib is Packt's online digital book library. Here, you can access, read and search across Packt's entire library of books.

Why Subscribe?

- Fully searchable across every book published by Packt
- Copy and paste, print and bookmark content
- On demand and accessible via web browser

Free Access for Packt account holders

If you have an account with Packt at www.PacktPub.com, you can use this to access PacktLib today and view nine entirely free books. Simply use your login credentials for immediate access.

Instant Updates on New Packt Books

Get notified! Find out when new books are published by following *@PacktEnterprise* on Twitter, or the *Packt Enterprise* Facebook page.

David's dedication:

This book is dedicated to the incredible team at I.B.I.S., Inc. It's a privilege to work with them each day.

Chris' dedication:

This book is dedicated to my incredible parents who have always taught me that by giving my all to everything I do, I could accomplish anything that I put my mind too. This book would not have been possible without their love and support.

Table of Contents

Preface

Microsoft Dynamics GP 2010 is a sophisticated Enterprise Resource Planning (ERP) system with a multitude of features and options. Microsoft Dynamics GP enables you to create and manage a variety of reports that help small and mid-size businesses effectively manage their financial and operational data.

This book will show you how to create and manage reports, know what tools to use and when, how to use them and where to find the data based on how it's being entered into the system with Dynamics GP.

It will empower you with the tools and reports necessary to use Dynamics GP data in making key business decisions. The book addresses the many challenges and frustrations a company may face when preparing to build new reports. Then it moves on to explain how to find your data in the GP system and company databases. The book then dives deep into topics such as SmartLists, SL Builder and Excel Report Builder, Report Writer, SSRS Report Library, and Analysis Cubes Design and Management Reporter amongst others. With this knowledge in hand, you will be capable of selecting the most effective tool for the current reporting environment.

What this book covers

Chapter 1, Meeting the Reporting Challenge: Our opening chapter will provide commentary on the many challenges and frustrations a company may face when preparing to build new reports. Developers tasked with report creation must be aware of these challenges and select the most effective reporting tool, or tools, to satisfy the company's reporting needs. In addition to using the discussion of challenges faced with reporting as a springboard for the rest of the book, this chapter will also provide commentary on recent reporting trends in the Dynamics GP space.

Chapter 2, Where Is My Data and How Do I Get To It?: Before we can begin utilizing many of the reporting tools covered in this book, we must have a better understanding of how Dynamics GP stores data. This chapter will provide users with helpful tips for finding and locating their data in the GP system and company databases. Knowing where to begin is a critical first step for any technical resource setting out to develop a new report, and this chapter aims to make the process of beginning a new report an easier one.

Chapter 3, Working with the Builders: SmartList and Excel Reports: This chapter begins our discussion of our first reporting tools as we introduce the SmartList and the "Builders": SmartList Builder and Excel Reports Builder. Users will briefly review how to use basic SmartLists for simple reporting. Readers will learn how to deploy the Excel Reports that duplicates the SmartList favorites in Excel format and offers a live data connection that makes the reports instantly refreshable. The final half of this chapter will focus on using SmartList Builder and Excel Reports Builder tools to create additional reports beyond the standard SmartList/Excel favorites.

Chapter 4, Report Writer: This chapter covers the built-in report-writing function of GP 2010 known as Report Writer. This chapter on Report Writer will introduce the reader to the basic layout and the various functions of Report Writer. By the end of this chapter, readers should be familiar with making basic modifications to standard GP reports. Additionally, readers will be exposed to the capabilities and limitations of the new GP 2010 Word Template functionality that allows existing reports to be rendered in Microsoft Word format.

Chapter 5, SSRS Report Library: This chapter introduces the concept of utilizing the well-known SQL Server Reporting Services (SSRS) tool with Dynamics GP data. This chapter opens with tips for installing SSRS in your environment before moving into a discussion on deploying the pre-defined SSRS Reports and Metrics designed specifically for GP 2010. Finally, we will cover the use of Visual Studio to make modifications to existing SSRS reports as well as to create new Report Metrics and KPIs that can be deployed on the GP 2010 Home Page.

Chapter 6, Designing Your Analysis Cubes for Excel Environment: This is the first of two chapters which will cover the extensive Analysis Cubes for Excel reporting tool. This chapter will cover the installation of Analysis Cubes and provide details on the various components that are created by the installation. Finally, this chapter will cover some simple modifications that can be made to the Analysis Cubes data warehouse and Analysis Services database to improve the end-user reporting experience.

Chapter 7, Utilizing Analysis Cubes for Excel for Dynamic Reporting: Many readers will be familiar with some of the concepts discussed in the early portion of this chapter. Excel PivotTables are widely used throughout many organizations, even those without GP 2010, but the first part of this chapter will explore the use of PivotTables specifically with the Analysis Cubes for Excel product. From here, we will explore the use of the lesser-known CUBE formulas that prove to be a useful skill-set to know when building static reports and dashboards based on Analysis Cubes data.

Chapter 8, Designing Financial Reports in Management Reporter: Like Analysis Cubes for Excel, content for the Management Reporter tool will span multiple chapters. This chapter will introduce readers to Management Reporter and basic report design. We will provide an overview of Management Reporter installations before providing tips for navigating the Management Reporter layout. Finally, this chapter will cover the use of the various building blocks of Management Reporter for report creation.

Chapter 9, Viewing Financial Reports in Management Reporter: This chapter continues the discussion on Management Reporter begun in Chapter 8. Here, we will cover information related to the Report Viewer component of Management Reporter. In addition to discussion on report-generation, this chapter also provides information on managing reports through the use of report packages and version control. Finally, this chapter provides some commentary on the differences between FRx and Management Reporter.

Chapter 10, Bringing It All Together: This chapter brings our book to a close by combining the discussion of reporting challenges and trends broached in Chapter 1 with the reporting tools discussed in the remaining chapters. Here, we will consider each challenge in light of the various reporting tools. By the end of this chapter and book, readers will not only be familiar with each reporting tool, but they will have a better understanding of how and when each reporting tool can be used most effectively in their organization.

Appendix A, Comparing the Dynamics GP Reporting Tools Against Different Reporting Challenges: The final section of this book contains a helpful table that can be used as a quick reference guide to see how the reporting tools measure up to the various reporting challenges we have already discussed. By presenting this data in table format, readers can quickly scan across a row to see how each tool meets a particular challenge, or they can scan down a column to see how a single reporting tool measures against each individual challenge.

What you need for this book

The required software is:

- Microsoft SQL Server 2005 or later (Database Engine, Analysis Services, Reporting Services, Integration Services)
- Microsoft SQL Server Business Intelligence Studio (Should be installed with SQL) or Visual Studio 2005 or 2008
- Microsoft Dynamics GP 2010 SP1
- Microsoft Dynamics GP 2010 Add-In for Microsoft Word
- Microsoft Dynamics ERP Management Reporter Feature Pack 1
- Analysis Cubes for Excel 2005 or 2008 (Depends on SQL version)
- Microsoft Excel 2007 or later.

Who this book is for

If you are a Microsoft Dynamics GP developer, consultant, or power user who wants to create and manage reports, then this book is for you. A working knowledge of Microsoft Dynamics GP is required. A basic understanding of business management systems and reporting applications such as Microsoft Excel and SQL Reporting Services is highly recommended.

Conventions

In this book, you will find a number of styles of text that distinguish between different kinds of information. Here are some examples of these styles, and an explanation of their meaning.

Any command-line input or output is written as follows:

```
=CUBESET("GP Receivables Cube","[Customers].[Customer Name].[All].
Children","Top 10 Customers",2,"[Measures].[Functional Amt - Receivables
Aging]")
```

New terms and **important words** are shown in bold. Words that you see on the screen, in menus or dialog boxes for example, appear in the text like this: "clicking the **Next** button moves you to the next screen".

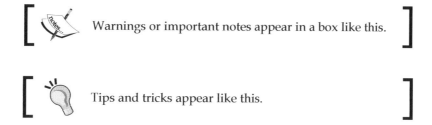

Warnings or important notes appear in a box like this.

Tips and tricks appear like this.

Reader feedback

Feedback from our readers is always welcome. Let us know what you think about this book—what you liked or may have disliked. Reader feedback is important for us to develop titles that you really get the most out of.

To send us general feedback, simply send an e-mail to feedback@packtpub.com, and mention the book title via the subject of your message.

If there is a book that you need and would like to see us publish, please send us a note in the **SUGGEST A TITLE** form on www.packtpub.com or e-mail suggest@packtpub.com.

If there is a topic that you have expertise in and you are interested in either writing or contributing to a book, see our author guide on www.packtpub.com/authors.

Customer support

Now that you are the proud owner of a Packt book, we have a number of things to help you to get the most from your purchase.

Downloading the example code

You can download the example code files for all Packt books you have purchased from your account at http://www.PacktPub.com. If you purchased this book elsewhere, you can visit http://www.PacktPub.com/support and register to have the files e-mailed directly to you.

Errata

Although we have taken every care to ensure the accuracy of our content, mistakes do happen. If you find a mistake in one of our books—maybe a mistake in the text or the code—we would be grateful if you would report this to us. By doing so, you can save other readers from frustration and help us improve subsequent versions of this book. If you find any errata, please report them by visiting http://www.packtpub.com/support, selecting your book, clicking on the **errata submission form** link, and entering the details of your errata. Once your errata are verified, your submission will be accepted and the errata will be uploaded on our website, or added to any list of existing errata, under the Errata section of that title. Any existing errata can be viewed by selecting your title from http://www.packtpub.com/support.

Piracy

Piracy of copyright material on the Internet is an ongoing problem across all media. At Packt, we take the protection of our copyright and licenses very seriously. If you come across any illegal copies of our works, in any form, on the Internet, please provide us with the location address or website name immediately so that we can pursue a remedy.

Please contact us at copyright@packtpub.com with a link to the suspected pirated material.

We appreciate your help in protecting our authors, and our ability to bring you valuable content.

Questions

You can contact us at questions@packtpub.com if you are having a problem with any aspect of the book, and we will do our best to address it.

1
Meeting the Reporting Challenge

In an increasingly digital world, utilizing proper reporting techniques is essential to making sense of the increasing mountain of data we find stored on our computers.

The task of reporting on and identifying trends in this data is an exciting field that will only grow in importance as companies continue to take advantage of cheaper disk space and the growing capability of applications and Enterprise Resource Planning (ERP) systems that can track and record every last detail of conducting business.

As developers and consultants tasked with report writing, our goal is to provide the decision-makers in our organization with the tools and reports necessary to use this data in making key business decisions. We can help our end users unlock the trends found within the data being analysed. By providing accurate reports that bridge the gap between disparate information systems, we can provide users across the company with accurate, reliable information. In other words, we can provide them with a single version of the truth so that multiple end users can make decisions from the same set of data.

This book is intended for anyone who might be tasked with developing and creating reports, whether they are for personal use or for use by other report consumers. The term "developer" invokes an image of someone who is technically adept and possesses a unique understanding of the inner-workings of a particular piece of software. But, in the context of report-writing (and this book), the term developer has a much wider meaning. Instead, report developers can include those with more application experience such as senior accountants and day-to-day operations personnel. It can also apply to application consultants who are well-experienced with an organization's ERP application.

As we reach the end of this chapter, we should possess a better understanding of the following:

- Taking advantage of the major trends facing report writers and developers in today's hyper-competitive environments
- The end user driven challenges or requirements that exist when designing a report according to an end user's specifications
- Organizational challenges that may help or hinder us from designing a report that meets the end-user's requirements
- Weighing the pros and cons of numerous trends and challenges in light of each other in order to select the most effective report or reporting tool possible

While the focus of this book will primarily rest on reporting tools associated with the Microsoft Dynamics GP ERP application, the concepts required to design and build reports apply to the entire spectrum of ERP applications and various data repositories in general.

Trends in reporting

As companies have adapted to new ways of capturing and recording business data, the techniques for reporting and making sense of this data have also changed. The best report developers are those who understand how these techniques have changed and are willing to update their own skill sets to capitalize on this.

Some of the most recent, important trends in the reporting space include:

- Increased flexibility
- Reporting through all levels of an organization
- Increased access to report generation process

Understanding how reporting techniques have changed in the last few years provides us an opportunity to improve our ability to produce relevant and useful reports. Developers and consultants who understand how to exploit these trends can position their organization's reporting capabilities to provide true competitive advantage against other industry laggards. Understanding past trends will provide us insight into the future of reporting so that we may begin taking steps to prepare for new tools and techniques.

Increased flexibility

Designing and developing reports has long been the domain of IT departments. If an end user identified a need for a particular report, he or she would typically have to submit a request to the IT department or some other functional group assigned to report development and creation. The process of designing and creating the report would then be assigned to a developer who, more than likely, had a number of other tasks waiting to be completed. Not surprisingly, the end user would not receive his or her report for several days, if not weeks or months! By then, it is entirely possible that the end user's needs may have changed and the anticipated report has become obsolete before it can even be used for the first time.

Is it any wonder then, that this inefficient practice has quickly given way to a more flexible process? While many situations still require the involvement of an experienced technical developer, in today's business environment, end users have a reasonable expectation that they will be provided with the tools necessary to create their own reports. As business software becomes more accessible and easier to use, end users increasingly expect to be equipped with the tools they need to create their own reports. This allows end users to design and create reports that match their specifications and to do this in a much quicker time frame than would be possible if this report were being designed by an individual in another department.

On the surface, this trend offers an extraordinary level of efficiency and flexibility that should be welcomed throughout all organizations. Certain challenges with this model do exist, however, and developers and consultants should be aware of these. Of course, end users who wish to create their own reports cannot have unfettered access to an organization's production database, nor will most of them understand the hardware and network requirements for working with reporting tools that handle large amounts of data. Therefore, while traditional IT departments are no longer the key designers and creators of most reports, they still have a key role to play in providing central oversight for the reporting needs of the entire organization. Additionally, developers and consultants must also expand their focus beyond the IT department to ensure that end users are well-equipped and trained in making the most effective use of their reporting tools.

Reporting through all levels of an organization

In years past, access to reports was typically limited to members of the Executive team. As the long-term decisions makers for the company, it was the Executive team that benefitted most from reporting tools that provided a snapshot of company performance over a period of time. Reporting at other levels of the organization was generally an afterthought if it was not ignored entirely. Of course, one reason for this may lie in the fact that ERP systems were generally not as adept in capturing information from all aspects of the business; instead, the focus was on capturing general ledger information, which is generally perceived to be the domain of the Executive and Accounting teams. Additionally, perhaps for reasons of security and trust, Executive team members often did not see a reason to share key metrics and information with lower level team-members.

In recent years, however, as ERP systems have become more adept at capturing a wider variety of information across all functions of business, reporting across all levels of the organization has become more important. Executive teams are no longer the exclusive focus of an organization's reporting efforts. Today, in an effort to gain competitive advantage, all levels of the organization must utilize reporting tools to improve their ability to make decisions on a day-to-day basis. In other words, organizations are now focused on putting their hard-earned business data in the hands of those who can benefit the most from it. They are also discovering that transparency can improve an employee's performance and focus. Employees can quickly and easily see how their individual and team performance is impacting the overall company performance. This leads to greater buy-in and focus from all levels of the organization.

As a developer or a consultant tasked with developing reports, the focus is no longer just on developing balance sheets and income statements for an Executive team. While such reports are still relevant and necessary, additional reports for lower levels of the organization are also important. The Sales manager expects improved insight into customer spending behaviour. The Warehouse manager demands access to reports that identify orders behind schedule. Developers must be aware of the various reporting audiences that exist within an organization, the types of reporting that are required by these audiences, and the security that is required to ensure that sensitive information is only seen by the right individuals.

Increased access to report generation process

Successful organizations are the ones that make their data available to all levels of the organization. One reason for this trend lies in the fact that newer, more effective reporting tools have improved the ability of users across all levels of an organization to access company data. In previous years, hardware and resource limitations meant that reports were generated at specific times such as month-end close. In a less-connected business environment, where decisions did not have to be made on a minute-by-minute basis, companies could afford to wait until certain points in time to generate and review their financial statements.

In today's hyper-competitive business environment, however, this is no longer a luxury that organizations can afford. Instead, any report, whether a key financial statement or an aging trial balance, must be capable of being generated at a moment's notice with near-to or real-time company data. Organizations' members cannot afford to wait until the weekly sales meeting or the quarterly Executive team meeting to review key reports; instead, they must be generating and reviewing these reports on a daily basis.

Developers and consultants must be aware of this trend and seek ways to make reports more readily available to an organization. Issues such as latency and hardware must be considered to ensure that reports can be generated at a moment's notice without any negative impact to transactional processing. One of the most effective ways to do this is to make a wide range of reporting tools available to all levels of the organization and then equipping team members with the knowledge necessary to utilize these tools effectively.

Challenges in developing and writing reports

Now that we have identified some of the common trends that exist in today's reporting domain, let's take a look at some of the challenges these trends pose to the developer or consultant setting out to create a well-designed report. As we've seen, each trend leads to a number of different challenges. Careful consideration of these challenges can be the deciding factor in whether or not a report gains acceptance from the intended audience of the report.

In our experience with designing reports, we have identified a list of nine common areas or challenges that we think are important to consider before setting out to design or build the perfect report:

- Intended audience
- Data sources
- Latency
- Formatting and presentation
- Ad hoc queries vs. traditional reports
- Security
- Network access and general IT infrastructure
- Developer resources

While this is certainly not a comprehensive list of challenges we'll meet while designing reports, it does include some of the most important to consider when developing and creating reports. The first five challenges relate to how the end user anticipates the report will be designed. Obviously, these challenges should be addressed based on feedback from the end user. The final challenges are less about end-user requirements and more about the environment in which we will be designing the report. Oftentimes, it can be a challenge explaining to an end-user why certain environmental challenges, such as lack of developer resources, may prevent you from building a report to his or her specifications.

Keep in mind that becoming a successful report developer does not always mean delivering a final report to the intended audience; instead, in many cases, the ultimate "deliverable" that will result from the report writing process will come from equipping the intended audience with the tools necessary for them to create their own reports. As we work our way through the rest of this book, remember that when we discuss "creating a successful report," we are really commenting on the overall reporting solution.

Intended audience

The intended audience is any individual or business entity that will use the report as a means to answer questions about specific business functions. A successful reporting solution will be one that is designed with the ultimate end user in mind. It will answer the question, or questions, set forth by the intended audience in a clear, concise manner.

Within an organization, an Executive team may request a cash flow statement in order to view the company's cash position and to understand how much cash is available for further investment. A Payables Coordinator for the same company may need a report that identifies vendor's terms and discounts to determine which vendors should be paid sooner rather than later. Although both audiences may come to the same internal developer for these reports, the developer must be capable of understanding the requirements of the target audience.

A developer also may be tasked with creating a report for an external audience. For example, auditors or external creditors will request reports from an organization as a means to understanding more about an organization's business practices. It is possible that these reports will need to be submitted to external auditors in a specific, pre-determined format.

In all cases, a report writer must be aware of the "Me-Me-Me" syndrome. Requests for reports are usually the result of a need to answer a question specific to the intended audience's immediate function. To an individual who needs a specific report, no report is more important than the one he or she has requested. Not surprisingly, the requesting user will go to great lengths to prove that his or her report should receive top priority over other, yet-to-be created reports. While more clever developers may use this to their advantage and request bribes in the form of cookies or more vacation time. Effective developers will be wary of those who place their reporting needs above all others. And of course, if your boss is the one requesting the report, then by all means, you better pay attention!

Developers may also want to be on the lookout for the "all-knowing" report. Either we have been asked to write a report of this nature or have heard horror stories of it from fellow developers. This is the report that is supposed to give the user every bit of information from the entire system in one report, hence its name "all-knowing". Now, this almost always turns out to be an impossible feat. Sure, it sounds easy enough to the user, but if—and that is a big "if"—the report can actually be created does it provide any true value or is it just a discombobulated mess. If tasked with writing this type of report, don't be afraid to question the need and find out if this really should be a single report or multiple reports that present the data in a meaningful way.

Data sources

While the goal of any ERP system is to provide a single comprehensive location for recording all functions of business, in reality, we find that most companies, in addition to the production ERP database, utilize a wide variety of different systems. Each system is incorporated with its own set of business logic, for recording data. These silos of information can range from entire database applications down to a static spreadsheet that an end-user keeps on his or her desktop. While a company's reasons for a lack of a single data repository can vary from lack of money required to combine systems to the inherent difficulty in transitioning from an older system to a newer system, the reality is that this kind of environment provides numerous challenges when it comes to accurate and timely reporting.

The challenge of having multiple data sources can be seen in the illustration below. Typically, there are multiple sources of data, being accessed and/or stored on one server or across multiple servers. In many cases, one way to address this challenge is to have a reporting server compiling all this data.

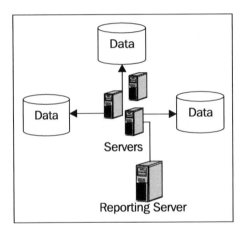

Let's think about what some of these challenges of reporting across multiple data sources might be:

- Data may be duplicated across multiple systems.
- The business logic utilized by the systems that captured information may differ from system to system, leading to differences in how the data is stored in each silo.
- Timing differences may exist between silos. Data in one system may be updated on a real-time basis whereas in another system, it's updated on a weekly basis.

Each of these challenges must be managed to provide accurate and effective reporting. First, developers and consultants must be careful to select a reporting tool that can bridge the gap between these disparate systems without adding another independent silo of information. Once this tool is selected, it must be used effectively to present one version of the truth to the end user. By this, we mean that it must provide users with a consistent and reliable look at the data in the report, regardless of how many data sources were used to generate the data in the report in the first place.

But, let's be honest, accumulating and storing data outside of the ERP database is not always a bad thing. A company cannot and should not expect to conduct all reporting against the production ERP database, which is where the majority of the transactional and statistical information resides. While this method is more likely to allow for real or near-real time reporting, it is also likely that it will cause a decrease in system performance for other users. A common technique for many companies who want to provide reporting tools to users without impacting production performance is to set up a separate data warehouse. This separate data warehouse contains data from one or more enterprise systems and provides a separate location against which users can generate reports and queries. Data in this warehouse is updated at pre-set intervals via extract, transform, and load tools such as SQL Server Integration Services (SSIS). Some companies take the concept of a separate reporting server one step further by creating a separate reporting server. This completely removes the performance impact of reporting away from the ERP system database.

Regardless of the reporting tool we select, we must be aware of the trade-offs in the various sources of data that may be used to generate the report. If we're reporting from a production database, we may encounter additional issues with security and hardware performance. Likewise, if we are extracting data for reporting from a separate data warehouse, we have to be aware that the data may not be in real time. Furthermore, if we plan to utilize multiple sources of data, such as when we want to combine data in an Excel spreadsheet with data stored in our ERP application, to generate our report, we must pay attention to such challenges as duplicate data, business logic, and more.

Latency

As we have discussed, trends in reporting have led to more users wanting more data in real time to gain a more competitive business advantage. When we speak of latency, we are referring to the delay between when source data is generated and when it can actually be used in a report. For example, if a journal entry is posted to a revenue account, but the President of our organization must wait until a scheduled report generation process to see the impact of this entry on an income statement for the organization, then we have a period of latency between when the source data was generated and when it was retrieved by a particular report.

As a report developer, one of the first questions that needs to be answered is, "Does the report need to be real-time or can it be generated after some arbitrary delay?" This can and usually does lead to other challenges. Many times users will want everything in real time.

Most often, true real-time reporting is either nearly impossible to achieve or can cause a real strain on the infrastructure. In addition to this, the developer must ask, "Is there really a true need for the report to be in real-time?" Take, for example, an Accounts Receivable manager who is requesting a real-time aging report. Is the benefit of having this run on real-time data going to make a dramatic difference in what is actually collected on these open receivables? Probably not! Now, if we take an example of a Sales Manager requesting a real-time report of open sales orders that have not shipped yet, having this information can make a difference. This will give that Sales Manager a report from which he or she can take immediate action by going to shipping and identifying the hold up on the orders.

It's important to note that the closer we get to real-time reporting, the cost of resources required to provide such real-time reporting will become greater, while the extra increase in added benefit from access to this real-time data will shrink. At the same time, the cost of accessing real-time data usually outweighs the extra benefit provided by having access to such data. When this happens, we face the challenge of convincing our report-users that the data latency they may experience in their reports must be acceptable.

An example of the concept of increasing costs for a decrease in latency is seen in the following image. As we move from high latency, for example, data provided the next morning, to low latency, real time data for instance, the cost of that goes up in terms of both lower performance and higher monetary cost.

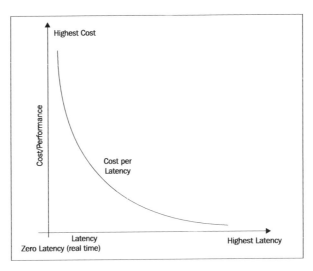

So, how does a report designer weigh the pros and cons of providing end users with access to real-time data? The main thing we want to ask ourselves as report developers when determining whether a report truly needs to be real-time is whether or not the data in the report is critical to spurring immediate action or changes in the day-to-day operations of our organization.

Formatting and presentation

Before selecting an appropriate reporting tool for a given situation, requirements for formatting and presentation must be given careful consideration. To some degree, the appropriate solution to this challenge will rely on the report's intended audience. External reports, such as those being sent to customers and clients will, in most cases, require company logos and other colourful visuals that represent your company in a professional manner. On the other hand, reports being designed for internal use, such as for a warehouse manager, may not require extensive formatting and presentation capabilities.

As can be seen in the below diagram, you can see how much more presentable the balance sheet on the right is when compared to the standard out of the box balance sheet on the left:

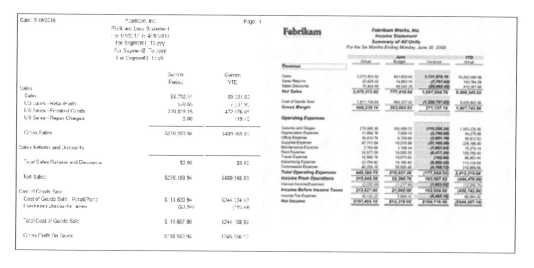

Understandably, this reporting challenge often takes a back-seat to other, more important challenges such as latency and security. Providing a clean, colourful report, however, can play a critical role in a user acceptance of a report and its contents. By going the extra mile to select a reporting tool that has the ability to easily control report formatting and graphics, report viewers are more likely to be influenced by the contents of the report in a manner of our choosing.

But, this challenge is not just about using fancy fonts or selecting pretty images and logos from a graphics repository. It is also about providing appropriate tools for improving the readability of your report. For example, if we are developing reports that display key financial metrics, we will want our reporting tool to have the ability to display data in straight rows and columns. Viewers of the finished product should be able to follow the logical flow of information presented in the report. Whether this means looking across columns to see how performance has changed over time or down the rows of an income statement to see how revenues compare to expenses over the same period of time, the report should be laid out in logical fashion.

Our report may also be required to meet certain standards for formatting. For example, publically traded companies must submit certain financial statements and these statements must be prepared according to certain principles and standards. A few examples of this includexBRL (eXtensible Business Reporting Language) reporting and GAAP/FASB/IASB regulations. If this is the kind of report we will be developing, then it should play a prominent role in the selection of the reporting tool.

Ad hoc queries versus traditional reports

In addition to the challenges covered thus far, we must also consider the kind of report we need to create. Is this a report that our users will create on an as-needed basis? Or, is it a report that users will need to create repeatedly over a period of time? Additionally, the selection we make here may impact how these reports are distributed among the various individuals who need to see the contents of the report.

The concept of ad hoc versus traditional reporting can be broken down into two components:

- The ease with which a report can be created; or, how easily the report can be modified after initial creation
- How easily the final version of a report can be distributed to other report viewers

Every organization has a need for viewing its financial performance at or over a period of time through the use of financial statements. Financial statements are traditional reports that typically require some effort during the initial setup to determine how they will be structured, how often they will be created, and so on. But, usually after this initial setup is done, the structure requires very little in the way of modification during future financial periods. Therefore, while it may be helpful, it is not always critical that the reporting tools we use to generate our financial statements offer us exceptional flexibility in changing or modifying reports.

In addition to reporting requirements that span multiple financial periods, individual users may have a unique reporting need that arises due to a specific business challenge. Rather than go through the effort of setting up a traditional report that can be used over and over again, our user simply needs a reporting tool that can quickly generate a report on an as needed basis in order to answer the specific question at hand. In exchange for this ad hoc capability, ad hoc report viewers may be willing to allow a trade-off in other areas such as formatting and presentation.

In this image, we see a sample of the PivotTable functionality from Microsoft Excel that provides users an opportunity to query their data in an ad hoc fashion:

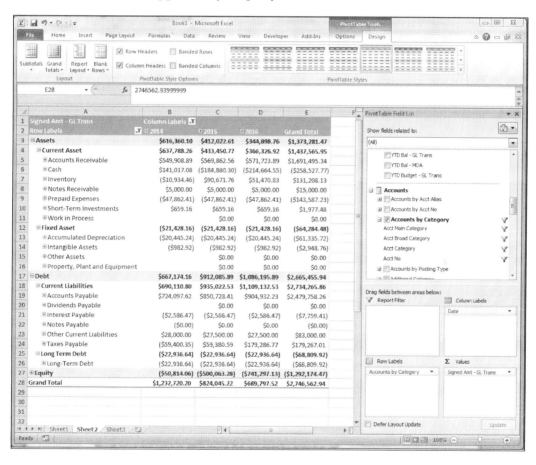

As we answer the challenges associated with ad hoc versus traditional reporting tools, we must also determine how the report will be distributed to those end users who do not have the ability to generate the reports. Will these users be reliant on a power user or the initial report requestor to generate the report and email the results in PDF format? In most, but not all, cases, we will find that traditional reports are more easily distributed than ad hoc reports. Traditional reports, such as financial statements, usually contain information that is useful across a wide variety of users. These reports contain data presented in a standard format, making the reports useful for users across a wide variety of backgrounds. If a report will be distributed on a regular basis, we must make additional considerations for how to manage security for these reports, the manner in which they will be distributed (for example, via email or via a central location like a company intranet), and how the process of report distribution will be scheduled.

On the other hand, reports generated through ad hoc reporting tools are not usually distributed to a wide variety of users. By their very nature, ad hoc reports are developed quickly, and for a single purpose. For example, an external auditor may request a list of all journal entries made by a company in a particular year. This is a typical request by external auditors as they prepare a company's audit report. However, it isn't really information for which a company will need a traditional report, nor is it a report that will be saved and re-distributed. Rather than expend time and energy developing a report that will be used only once, we may be better off utilizing an ad hoc reporting tool to meet our needs.

A good report developer or consultant will be able to pick up on key requirements from the report requestor and quickly determine whether the information being requested is better pulled in the form of an ad hoc report or some other type of traditional report.

Security

Few reports exist that can be distributed to anyone and everyone inside and outside of an organization without regard for security. Instead, most reports contain sensitive data that must be tightly controlled to ensure it does not fall into the wrong hands. At the organizational level, companies must have control over their data to ensure that it does not fall into the wrong hands outside of the organization. Within an organization, reports developed for one department may not be suitable for employees in another department. For example, consider a report on year-to-date payroll amounts developed for the Director of Human Resources. This type of report is usually considered sensitive information that should not be seen by others in the organization.

When selecting a reporting tool, developers and consultants must consider how effective that reporting tool will be when it comes to managing user access to the data contained in the report. Will entire reports be restricted to certain users? Or, will one format be provided to all users with the select data being displayed based on the user viewing the report? It is also worth considering which attributes will be used to determine security. In some cases, it may be the department that a user belongs to, or it may be that user's functional role within the organization that allows him or her access to certain reports. In other cases, still, it may be that reports will be password protected, and only those with the password will be allowed access to reports.

As developers and consultants tasked with report writing, we often find ourselves with greater access to company data than that of the average end user. With this access comes a high level of responsibility. One of the greatest proprietary advantages a company has over its competitors is the data that it carefully maintains. By selecting reporting tools with security in mind, we take a critical step towards ensuring that hard-earned company data will continue to provide an extra advantage over our competitors.

Network access and general IT infrastructure

Access and infrastructure play multiple roles in determining our reporting solution. Not only do we need to determine whether our infrastructure will allow the type of reporting we are going to be utilizing from a performance perspective, but we also need to determine if it will provide the necessary access to our intended audience.

Some of the questions we might ask with regard to this reporting challenge include:

- How will our intended audience access the reporting tool?
- How much data is being transmitted across the network?
- Do we have a dedicated server for reporting purposes?
- Do we have sufficient disk space to support a data warehouse?
- Will the reports be memory intensive?

By asking these questions and more, we can make a more accurate selection of a reporting solution.

As the following diagram shows, users in our organization may require external access to the reporting server. This requires taking firewalls and network access into consideration as we select a reporting tool. Additionally, we may have users who will be asking for reports internally, and those users may be able to take advantage of a completely different reporting tool.

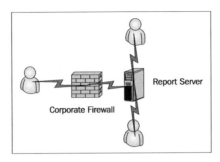

With the advent of such technologies such as Citrix and Terminal Server, the ability to give either internal or external access to users on a large scale has been made easier. Many companies that run some type of ERP system will usually already have one of these solutions in place to grant their users remote access. In addition, this type of infrastructure allows companies to centralize their servers, keep maintenance down to a minimum, and keep the systems standardized. In these types of environments, we can easily add on our reporting solutions.

In deciding what the most appropriate reporting solution is, we must also consider how much data is being transmitted across the network. If, for example, we are trying to pull down large amounts of data in the middle of business hours, what kind of effect is that having on our network? Do we need to add bandwidth to our network or can we work within the current bandwidth we have? The answer to this question is usually imperative to deciding on the most appropriate reporting solution.

We have talked about various areas of infrastructure that need to be considered when writing reports. Another important area is available disk space. Whatever reporting solution we ultimately decide on, will, to some degree, require additional disk space. Whether or not the reporting tool requires enough space for an entire data warehouse or if it can rely on something as simple as enough local disk space that contains a report depository or data store, the report developer or consultant needs to be aware of this. We must also determine how much anticipated growth in the data there will be so that disk space can be planned accordingly. One thing we want to avoid is recommending and building a solution that has a short lifespan because it runs out of disk space and crashes the server! As report developers and consultants, it is our job to figure out how long the lifespan of the solution needs to be based on the customers' needs and plan for that growth, ensuring that end solution indeed fills that need.

The last thing we want report developers and consultants to be aware of from an infrastructure standpoint is how memory intensive the reports can be. We have discussed this briefly in terms of dedicated reporting servers, but in addition we want to point out that even with sufficient memory, some reports will just take time to run. A perfect example is a heavy distribution company with thousands of orders. To run an open order report against thousands of orders that might have a large number of line items, we are looking at a potentially long report generation time. It is in these types of reports we must decide on how frequently this report will be generated. Is it something we can schedule to run overnight to be ready first thing in the morning? Or, is it something we can break down into smaller runs, with filters/ parameters to spread out the load? These are just some of the things to think about and discuss with the report requestor.

Developer resources

So far, we have mainly discussed challenges having to do with choosing the proper reporting solution. Another piece of the puzzle is the resources that will be tasked with actually developing the reporting solution.

Many times equipping our intended audience with the tools necessary for them to create their own reports is the right course of action. In this model, these "power users" are users who are less technical, but they understand the data they are working with and the output that they need very well. One thing we as report developers and consultants need to take into account is whether this model works for the organization as a whole and that the IT department understands that they are going to have less control over the solution as a whole. We also need to make sure that we don't lose corporate governance over sensitive information.

Though empowering users to be able to generate their own reports has grown more and more acceptable, many IT departments don't want to lose control of the management of the data and are concerned that they will lose corporate oversight and create multiple silos of data. Because of this, report development is usually assigned to a dedicated report developer, be that either an internal resource in the organization, or an outside developer or consultant.

Organizations will often determine whether to develop reporting solutions in house or to outsource it based on many factors. The main factors for our purpose are who is available to develop the reports and whether there are any time and budget constraints. Even if the organization has the required skill set in house, the resource might not necessarily have the time to dedicate to developing the report. This is when companies will often look to outside resources to get the job done. The flip side of this may be if there are budget constraints that prohibit an organization from going outside to get the reporting solution developed, and this is when we typically see organizations keep it in house.

Summary

As we work our way through the rest of this book, always keep in mind that our goal is to provide our end users with accurate and reliable ways to mine the data found in our reporting systems. If we cannot maintain accuracy and reliability, then our end users will quickly seek out another report developer who can meet their needs!

Creating accurate and reliable reports requires the ability to properly identify the end user and corporate requirements. The ability to identify the requirements for a report or reporting tool is a valuable skill to have in today's business environment. But, this skill doesn't come easily! Instead, developers and consultants must constantly ask challenging questions of end users and the corporate infrastructure to select the most effective reporting tool for the circumstances.

Not surprisingly, the process of creating a report is not often as easy as creating a data connection to a database and throwing data up onto a computer screen or a PDF file. But, in order to make it easy, we've provided you with information to set you along the way towards identifying the requirements for your report.

As we begin to cover specific reporting tools for Microsoft Dynamics GP, keep the trends and challenges we've discussed in this chapter in the back of your mind. Continue to ask yourself how each reporting tool can help you meet the challenges that we've presented in this chapter.

In the next chapter, we will begin by looking at some tips and tricks to locating our data in the Microsoft Dynamics GP system. Then, we will look at certain tools that can help us in finding the specific data we need to begin writing our reports.

2
Where Is My Data and How Do I Get to It?

Now that we have looked at the latest trends in reporting and have an understanding of the many challenges that go along with report development, we are ready to start gathering our data and writing our report. As any developer or consultant that has been tasked with filling user requests for reports is aware, ultimately the very first question after deciding on the reporting tool is "Where is my data and how do I get to it?"

Knowing where to begin is a critical first step in the development process. The aim of this chapter is to provide helpful tips for finding and locating data in the Dynamics GP 2010 ERP system and company databases. Although we'll discuss some reporting tools that do not require us to know the SQL database structure for Dynamics GP companies, it is still helpful to understand how GP stores its data.

In this chapter, we will discuss the following:

- Differences between the DYNAMICS database and company databases
- Conventions that are helpful to know and understand when it comes to Microsoft Dynamics GP 2010 data and how it is stored
- Using Resource Descriptions as a tool for finding data from within GP 2010
- Utilizing additional tools, such as the GP 2010 SDK and Support Debugging Tool, to find our data

DYNAMICS database versus company database

The first task of identifying where our data is located is making sure we are using the correct database! Microsoft Dynamics GP 2010 utilizes the Microsoft SQL Server platform as its database engine. When Dynamics GP 2010 is installed on our environment and a new company is created, the installation process creates several databases on a server that has been designated during the install. These databases will store all the information entered through the Dynamics GP 2010 application, and we can use SQL Server Management Studio to access the underlying tables that store this data.

Microsoft Dynamics GP has two types of databases: a system database (DYNAMICS) and company database(s). For first-time report developers and seasoned writers, knowing which of these databases stores a particular piece of information we need is crucial for an accurate report.

What is the DYNAMICS database?

When Microsoft Dynamics GP is first installed and some initial settings are provided, a system database will be created. This database is the DYNAMICS database. It includes such things as records for each company that you create, the organizations registration information, the maximum account framework, and so on.

> Regardless of how many company databases we have, they will all share a single DYNAMICS database.

From a reporting standpoint, there is certain information located in the system database that we may need to report on at one time or another. We have provided a quick reference for this information below:

- Multicurrency System Setups – This includes the setup of the currencies, the exchange rates, and the currency symbols for those organizations that process transactions in any number of foreign currencies.

- Intercompany Setup – This is where the intercompany relationships are stored and the specific due to/due from accounts are mapped.

- Organizations Structures – This will include the organizational levels and entities that have been created for those organizations that use this feature.

- User Master – This table stores information about the users in the ERP system, including their user ID and username.

- User Tasks – This table stores the tasks that users set up in Dynamics GP. These are the tasks that are displayed on the users' Home screens in GP.

- Company Master – Stores company setup information such as whether security is enabled, the company ID is in the form of the company database ID in SQL Management Studio, primary address information, tax schedule defaults, and any number of options for the company.

- Security Setups – This includes all of the security tasks, security roles, and user security assignments.

- User-Company Access – Includes the companies that each user has access to.

Company database

Each company that we create in Dynamics GP has its own company database. As information such as transactions, accounts, and customer or vendor data is entered through GP, this information is recorded in individual fields. These fields comprise the smallest unit of data stored. All of this data makes up a record and a record is grouped with similar records and stored in a table.

For obvious reasons, this data is segmented by company database so that each company can maintain unique records. In addition to this transactional data, numerous additional company setups exist in the company database. As with the DYNAMICS database, we may need to report on some of these company system setups. Here is a quick reference to the more common company setup tables:

- Account Formats – Stores the chart of accounts format for the company.

- Posting Definitions – Stores how the individual modules post to the General Ledger.

- Company Locations – Lists additional addresses for each company.

- Source Document Master & Audit Trail Codes – Every transaction is assigned both a source document and an audit trail code. This table can be used to report on the full description of these codes.

- Shipping Methods Master – Stores the setup details of the shipping methods for the company.

- Payment Terms Master – Stores the setup details of the payment terms created for the company.

- Record Notes Master – Stores all of the record level notes for the particular company.

- Comment Master – Stores predefined comments to be used across multiple series in Dynamics GP.

- Electronic Funds Transfer – Stores the EFT setup information for the company for both Payables and Receivables modules. This includes customer and vendor banking information.

- Period Setup – Stores the fiscal period setup for the company.

- Sales/Purchases Tax Tables – These tables store the tax detail and tax schedule records as well as the tax summary amounts.

Dynamics GP table naming/numbering conventions

Dynamics GP has a rather interesting and sometimes frustrating table naming structure. When developers or consultants first see this, they are overwhelmed, to say the least. However, once you learn that there is a rhyme and reason to the madness, it actually makes a lot of sense and it is quite easy to follow and locate the tables that we need.

Tables versus table groups

When data is entered into windows via the Microsoft Dynamics GP application, that data is stored in tables in the underlying SQL database. In most cases, data entered via a single process can be stored in two or more tables. In such cases, it is common for these tables to be grouped together by a certain naming convention. For example, entering journal entry information may update the Transactions Work table (contains General Ledger transaction header information), the Transaction Amounts Work table (contains the General Ledger transaction distributions), and the Transaction Clearing Amounts Work table (contains the General Ledger clearing transactions distributions). These make up what are called Table Groups. These table groups are also referred to as logical tables.

Each Microsoft Dynamics GP table has three names: a technical name, a display name, and a physical name. The technical name is used solely by the software and will usually be seen in some alert messages instead of the display name. The display name is the name that will appear in most of the alert messages generated by the system and is typically the name used for a given table when referring to it in speech, for example, Vendor Master. The physical name is the name that will be found in the SQL database when looking in Microsoft SQL Server Management Studio.

Physical table naming/numbering conventions

When working within the context of a SQL database to generate reports, developers and consultants will make use of the table physical names. A quick scan through the various tables in a standard GP install reveals a bewildering array of table numbers. How can there possibly be any rhyme or reason to these table names? Surprisingly, it does actually follow a certain pattern. For the most part, the table numbering follows a special convention. This schema packs a lot of information into a small number, and it can help developers and consultants know where to begin looking for their data.

As Dynamics GP has grown into a more comprehensive accounting solution, it has expanded, in part, by incorporating third-party applications into the solution. While many of the third-party programmers tried to stick within the relative bounds of the GP physical table naming conventions, as we will soon see, this is not always the case. So, while many of the tables that belong to the core GP modules maintain a fairly standard numbering convention, we will find that this does not hold true for all GP modules.

Generally speaking, GP table physical names contain a two or three digit alpha prefix followed by a five digit number. The three digit prefix represents the module for which the table holds data. The numbers that follow identify what type of data is held in the table. For example, is it posted transaction data? Or, is it information related to the module setup?

As we see in the next image and following sections of this chapter, the numbering schema for a Dynamics GP physical table can be broken down to reveal information about the kind of data that is found in that table.

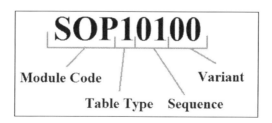

Alpha code

Let's begin by taking a look at the alpha-prefix for these tables. We have put together a handy reference of some of the most common prefixes and the modules that they represent:

Prefix	Module	Prefix	Module
AA	Analytical Accounting	MRP	Material Requirements Planning
AF	Advanced Financials	MXLS	Audit Trails/Electronic Signatures
ASI	SmartList	NLB	Navigation List Builder
BM	Bill of Materials (Mfg)	OC	Sales Configurator (Mfg)
CFM	Cash Flow Management	OSRC	Outsourcing (Mfg)
CLM	Certification Manager	PA	Project Accounting
CM	Checkbook Master	PDK	Personal Data Keeper (Proj. Acct.)
CN	Collections Management	PM	Payables Management
CP	Capacity Requirements Planning (Mfg)	POP	Purchase Order Processing
DD	Direct Deposit	PP	Revenue Expense Deferrals
EC	Engineering Change Management (Mfg)	QA	Quality Assurance (Mfg)
ERB	Excel Report Builder	RM	Receivables Management
EXT	Extender	RT	Routings (Mfg)
FA	Fixed Assets	SC	Sales Forecasting (Mfg)
GL	General Ledger	SLB	SmartList Builder
HR	Human Resources	SOP	Sales Order Processing
ICJC	Job Costing (Mfg)	SVC	Field Service
IV	Inventory	SY	System/Company Setup
IVC	Invoicing (Sales)	UPR	Payroll
MC	Multicurrency	VAT	Intrastat
ME	Electronic Reconcile (EFT)	WC	Work Centers (Mfg)
MOP	Manufacturing Order Processing	WO	Manufacturing Orders

In some modules, such as Manufacturing, tables are broken down even further with Routing tables represented by one set of digits while Material Requirements Planning data is found in tables represented by another set of digits. More commonly, however, entire modules are generally represented by a single alpha code, such as is the case with Project Accounting where all project transactions, billing, and revenue recognition tables are represented with the same alpha code.

Table type

Once we've identified the module in which our data might be stored, our next thought should be towards the type of data that we are trying to find. Before we return to the numbering convention, let's take a look at the various types of data that exist in GP tables:

- Setup: Almost all modules in GP have set up windows that allow users to define default options or other settings for how that module will be used. The options selected in these windows can be found in the Setup tables.

- Master: Some modules, such as Payables Management, allow users to record master records. These master records represent permanent records, such as vendors, for the company. Typically, master records must be entered prior to using a module, as transactions will utilize these master records.

- Transaction: These tables contain the transaction-level data from Dynamics GP. These include the most basic of GP transactions, the journal entry, to transactions entered in sub-ledgers, such as the distribution records of a posted Receivables invoice. Transactions entered in various modules will, depending on their status, be stored in one of three types of transaction tables:

  - Work: Un-posted transactions can generally be found in work tables. The name is appropriate, as these transactions can be considered a "work-in-progress". They have not been committed to the sub or general ledgers via posting processes, so we should factor this into our thinking when deciding whether or not to include these records in our reports.

  - Open: Generally speaking, records in these tables have been posted, but are awaiting an additional action before they can be considered "closed" or "history". In the General Ledger module, the open table represents all journal entries for the current open year. In other modules, such as Receivables Management, open tables contain data for receivables transactions that have not yet been fully applied.

  - History: Transactions that are "completed" generally end up in the history tables. Again, this depends on the module. For example, in Payables Management, fully applied invoices are moved to history. In Purchase Order Processing, however, a routine exists to move completed purchase orders to history. Until this routine is run, records will not be moved to history.

- Cross Reference: Some tables represent data that spans multiple modules. For example, GP users can link purchase orders to unfulfilled sales order line items via Sales Order Commitment. The prefix of the table that contains these links indicates that this is a Sales Order Processing table, but in actuality, it contains data from Purchase Order Processing, as well.

- In addition to these main table types, other table types exist that are less commonly used for reporting purposes. Nonetheless, it is helpful to understand what these table types contain:

  ○ Report Options: Before users can generate a report from the Reports menu, a series of options must be designated for that report. These report options are recorded in a series of report options tables.

  ○ Temp: As the name implies, data is only stored in these tables temporarily. Temporary tables can be used in a variety of situations, such as when a user presses the "Post" button for a transaction. Although rare, it may be necessary to use a temp table when designing a report that should contain data from the time of posting. For example, a sales invoice can be generated at the time the user posts the invoice and can be based on data stored in a temp table at the time.

In terms of the physical naming convention for GP tables, the data type is represented by the first digit following the module code. The following table contains the various table types and their associated number in the numbering convention:

Table Type	Number
Master	0
Work	1
Open	2
History	3
Setup	4
Temporary	5
Cross Reference	6
Report Options	7

Sequence

The next two digits in the numbering convention make up the sequence number. This number indicates the logical table to which the table belongs. As we discussed earlier in the chapter, logical tables are related tables, or table groups, that share similar data. Not only do these table groups share similar data, but they also share the same data type and sequence number when it comes to the physical table numbering convention.

For example, let's consider the following set of logical tables:

- PM00200 (Vendor Master)
- PM00201 (Vendor Master Summary)
- PM00202 (Vendor Master Period Summary)
- PM00203 (Vendor Accounts)
- PM00204 (Purchasing 1099 Detail)

These tables comprise the Payables Vendor Master Logical File table group. We can easily see this by the numbers that follow the module code. First, we see that these tables share the same data type—remember, 0 means these are Master tables—and second, we see that these tables share the same sequence number. Although we need other tools to help us determine the name of the table group, we are able to easily scan through a list of table physical names in SQL Management Studio and see that these tables are in the same table group.

Variant

The final two digits of the physical numbering convention represent the logical group variant. Within a logical group, numbers are incremented sequentially. This is evident in our example using the Payables Vendor Master Logical File above; as we see the final two digits of each table increment by one.

In table groups related to transactions, the variant often distinguishes between header tables, detail tables, distribution tables, and other related tables.

Keep in mind, what we have discussed is only a general naming and numbering convention for GP tables in their SQL databases. Unfortunately, to the frustration of developers and consultants everywhere, these conventions do not hold true in all cases! At the very least, knowing this convention can point us in the right direction. We can rely on other tools and resources to help us pinpoint the right table when these conventions fall short.

Locating Dynamics GP data using the Resource Descriptions windows

One of the most useful tools for locating data when being tasked with writing reports against Dynamics GP data is the Resource Descriptions tool within the application itself. Resource Descriptions are broken into three distinct windows: **Tables**, **Windows**, and **Fields**. Typically, we find ourselves using a combination of these three windows to locate the specific data we are looking for. There is not really a right or a wrong way to use these windows. Each report developer or consultant could argue that the way he or she uses the windows is the correct way, but ultimately, as long as we are able to identify and find the data we need, we will be that much closer to creating an accurate report that fills our users' needs.

The various **Resource Descriptions** windows are located by browsing to **Microsoft Dynamics GP | Tools | Resource Descriptions**.

Tables

Table Descriptions let us select a **Product** (Microsoft Dynamics GP, Fixed Assets, and so on) as well as the **Series** (Financial, Sales, and so on). We are then provided a list of all the tables for the selected product and series. By default, the list of tables is by **Display Name**. We do have the option to change how the tables are sorted by changing the **View By** field. The options are **Table Display Name**, **Table Group Technical Name**, **Table Physical Name**, or **Table Technical Name**. The method we choose will depend on how familiar we are with the table structure. For example, we might select **Table Physical Name** once we are familiar with the naming convention guidelines provided earlier in this chapter. There is also a **Find** button that allows us to search for the table based on any one of its three names.

To access Table Descriptions follow these steps:

1. Open Microsoft Dynamics GP.
2. Click the Microsoft Dynamics GP Menu from the toolbar.
3. Select **Tools.**
4. Select **Resource Descriptions.**
5. Select **Tables**.
6. Click the **Ellipses** button and find your table. In the image below, we are searching for the **PM Vendor Master File** table, which is found under the **Microsoft Dynamics GP Product** and **Purchasing Series**.

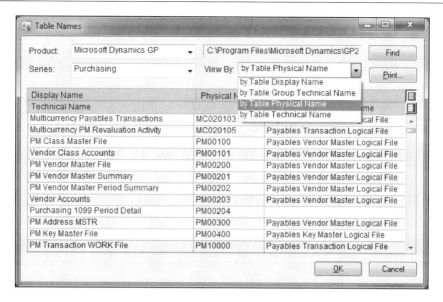

Once we have found the table we are looking for, we can drill into that table and get additional information for that table. This view includes all of the fields in the selected table, their physical names (as would be seen in the SQL tables), the storage type of the field, and the position.

We can access this additional information by double clicking the table record in the **Table Names** window. This opens a new window called **Table Descriptions**:

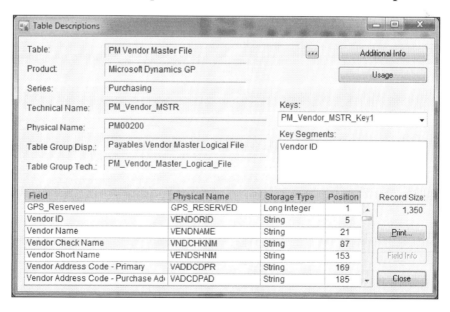

From the **Table Descriptions** window, we can further drill into each field and get information such as the **Format Type**, the **Keyable Length** of the field and if applicable, any **Static Values** if it is a dropdown field.

We can access this detail by double clicking a field or selecting the field and clicking the **Field Info** button to open the **Additional Field Information** window:

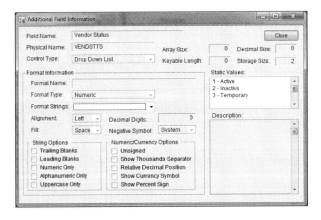

Returning to the **Table Descriptions** window, the last pieces of information we can access from this window are additional info such as any secondary tables, the secondary tables' keys, what the related fields are for the tables, and what the relationship type is. We can also see the usage, which gives us all the forms and reports that use this table.

Most of this information can be found by returning to the **Table Descriptions** window and clicking the **Additional Info** button. This opens the **Additional Table Information** window as seen in the following image:

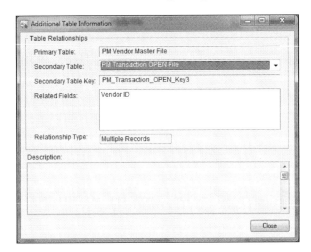

Also, from the **Table Descriptions** window, we can access the **Table Usage** window by clicking the **Usage** button on the **Table Descriptions** window:

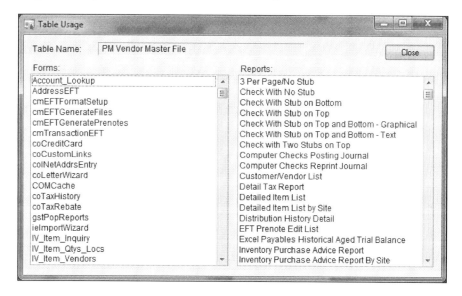

Typically, we use **Table Descriptions** when we know the name of the table needed and we need to find additional information about that table.

Fields

Field Descriptions gives us the ability to again select both the **Product** and the **Core** (Series), which contains the field we are looking for. Once both these fields are selected, we are provided with the field list. Similar to how we could look at field info in **Table Descriptions**, we can look at field info here as well.

To access Field Descriptions, follow these steps:

1. Open Microsoft Dynamics GP.
2. Click the Microsoft Dynamics GP Menu from the toolbar.
3. Select **Tools**.
4. Select **Resource Descriptions.**
5. Select **Fields**.
6. Select a Product and a Core.

For example, in the following image, **Microsoft Dynamics GP** has been selected as the **Product** and **System** has been selected as the **Core** value. This shows us a list of fields that meet this criteria and a list of the tables that contain the selected field:

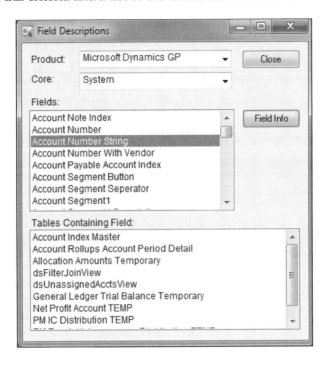

The one added benefit of using this window over others accessible via **Resource Descriptions** is that once we select the field we are looking for, a list will be provided showing us all the tables that contain that field.

This window is typically used when we are not sure exactly which table(s) a requested field resides in. We can use this window to tell us all the table display names that contain the selected field, then we can go to **Table Descriptions** and find the physical (SQL) table name based on results returned in the **Field Descriptions** window.

Windows

Windows Descriptions provides us with the ability to view the windows where the data is being recorded or viewed. As with the other **Resource Description** windows, we select the **Product** and **Series**. Once we locate the window we are looking for, Purchase Order Entry for example, we will be provided a list of both the fields on that window and the tables used by the window. We can also use the **Form** name in this window to find the related fields and tables.

To access **Window Descriptions**, follow these steps:

1. Open Microsoft Dynamics GP.
2. Click the Microsoft Dynamics GP Menu from the toolbar.
3. Select **Tools**.
4. Select **Resource Descriptions**.
5. Select **Windows**.
6. Select a **Product**, **Series**, and **View By** from their dropdown lists.

As the following image shows, selecting **Microsoft Dynamics GP** as the **Product**, **Purchasing** as the **Series**, and **by Window Display Name** as the **View By** option presents us with a list of all windows available in this unique combination:

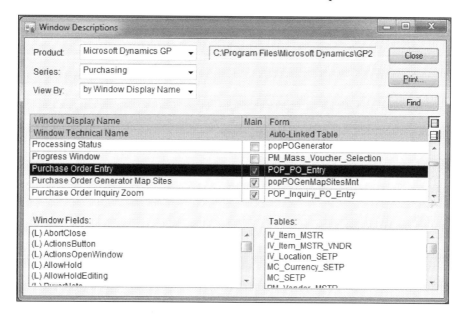

We typically use **Window Descriptions** when we know where the requested information is being entered or displayed in Dynamics GP, but we are unsure of the field name(s) or the table name(s) used to store said data. As with **Field Descriptions**, once we have a list of possibilities, we can cross reference to **Table Descriptions**.

This window is a bit constrained in size, and when dealing with a **Product** and **Series** with numerous tables, it can often be time-consuming to scroll through the list to find the right window. Don't neglect the **Find** button in the upper-right hand corner of this window. After selecting this button to open the **Find** window, we can type in the **Display Name** we are looking for and the window will auto-focus on this row in the scrolling window. Remember, the **Display Name** corresponds to the name of the window as it appears in the menu bar attached at the top of the window in GP. Of course, this requires knowing and selecting the **Product** and **Series** to which the window actually belongs prior to opening the **Find** window.

Table Import

Another very useful resource for finding the data that we need to begin writing our reports is the Table Import utility. From any window in Dynamics GP, we can open the table import utility and be provided with all the friendly table display names that are used by this window. For example, opening the **Table Import** window from the Sales Transaction Entry window yields the following information:

To access the Table Import from any window, follow these steps:

1. Open Microsoft Dynamics GP.
2. Open the Dynamics GP Window you are looking for.
3. Select **Tools**.
4. Select **Integrate**.
5. Select **Table Import**.

Once we know which table we want to go find our data in, we can again cross reference the Table Resource descriptions to find the physical SQL table name. This utility is very useful if the user tells you that they need a report that includes information they are entering on a particular screen.

Accessing data at the table level using SQL Management Studio

Once we have identified our physical table name, we can begin to use SQL Management Studio to view the data in the table. To accomplish this, we can write simple select statements to view the data. This can be very useful, as it allows us to see actual data in the underlying table. So, if a user tells us they need information they are entering in Sales User defined fields, we can view that data directly in the table to be sure we are capturing the requested data. A helpful tip for this is to open the **Sales User-Defined Fields Entry** window in Dynamics GP for a specific document number. Then, in SQL Management Studio, we can select the record from the table (in this case, the SOP10106 table) that equals the same document number we are looking at in the screen. This allows us to ensure we are looking at the correct data.

> One thing to keep in mind if we are working on a production database or even a test database with large amounts of data is that we can use commands such as NOLOCK, TOP 1, TOP 10, etc. to keep us from putting inadvertent locks on the table and to limit the amount of data returned by our queries. We don't necessarily need to select all records from a Sales Transaction table to see the data in that table and begin writing our report. It is much more efficient to use small selections of data at this point in our data gathering.

A sample of these TSQL statements can be seen in the following image:

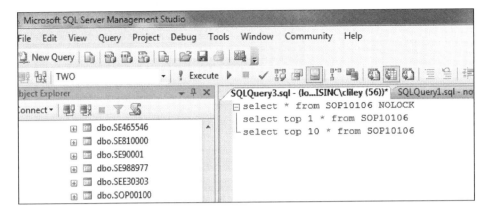

In SQL Management Studio, there is another very useful command that we have at our disposal. This command is called SP help and is very easy to use. We simply open a new query window and type in `sp_help` and our table name (`sp_help SOP10100`). This will return information such as the owner of the table and the created data, along with all of the columns in the table, their names, types, whether they are computed, their length, and if they are nullable amongst other things. We will also be provided with the indexes on the table. All of this information can be helpful to us when we begin writing our reports.

Locating Dynamics GP data with additional tools

Earlier in this chapter, we discussed a logical way for finding data for our report by starting at the database level and working our way down to the field level within the SQL database tables. While this approach utilized the GP naming and numbering convention, as well as the Resource Descriptions and Table Import tools within Dynamics GP, several other tools exist outside of the standard GP application that can help us better understand where our data might be located.

Dynamics GP 2010 Software Development Kit

Another useful tool for report writers and developers to use when trying to determine which tables should be used in building a report is the Software Development Kit or SDK, for short. Unlike the Resource Description windows, this tool resides outside of Dynamics GP and requires a separate download, meaning that you don't need a workstation installation of Dynamics GP to use this tool.

Downloading the Software Development Kit

New releases of the SDK are timed to coincide with new releases of the Dynamics GP application. The 2010 version of the SDK was released around the same time as Dynamics GP 2010. Microsoft Partners and customers can find the download under the Product Releases section of PartnerSource and CustomerSource, respectively. Additionally, the SDK can be installed from the original Dynamics GP 2010 CD software.

On PartnerSource, however, several SDKs exist, many of which contain information related to additional products and tools that can be integrated with the core Dynamics GP application. For example, users can find SDKs for Business Portal 5.0 for GP 2010 as well as for eConnect for GP 2010 on the same Product Releases page. Our focus will be on the SDK designed for the core application, which is labeled on the Product Release page as the "Software Development Kit (SDK) for Microsoft Dynamics GP 2010".

After downloading the file, extract the contents and run the executable to begin the SDK installation. Accepting defaults will install the program so that it can be opened from the Microsoft Dynamics folder under the Start menu.

Using the Software Development Kit

The Software Development Kit (SDK) is broken up into several sections containing information related to customizing Dynamics GP 2010 and working with the various database objects that exist in each company's SQL database. Among these sections, we will find the following:

- Table Integration, Database Diagrams: This section provides diagrams of tables related to the selected module. While information about specific fields is not found in this diagram, this documentation can be helpful in displaying a list of tables related to a specific module.

- Table Integration, Design Documents, and Transaction Flows: Documents in this section describe how data flows from one table to the next as transactions are conducted in GP.

- Additional Products: Additional modules, such as Manufacturing and Project Accounting, are not included with the information described in the preceding sections. Check this section to find documentation describing the tables and fields related to these modules.

We can use the SDK when we want to get a better understanding of how data flows through the various tables. Data in GP flows through many SQL tables as transactions are conducted in the overlying GP application. Often, we are asked to develop reports that capture data at a certain point in the transactional process, and we can use the SDK to help us determine where to locate this data.

Support Debugging Tool

The Support Debugging Tool is another valuable tool to have in our toolbox as we seek out our data in GP and its accompanying SQL databases. The Support Debugging Tool is a relatively new tool in the world of Dynamics GP, and as such, it's still gaining traction among users as a go-to tool for troubleshooting of any kind. Although the Support Debugging tool offers a wide range of functionality, not all of it is useful in terms of developing and writing reports. Nonetheless, we can use several components of the Support Debugging Tool during the report writing process.

Downloading the Support Debugging Tool

Although it existed for previous versions, the Support Debugging Tool was updated in May 2010 to coincide with the new release of Dynamics GP 2010. By the end of the year, Build 14, including some new and improved features, was released. This tool, primarily developed by David Musgrave of the Microsoft Dynamics GP Asia Pacific Support team, is a free tool, but it can only be downloaded by Microsoft Partners via PartnerSource.

For a list of resources and links related to the Support Debugging Tool, check out the "Support Debugging Tool Portal" at the following link: `http://blogs.msdn.com/b/developingfordynamicsgp/archive/2009/08/07/support-debugging-tool.aspx`.

After downloading the tool, the install process requires users to add a chunk (`.cnk`) file to the Dynamics GP root directory, launching Dynamics GP, and selecting to include the new code when prompted. Upon install, the tool is accessible from the GP application via the Tools menu.

Using the Support Debugging Tool

The primary Support Debugging Tool component that we will explore is the **Resource Information** window. This can be accessed from Support Debugging Tool by selecting **Options | Resource Information** from the navigation menus. This functionality is an extended version of the **Resource Descriptions** window that we covered earlier in this chapter.

Like the **Resource Descriptions** window, this tool provides insight into display, technical, and physical names for all windows, tables, and fields in the Dynamics GP application. Unlike the **Resource Descriptions** window, however, this tool combines three windows (**Window Descriptions**, **Table Descriptions**, and **Field Descriptions**) into one! Additionally, we can come to the **Resource Information** window with limited information, and the Support Debugging Tool will fill in the rest for us!

Let's use an example to consider one way in which this tool can be used to find our data.

Suppose we want to include the **Text Field 1** field from the **Sales User-Defined Fields Entry** window (**Transactions | Sales | Sales Transaction Entry | User-Defined button**) in our report:

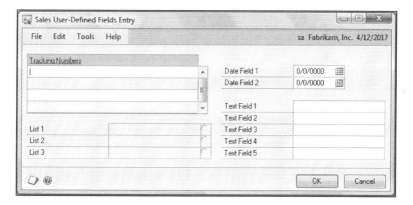

From the Support Debugging tool, we can open the **Resource Information** window and select **Forms, Windows & Fields** in the **Resource Type** drop down. Near the bottom of the window, we can type the **Display Name** of the window we want to know more about; in this case, we enter **Sales User-Defined Fields Entry** and tab off of the field:

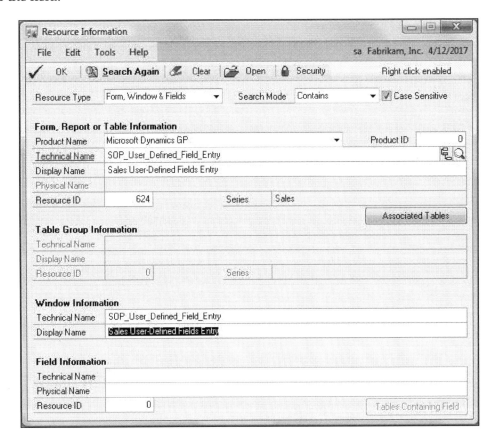

Remember, the display name is the name as it appears at the top of the window in GP.

The **Associated Tables** button becomes available, and the Support Debugging Tool auto-populates the Technical and Display names for this form in the **Form, Report or Table Information**. Selecting the **Associated Tables** button opens a window displaying information about SQL tables containing data used by this window. This is similar to using the Table Import trick that we discussed earlier in this chapter.

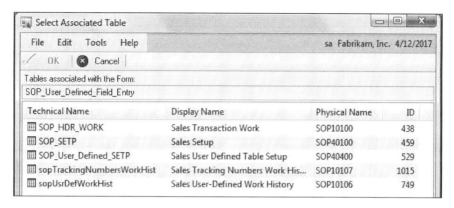

Back on the **Resource Information** screen, with the technical and display name information displayed, we can select the **Lookup** button beside the **Technical Name** field to open the **Resource Explorer** for this form. This allows us to select the **Main** form, and shows us a list of all of the fields in this window. We can scroll through this list until we find the field that corresponds to the one we are looking for. In this case, the name does not exactly match what appears in the window in GP, but **User Defined Prompt 1** is close enough to the **User Defined Entry** window and the **Text Field 1** that we know we have found the right field.

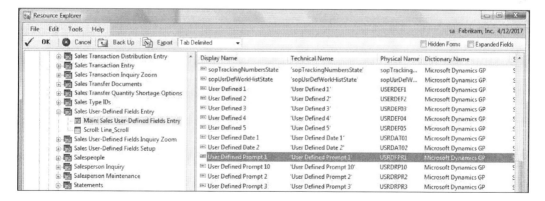

Double-clicking the line containing our field causes the **Resource Information** window to appear again, this time with the **Field Information** fields populated. Additionally, we notice that the button for **Tables Containing Field** at the bottom right-hand corner of this window can be selected. Selecting this button shows us a list of SQL database tables that contain a field called **USERDEF1**:

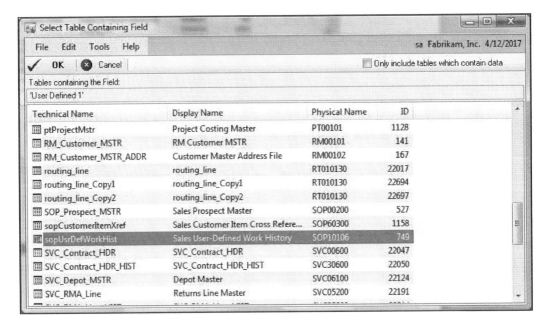

Of course, numerous tables contain a field as generically named as **USERDEF1**, but we can easily scroll through this list and determine that the table that we are probably looking for is the Sales-User Defined Work History table, or SOP10106.

By using the Support Debugging Tool, we can significantly reduce the amount of time spent searching for our data. Because it allows us to begin with limited amounts of data, it is a great tool to use as we initially set out on our quest for data. If you haven't tried out the Support Debugging Tool yet, what are you waiting for? Check with your Microsoft Partner for more information!

Summary

In this chapter, we discussed the various challenges of developing reports. Once those challenges have been considered, the next step is finding our data. Even though some reporting tools do not require understanding the SQL database structure of GP company databases, we can still use our knowledge of GP data structures to build better reports.

To that end, we've used this chapter to explore some of the conventions surrounding how GP data is stored. We began at the database level by exploring the differences between the DYNAMICS database and the various company databases. Then, we moved on to understanding the naming and numbering convention for tables found within these databases. At first glance, the numbering convention used for GP tables can be confusing, but by this point, we are familiar with some general naming conventions that can help us in most cases.

Finally, we looked at some tools that can be used for finding this data. Some tools, such as Table Resources, Table Import, and SQL stored procedures can be used with any standard install of GP. Other tools, such as the SDK for Dynamics GP 2010 and the Support Debugging Tool can also be used with GP data, but they require separate installs.

In the next chapter, we'll begin exploring and using our first reporting tool! SmartList is a tool that comes with the standard install of Dynamics GP. We'll also look at additional add-ons SmartList Builder and Excel Reports Builder. These tools will allow us to extend the concept of SmartLists and create or customize our own SmartLists and Excel Reports.

3

Working with the Builders: SmartList and Excel Reports

In the last chapter, we explored some of the many methods available to us for locating our data in the ERP system. We started with some background on how the data is stored and then we moved on to some additional tools that can help us understand how the data flows and ends up in the tables that it does.

Now, it is finally time to begin writing our new reports. There are many reporting tools available to us in Dynamics GP 2010, and in this chapter, we will be introducing four of the tools that we consider beginner reporting tools:

- **Default SmartLists**: These SmartLists are included out-of-the box along with every install of Dynamics GP
- **Excel Reports**: These reports, which mirror the default SmartLists, must be deployed before they can be used
- **SmartList Builder**: This tool allows users to extend the functionality of the default SmartLists
- **Excel Report Builder**: This tool, like the SmartList Builder, allows users to extend the functionality of SmartLists and Excel Reports in an Excel format

Satisfying basic reporting needs with canned SmartLists

Before we begin using SmartList to create simple reports, it is important to understand what SmartList is. SmartList is an out-of-the-box module within Dynamics GP that lets developers, consultants, or endusers create lists of data within Dynamics GP. As we will see, it is a very easy-to-use tool.

Structure of SmartList

SmartList is laid out in a fairly simple fashion. It is made up of SmartList Objects and SmartLists organized by Series. Upon opening SmartList and expanding one of the Series folders on the first level, all of the folders we see grouped under this level are referred to as SmartList Objects. We can think of them as a container for similar SmartLists. For instance, theSmartList Object called Account Transactions contains a series of SmartLists related to transactions posted to the General Ledger. Once we expand one of these objects, we will see any number of SmartList Favorites that were either installed with Dynamics GP or were created by users. SmartList Favorites allow us to make minor modifications to a default SmartList and then save our changes so we can simply come back in SmartList at any time and retrieve a refreshed list of the data without having to set up all our columns and search criteria again.

The easiest way to access the SmartList is to click the Microsoft Dynamics GP menu and choose **SmartList**, as seen in the following screenshot:

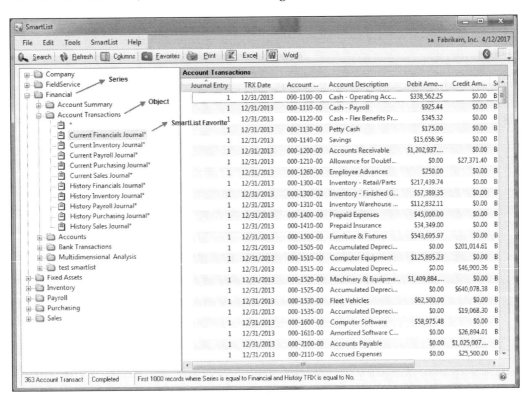

Across the top of the SmartList window are the following buttons that allow us to customize and/or create SmartListFavorites:

- **Search**: This button allows up to four search criteria for our lists.

- **Refresh**: This button forces a refresh of our list. This is useful if we know the data has changed since we saved or opened the SmartList.

- **Columns**: This button allows for changing the columns being shown on the list, the order the columns are in, how the lists are sorted and allows us to add any field that is already built into the object.

- **Favorites**: This button allows us to save our current list as a favorite. There are four types of favourites: System, Company, User Class, & User ID.

  - ° **System**: Saves the SmartList so any user has access to the Favorite from any company database

  - ° **Company**: Saves the SmartList in the current company database only. All users can access it

  - ° **User Class**: Saves the SmartList so any user in the same user class as current user that created the SmartList can access it

  - ° **User ID**: Saves the SmartList so only the user that created it can access it

- **Print**: This button allows for printing the list out to the screen or printer, or exporting it in text, comma delimited, tab delimited, HTML or XML data file formats.

- **Excel**: This button allows for exporting the list directly to Microsoft Excel.

- **Word**: This button allows for exporting the list directly to Microsoft Word in a table format.

Basic SmartList tools

Now that we have a basic understanding of the structure of SmartList, we can begin using some basic tools to build our SmartList report. The areas we will cover are:

- Narrowing our result list with search criteria

- Adding new columns

- Changing the number of records returned

- Modifying a `dex.ini` switch for faster export to Excel

Narrowing our result list with search criteria

Probably the most important concept of SmartList is the Search function. This is what allows us to narrow our result set to the exact data we are looking for. To use the search criteria, we simply click the **Search** button after selecting an existing Favorite or the default SmartList represented by an asterisk (*). Let's use the **Past Due Payables** Favorite to see how search criteria are utilized:

1. Open SmartList by clicking the **Microsoft Dynamics GP Menu**.

2. Select **SmartList**.

3. Expand the **Purchasing** folder.

4. Expand the **Payables Transactions** object.

5. Click the **Past Due Payables** SmartList.

6. Click the **Search** button from the toolbar.

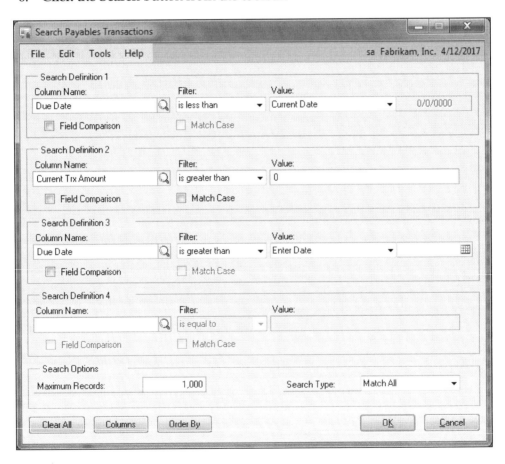

Here, we can see that the SmartList is set to return data where the **Due Date** is less than the **Current Date** and the **Current Transaction Amount greater than 0**. We also notice that the **Search Type** field at the bottom is set to **Match All**. This means that for the data to be returned, all of our search criteria must match. The other option is **Match1 or More**. This means one or more of the search criteria must match for data to be returned. We must be sure we know what this type means, as choosing one versus the other can give us an entirely different set of data.

Let's say that we want to add one more search criteria to our SmartList. We can easily accomplish this by following these steps:

1. From our search window, click the lookup magnifying glass on any of the four search definitions:

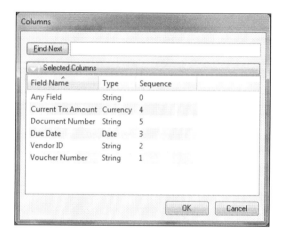

2. We are provided with the list of selected columns on the SmartList. Select a column or click the **Selected Columns** bar and choose **All Columns:**

3. We are now provided a list of the columns available in this object. This gives us the ability to filter our data on columns that we don't necessarily have on our SmartList. For example, if we included **Document Type** in our SmartList, but filtered on the type of **Invoice**, we would see the word "Invoice" on every line. This redundancy is unnecessary, so we can remove this column from our SmartList.

4. For this SmartList, let's select **Current Balance** as our third search definition with a filter type of **is greater than** and enter a value of **5,000**. This will give us all Past Due Payables where the vendors' current balance is over $5,000.

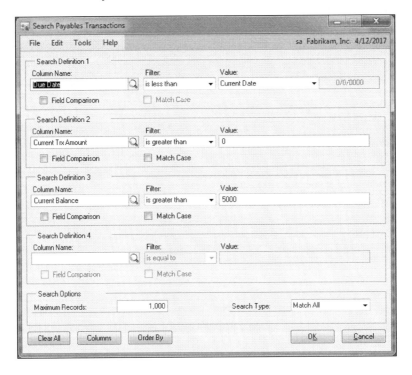

Adding new columns

Another important concept of SmartLists is adding columns. We can add any column to our SmartList that is available to us. These columns all come from the source of the object whether it is an out-of-the-box object that joins Dynamics GP tables or whether it is a custom object that we will discuss later when we explore SmartList Builder and Excel Report Builder. Looking back at our Past Due Payables SmartList, we can see the columns being utilized are **Voucher Number**, **Vendor ID**, **Due Date**, **Current Transaction Amount**, and **Document Number**. Let's look at how easy it would be to add a new column to this SmartList for the Vendor's 1099 Type and their current balance:

1. Open **SmartList** from the **Microsoft Dynamics GP Menu**.

2. Expand the **Purchasing** folder.

3. Expand the **Payables Transactions** object.

4. Click the **Past Due Payables** SmartList.

5. Click the **Columns** button from the toolbar to open the **Change Column Display** window:

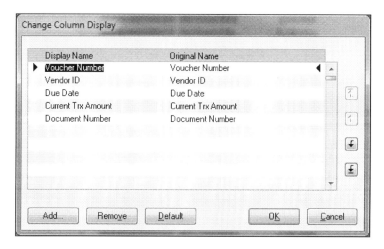

6. We are provided with a list of the columns selected for our SmartList.

7. Click the **Add** button:

8. As with adding search criteria, we are provided a list of all available columns in the object. We can select multiple columns simply by holding the *Ctrl* key as we click fields. Let's select **1099 Type** and **Current Balance**.

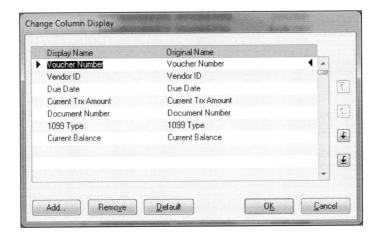

9. We now see our two new fields in our list. Before closing, we can reorder the fields with the **Move Column** buttons on the right, or we can remove unnecessary columns.

10. Click **OK** to return to the SmartList.

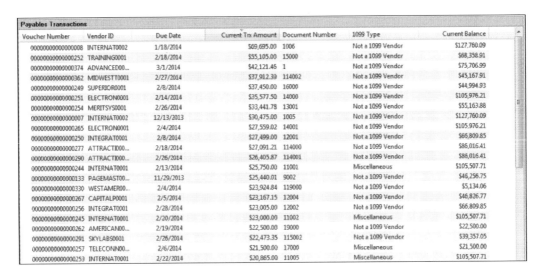

11. We now have our Past Due Payables SmartList showing us our new columns. From here we can **Print**, export to **Excel** or **Word**, and save this as a **Favorite**.

Changing the number of records returned

By default, the maximum records returned for a SmartList is set to 1,000. As mentioned, this can be changed on our search criteria window. Typically, it is a good idea to keep this setting small while building our SmartLists until we are sure we are returning the data we are actually looking for. Once we are sure of the data being returned, we can then increase the Maximum records on our SmartListFavorite, or we can adjust the Maximum Records for the object. A word of caution on this, it will make the value we set here, the default for ANY SmartList we create from that particular object. Let's look at how we can change this default value for multiple SmartLists at the same time:

1. Open the Microsoft Dynamics GP Menu.
2. Select **Tools**.
3. Select **System**.
4. Select **SmartList Options**.

From this window, we will select the **Category**, which corresponds to the SmartList object. We can then change the value in the **Maximum Records** field to increase (or decrease) the number of records allowed when viewing a default SmartList.

Achieving faster export to Excel with a simple dex. ini switch

One of the most well-known facts that any user, consultant, or report developer who has used SmartList to mine large sets of data and export those to Excel can tell us, is that the export process is extremely time consuming. The main reason for this is how Dexterity communicates with Excel. In short, because SmartList exports records row by row and sets each cell individually and each cell being written is done by a single Dexterity call for that particular cell, the export routine is very slow.

There is a solution for this. In the program files folder for Dynamics GP 2010, there is a configuration file called `dex.ini`. This file can control many settings in GP, but for the purposes of this book, we are focusing just on the switch that will greatly increase our Export to Excel performance.

To make this change, you can simply follow these steps:

1. Open Windows Explorer.
2. Browse to **Program Files | Microsoft Dynamics | GP2010 | Data**.
3. Double Click the `Dex.ini` file to open.
4. Add a line in the file with the following text:

   `SmartlistEnhancedExcelExport=TRUE`

5. Save and Close the `Dex.ini` file.

Essentially, what this switch does is instead of exporting row by row, the system will now batch the rows for export together. We will notice a slight delay when we click the export button as the system batches the data, but then it flies as it exports. Beware though, while usually rare, using this switch may cause a loss of formatting with some of the column values. But, for many, this is a small price to pay for increased SmartList exporting speed!

If we are using SmartList to design a report that reads thousands of records and then will be exported to Excel, this switch is almost a necessity.

Extending SmartList data to Excel by deploying Excel reports

As we have just seen, one of the common complaints about the default SmartList tool is that they take too long to export to Excel. This is especially true when viewing a transaction related SmartList, such as the default SmartList for Sales Transaction Line Items with no filter applied. Depending on our environment, this particular SmartList could have thousands, if not hundreds of thousands of records. When selecting to export this to Excel without using the dex.ini switch trick for faster exporting, this could take some time. Also, what happens once we get our data into Excel? What do we do the next day after new Sales Transactions have been added into GP? We have to run the SmartList and export to Excel all over again just to grab a few extra lines of data. Or, we could apply a filter to find only transactions with a certain date, but this procedure just opens the possibility of data falling through the cracks.

Fortunately, beginning with Microsoft Dynamics GP 10.0, Microsoft has provided the default SmartLists in pre-defined Excel formats. These Excel Reports are duplicates of the default SmartLists, with the one exception being that they are accessed directly from Microsoft Excel. Within the Excel document, an Office Data Connection (ODC) allows the user an instant connection to the data source. Refreshing data within the Excel Report then becomes a simple matter of selecting **Data | Refresh** from within Excel. No more waiting for thousands of lines to export to SmartList! These reports can be stored in a central file share location, allowing all users with access to that location to browse these reports, just as they would browse SmartList reports in GP.

In this section, we'll take a look at how these reports are deployed, how security to these reports can be controlled, and how to view and modify the deployed reports. Additional information about this process can be found in Chapter 32 of the GP 2010 System Setup guide.

Deploying Excel reports

Taking advantage of the Excel Reports functionality first requires that they be deployed to a shared location. This shared location can be a shared folder in a secure server location, or this shared location can be a SharePoint Server document library. Depending on the modules already installed in GP, the deployment process creates each Excel report and a corresponding data connection file for each report in the share location.

In the sample deployment to follow, we will address deploying the Excel reports to a shared network location. Prior to beginning the deployment process, create the folders and check the security permissions on that folder. It is helpful to have one folder dedicated to storing the reports (for example, "Reports") and another folder dedicated to storing the data connections (for example, "Data Connections"). At a minimum, the Windows user performing the install (note: NOT the GP user!) should have the ability to read and write against content in this folder. Allowing "Full Control" is preferred, at least for the administrator's Windows user account.

The deployment process is initiated from within GP 2010:

1. The Reporting Tools Setup window is accessed via **Microsoft Dynamics GP | Tools | Setup | System | Reporting Tools Setup**.

2. Click on the **Data Connections** tab.

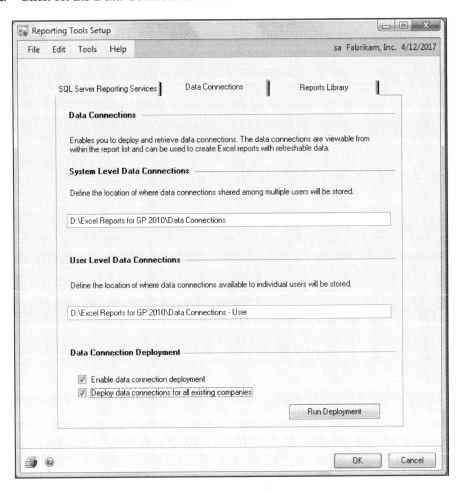

3. Data Connections must be deployed prior to deploying the actual reports. In the **System Level Data Connections**field, enter the path name of the shared folder location where the data connections will be stored. Although a mapped drive location can be listed here, it is recommended to use the Universal Naming Convention (UNC) format to identify the location (for example, `\\computer\Excel Reports for GP 2010\Data Connections`). Before tabbing off of this field, the system will check to ensure that a valid pathname has been entered.

4. In the **User Level Data Connections** field, enter the folder path that can be used should users decide to modify the system-wide data connections for personal use. In this field, a mapped drive location or UNC path can be listed here. The percentage symbol (%) can be used as a wild card in this path (for example, `\\servername\Documents and Settings\%\Data Connections`).

5. Under **Data Connection Deployment**, mark **Enable Data Connection Deployment**. This will enable the **Run Deployment** button at the bottom-right-hand corner of this window.

6. To complete the deployment of data connections for all companies, mark the **Deploy data connections for all existing companies**. Not marking this means the deployment process must be run individually for each company database.

7. Once all settings are identified, click **Run Deployment** to build the data connections in the specified directory. Data connections will only be deployed to the folder path listed for the **System-Level Data Connections** path.

8. When deployment is complete, select **Yes** to view the Data Connection Excel Report Deployment report. Review this report to see which data connections were installed and if any errors were encountered during the deployment process.

9. Assuming all data connections have been deployed successfully, return to the Reporting Tools Setup window (**Microsoft Dynamics GP | Tools | Setup | System | Reporting Tools Setup**). Select the **Reports Library** tab.

10. The process for deploying the actual reports is similar to deploying the data connections. In the **System Level Reports** field, enter the path name of the shared folder location where the Excel reports will be stored. Although a mapped drive location can be listed here, it is recommended to use the Universal Naming Convention (UNC) format to identify the location (for example, \\computer\Excel Reports for GP 2010\Reports). Before tabbing off of this field, the system will check to ensure that a valid pathname has been entered.

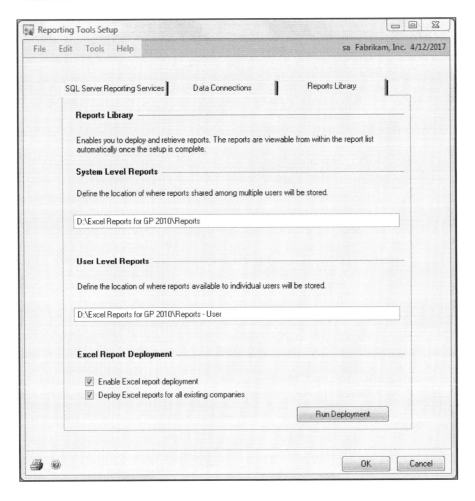

11. In the **User Level Reports** field, enter the folder path that can be used should users decide to modify the system-wide reports for personal use. In this field, a mapped drive location or UNC path can be listed here. The percentage symbol (%) can be used as a wild card in this path (for example, \\servername\Documents and Settings\%\Reports).

12. Under **Excel Report Deployment**, mark **Enable Excel report deployment**. This will enable the **Run Deployment** button at the bottom-right-hand corner of this window.

13 To complete the deployment of reports for all companies, mark the **Deploy Excel reports for all existing companies**. Not marking this means the deployment process must be run individually for each company database.

14. Once all settings are identified, click **Run Deployment** to build the Excel reports in the specified directory. Reports will only be deployed to the folder path listed for the **System-Level Reports** path.

15. When deployment is complete, select **Yes** to view the Data Connection Excel Report Deployment report. Review this report to see which reports were installed and if any errors were encountered during the deployment process.

Now that we have successfully installed the Excel reports and their data connections, let's take a look at how security is managed for these reports.

Maintaining security for Excel reports

Unlike maintaining security to GP modules and windows via GP user logins, security for Excel reports is maintained strictly through Windows Active Directory User accounts. Security must be controlled in two places:

- Security permissions for shared network folder
- Security permissions for company databases

Shared network folder permissions

As we discussed earlier, a shared network folders must be set up so that reports and data connections can be deployed to those folders. To grant users access to these folders, first right-click the folder in Windows Explorer and select **Properties**. This opens the folder properties window from which security privileges to the contents of the folder can be granted or revoked. At a minimum, users should be granted the ability to read and write the contents of the folder.

Once users are granted permission to a particular folder, they can browse to the folder containing the deployed reports and see each of the reports that have been deployed. Double-clicking the report will open the report in Excel. However, if the Windows user for the user opening the report has not also been granted security permissions at the database level, then a warning message will appear, letting the user know that he or she does not have database level permissions.

Although a user with folder access can open the Excel reports, if he or she does not have the appropriate database permissions required to view the content of that report, then the user will not be able to refresh the report.

Database level permissions

As part of the Excel Reports deployment, new database roles are created in each company database for which reports are deployed. The database roles, all of which begin with an `rpt_` prefix, govern user access to database objects such as views, tables, and stored procedures that are necessary for viewing the data in the Excel Reports.

The roles are named in such a way that it becomes fairly intuitive for someone setting up security to understand which roles allow access to which reports. For example, in order for a user to access data for the Payroll-related Excel Reports, the Windows User account for that user must be assigned to the **rpt_payroll** role.

For a more detailed list of which role allows access to a particular report, check Knowledge Base article #949524 on Customer Source or Partner Source. This is a protected Microsoft website, so you will need either a customer or partner login.

Also, note that a security role called **rpt_power user** is created by the install. This role has been made a role member of every other role, meaning any users assigned to the **rpt_power user** database role will have access to all database content required to view the Excel Reports data.

Granting user access to these roles requires creating a Windows logon for the user or group in SQL Management Studio and then adding that user or group to the appropriate `rpt_` roles. In the case that multiple users will be using the Excel Reports, we recommend setting up a Windows Active Directory Group to which individual users can be added. The security privileges described below can then be granted at the group level, making for a much less time-consuming process!

To grant database role access to a user or group, follow these steps:

1. Open SQL Management Studio.
2. Connect to the GP server.
3. Expand the **Security** node.
4. Right-click the **Logins** folder and select **Properties** to open the **Login – New** window.

5. Create a new Windows login for the user or group by selecting the **Windows Authentication** option and searching for that user or group in the directory.

6. Once all fields in the **General** tab have been completed, select the **User Mapping** tab to map this user to the various GP-related databases.

7. Click the **Map** checkbox next to the database to which the user should have access.

8. With a company database selected, in the **Database role membership** pane at the bottom of the window, select the database role to which the user or group should be assigned (remember, the reporting roles are all preceded by `rpt_`).

9. Map the user to additional company databases and reporting roles, as needed. Several Excel Reports use SQL views that refer to tables in the DYNAMICS database, so don't forget to map users and groups to reporting roles in this database, too!

Assuming these users also have the appropriate permissions on the folders containing these Excel Reports, then they should now be ready to access and use the Excel Reports!

Accessing and using Excel Reports

Deployed reports can be accessed in one of two ways: through Windows Explorer or through GP 2010. Security must be set appropriately before reports can be opened or refreshed.

Connecting to Excel Reports via Windows Explorer

To connect via Windows Explorer, users can browse to the appropriate share folder identified during the deployment in the **System Level Reports** field. Under this folder, another set of folders has been created by the install; these folders correspond to the company databases for which reports and data connections were deployed. If more than one company database was included in the deployment, then a separate folder will exist for each company database.

Underneath each company database folder, another layer of folders has also been created. These folders correspond to different modules in GP such as Financials, Purchasing, Project, and so on. They are created depending on which modules are installed in the selected GP company database. Users will also notice that the list of folders at this level corresponds to the same folder grouping list that exists when opening the SmartList from GP. This folder structure is further illustrated in the following images:

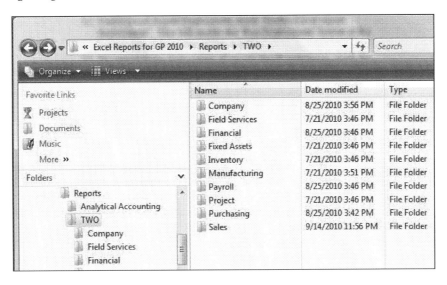

Clicking into each folder will reveal a series of Excel documents, each corresponding to one of the default SmartLists that can be found in GP. Even the content of the Excel documents, such as columns and filters, mirror the content of the similarly named SmartList from GP. These Excel Reports provide users with advantages over the default SmartList in that the data is already stored in Excel, and it can be refreshed instantaneously.

If a user accesses a report on the shared, system level directory, makes changes to that report, and then saves it in the same location, those saved changes will be accessible to all other users who access that same report. If a user wants to save that changed report so that only he or she can see the changes, then the report should be saved to the path defined in the **User Level Reports** field of the deployment.

Note that reports are only deployed to the **System Level Reports** path during the initial deployment. Nothing is actually deployed to the **User Level Reports** path. Instead, the User Level Reports Path is designed to be a repository for users who wish to save the default reports without impacting the original report.

These reports are deployed in Microsoft Excel 2007 format (`*.xlsx`), so users who are still on Microsoft Excel 2003 will need to install the Microsoft Office Compatibility Pack for Word, Excel, and PowerPoint 2007 file formats.

Connecting to Excel Reports via GP 2010

Users can also view these reports from directly within GP. After Excel Reports have been deployed, users can select **Excel Reports** from the list of available Report Lists. This will open up the Excel Reports list detailing each report and data connection to which the Windows User account has access. Selecting to open a report will open the System Level report in Excel format, just as would happen if the user browsed out to that report via the Windows Explorer.

Creating and publishing new SmartLists by using SmartList Builder

Earlier in this chapter, we discussed modifying the canned SmartLists that are included with any base install of GP. As wonderful and helpful as these default SmartLists can be, there comes a time in every GP user's life that no SmartList exists to satisfy a particular reporting need. Perhaps an existing SmartList provides some of the data, but it's missing a join to a particular table that provides critical information that is required by an end user. In times like these, where the ease-of-access and easy-to-use functionality of SmartList is still desired, developers and consultants can use SmartList Builder to extend the basic reporting functionality offered by the canned SmartLists.

The beauty of SmartList Builder is that it allows us to replicate the same functionality of regular SmartLists while connecting to data sources beyond just the standard Microsoft Dynamics GP tables. In fact, developers and consultants have the ability to connect to one of four data source objects when developing a new SmartList in the Builder:

- Microsoft Dynamics GP tables: includes tables defined in the Microsoft Dynamics GP and third-party dictionaries
- Microsoft SQL Server tables: includes tables found outside of the Dynamics GP dictionaries as well as views written against tables inside and outside the GP dictionaries
- Data Connections: includes SQL views for common fields and tables found in Dynamics GP
- Extender Resources: includes Extender objects that have already been defined via Extender functionality

When a standard, out-of-the-box SmartList Object doesn't do the trick, we can create our own SmartList Object using Dynamics GP tables or by writing a SQL view that serves as the underlying data source! The possibilities become limitless once SmartList Builder is included in our reporting toolbox.

Understanding the SmartList Builder window

SmartList Builder is accessed directly from GP:

1. Open the Microsoft Dynamics GP Menu.
2. Select **Tools**.
3. Select **SmartList Builder**.
4. Select **SmartList Builder** for a second time.

This opens the SmartList Builder window. Across the top of the Builder, we see the following buttons:

- **Save**: Allows the user to save the current SmartList Object.
- **Clear**: Clears the contents of the SmartList Builder, allowing the user to begin creating a new SmartList Object.
- **Delete**: Deletes the selected SmartList Object.
- **GoTo**: Allows the user to set up a GoTo action that can be used to execute a particular action when selecting a record in the SmartList. For example, a GoTo can be set up to open the **Customer Maintenance** window for a customer identified in the selected SmartList record.

- **Restrictions**: Allows users to set up default restrictions on a SmartList Object so these restrictions do not have to be entered as filters in the resulting SmartList. For example, a restriction can be placed on a new SmartList Object so that only transactions after a certain date will be displayed.

- **Calculated Fields**: Allows users to add calculated columns to the new SmartList that perform mathematical operations using one or more fields found in the underlying source data for the SmartList.

- **Options**: Several different options exist in this window, including one option to create a Summary SmartList that allows users to group records by certain criteria and perform other mathematical operations that can summarize large volumes of data. Additionally, from this window, users can select the **MulticompanySmartList** checkbox to combine data from multiple company databases.

Most of the buttons at the top of the SmartList Builder window are used to access unique SmartList Builder functions; however, the actual work of creating SmartLists occurs in the fields and panes below these buttons. We will explore the use of these fields and panes in the next section as we create a sample SmartList.

Creating a new SmartList via SmartList Builder

With the advent of Dynamics GP 2010, GP users have even more control over emailing statements to customers. In fact, when setting up customer-related information, email addresses can be assigned to each address setup for that customer via the Internet Addresses window (**Cards | Sales | Customer | Internet Addresses** button). In this window, users can identify the default e-mail address that will appear when accessing the **Receivables E-Mail Detail Entry** windows for transactions using this customer and address.

Unfortunately, however, the email address information entered in these fields cannot be accessed via any of the default Customer SmartLists. Instead, if the Accounts Receivable coordinator wants an easy way to look-up which email address will default for a given customer-address combination, he or she must look through each individual customer card. A new SmartList must be created to allow this information to be viewable in SmartList.

First, we must use the data-seeking skills that we learned in the last chapter to find out what Microsoft Dynamics GP tables contain the basic customer information and the email addresses we need. In GP terms, the data we are seeking can be found in the **Customer Maintenance**, **Customer Address Maintenance**, and **Internet Addresses** windows. Before continuing on through the rest of this exercise, try and see if you can find the Display Name for the Microsoft Dynamics GP tables that contain the information found in these windows.

If you attempted this exercise, hopefully by now you've discovered that the data we need is found in three tables (note: the table display name is listed with the physical name included in parentheses):

- RM Customer MSTR (RM00101): This table is located in the Sales series and contains one record for each individual customer record in GP 2010.

- Customer Master Address File (RM00102): This table is located in the Sales series and contains one record for each individual customer-address combination that exists in GP 2010.

- Internet Addresses (SY01200): This table is located in the Company series and contains the Internet address records for a variety of different record types such as Items, Customers, Vendors, and more. Email addresses entered in the **Internet Addresses** window for customers are stored in this table with a Master Type of "CUS".

Now that we've identified the tables we are going to use, let's use them to create a new SmartList in the SmartList builder:

1. Open the Microsoft Dynamics GP Menu.

2. Select **Tools**.

3. Select **SmartList Builder**.

4. Select **SmartList Builder** for a second time.

5. In the **SmartList ID** field, enter **CUST_EMAIL** as the identifier for this SmartList.

6. In the **SmartList Name** field, enter **Customer Statement Email Addresses** as the name for this SmartList. This name will appear in the left-hand pane of the SmartList window and will appear in the menu bar above the SmartList as it is being browsed.

7. In the **Item Name** field, enter **Customer Statement Email Addresses**. The Item Name can be the same as the SmartList Name and is what will appear in the lower left-hand corner of the SmartList window where the number of records found in the SmartList is displayed.

8. Enter **Microsoft Dynamics GP** as the **Product** and **Sales** as the **Series** for this SmartList. These options will determine what folder grouping the SmartList will fall under. In this case, our SmartList will be grouped under the Sales folder in the SmartList pane. At this point, your SmartList header should appear as follows:

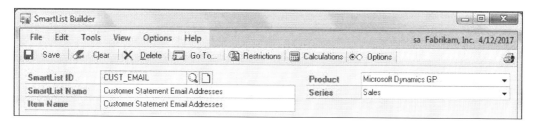

9. On the left-hand side of the **SmartList Builder** window, select the **Add Table** button. This button looks like a plus sign and appears at the top of the left-most pane in this window. Select **Microsoft Dynamics GP Table** to open the **Add Table** window.

10. In the **Add Table** window, select **Microsoft Dynamics GP** as the **Product**, **Sales** as the **Series**, and **RM Customer Master** as the **Table**.

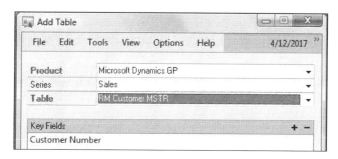

11. We are then given the option to select key fields for this table. Key fields represent a unique combination of values for each record. In this table, each record contains a unique Customer Number, so we will use this as the key field. Notice that SmartList Builder has already listed the key field in the**Key Fields** pane, so we can select the **Save** button to return to the main SmartList Builder window.

12. In this window, we see our newly added table, along with a list of columns from the table that can be included in our SmartList.

13. Leaving a checkbox checked in the **Display** column means that after the SmartList is created, these columns will be available for user selection by clicking **Columns | Add** from the SmartList window. We will leave all checkboxes checked.

14. Checked boxes in the **Default** column represent fields that will appear in the SmartList by default. Check the Default box for the **Customer Number** and **Customer Name** columns.

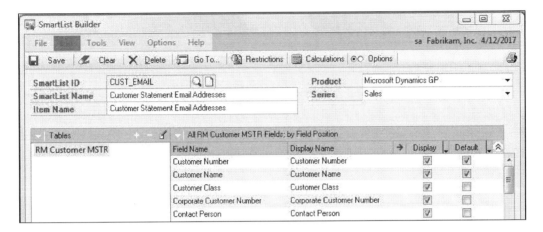

15. Now, we need to add an additional table to the first table. Click the **Add Table** button again and select to add a **Microsoft Dynamics GP Table**.

16. This time, we will add the Customer Master Address File table. Select **Microsoft Dynamics GP** as the **Product**, **Sales** as the **Series**, and **Customer Master Address File** as the **Table**.

17. Because we are adding a new table to the first one, we have to tell SmartList Builder how to link the two tables. Because we want all customers from the first table to display in the SmartList, regardless of whether or not they have been assigned an address, we will select **Left Outer** as the **Link Method**.

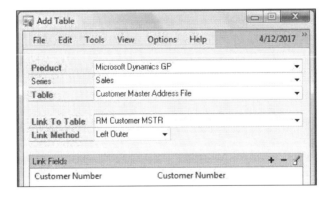

18. SmartList Builder identifies common fields between the two tables, and, in this case, Customer Number is listed in the **Link Fields** pane. Click Save to return to the SmartList Builder window.

19. With Customer Master Address File selected in the left-hand pane, select to include the Address Code field as a **Default** value in this SmartList.

20. Now, let's add our final table to this SmartList. Again, with Customer Master Address File selected in the left-hand pane, click the **Add Table** button.

21. This time, we are going to add the Internet Addresses table and link it to the Customer Master Address File table. To do this, we can select **Microsoft Dynamics GP** as the **Product**, **Company** as the **Series**, and **Internet Addresses** as the **Table.**

22. Because e-mail addresses are stored for each customer-address relationship, we need to link the Internet Addresses table to a table with similar fields. In the **Link to Table** drop-down, select the "Customer Master Address File" table. Again, because we want all customer-address combinations to appear in our SmartList, we select "Left Outer" as our **Link Method**. Note that, if we only wanted customer-address combinations that contain a value in the e-mail address fields to display in our SmartList, we would use the "Equals" option for **Link Method**. This decision often requires consideration of the end-user's needs and can be changed at a later time, if necessary.

23. Now we need to link our two tables together. The connection between Internet Addresses and Customer Master Address File is a bit trickier than the previous connection between two tables. SmartList Builder is intelligent enough to notice that Address Code is a commonly linked field between the two tables, but it fails to make a similar connection for the customer number. If we were to leave Address Code as the only link, our report would not be effective, as numerous customers may share similarly named address codes. To link the Customer Number, we have to join the Customer Number field from the Customer Master Address File to the Master ID column in the Internet Addresses table. To add this link, click the **Add Link** button (plus sign next to **Link Fields**) to open the **Add Link window** and make the selections that we've just identified.

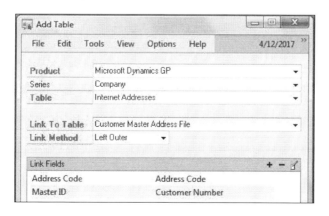

24. Click **Save** twice to return to the SmartList Builder window.

25. With Internet Addresses selected in the left-hand pane, select to include the **Email To Address** field as a **Default** value in this SmartList.

26. We are now ready to use our SmartList! **Save** the SmartList and close the SmartList Builder window.

27. Open the regular SmartList window by clicking **Microsoft Dynamics GP | SmartList.**

28. Any time that changes are made via SmartList Builder, a message will appear the next time the standard SmartList window is opened:

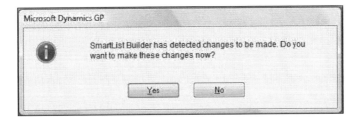

29. Click **Yes** to allow SmartList Builder to apply the new changes to the existing SmartList.

30. Once SmartList is open, expand the **Sales** folder, and then expand the **Customer Statement Email Addresses** folder to see the newly created SmartList. Congratulations, you've created your first SmartList using SmartListBuilder!

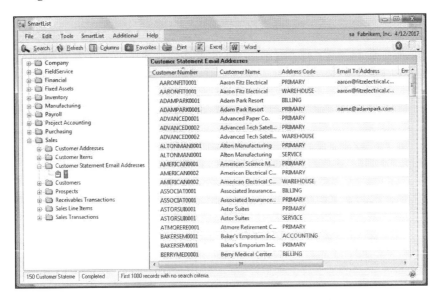

Creating and publishing new Excel Report formats using Excel Report Builder

As with SmartList Builder, Excel Report Builder is another powerful tool in our reporting toolbox. Though many of the same concepts that exist for SmartList Builder hold true for Excel Report Builder, we are not building a new SmartList Object that will be accessed through SmartList. Instead, as we discussed earlier in the chapter with the deployment of Excel Reports, we are creating our own Excel Reports, Office Data Connections, or both.

The advantage this tool gives us is that we can designate that our resulting report will either be a simple list of data or it will be a Pivot table in Excel. It basically takes out the step of our users needing to first extract the list of data, and then create the Pivot Table. Essentially, the user will open the resulting Excel file and be provided the fields they can select in their Pivot Table. They will not be provided with the list of raw data, but instead will select their fields in the Pivot Table, the data will refresh and be saved so that next time the spreadsheet is opened it will be refreshed with the latest data without the Excel Report needing to be republished each and every time. And if we are using SharePoint, we can also publish the Excel Reports and/or Office Data Connections directly to our SharePoint site.

Also, in common with SmartList Builder, Excel Report Builder allows us to replicate the same functionality of regular SmartLists while connecting to data sources beyond just the standard Microsoft Dynamics GP tables. As with SmartList Builder, Excel Reports Builder can connect to several data source objects; among those are Microsoft Dynamics GP tables, SQL Server tables, Data Connections, and Extender Resources. Refer to our discussion in the SmartList Builder section for a description of each of these data sources.

When a standard, out-of-the-box Excel Report doesn't do the trick or doesn't even exist, we can create our own refreshable Excel Report using Dynamics GP tables or writing a SQL view that serves as the underlying data source! The possibilities become limitless with the Builder!

Understanding the Excel Reports Builder window

Excel Report Builder is accessed directly from GP:

1. Open the Microsoft Dynamics GP Menu.
2. Select **Tools**.
3. Select **SmartList Builder**.
4. Select **Excel Report Builder**.
5. Select **Excel Report Builder** for a second time.

This opens the Excel Report Builder window. Across the top of the Builder, we see several buttons. Several of these buttons are similar to the ones found in the SmartList Builder window that we discussed earlier in this chapter. Several of these buttons, however, offer functionality specific to Excel Reports Builder only:

- **Options**: Several different options exist in this window, including one option to **Create a Summary Page** that allows users to group records by certain criteria and perform other mathematical operations that can summarize large volumes of data. Additionally, from this window, users can select the **Multicompanyreport** checkbox to combine data from multiple company databases, choose to **Display totals at the end of each list**, or **to consolidate all reports into a single worksheet**.

- **Drill Down**: Allows the user to set up a Drill Down to GP when selecting a record in the Excel Report. For example, a Drill Down can be set up to open the **Customer Maintenance** window for a customer identified in the selected Excel Report record.

- **Publish**: Allows the user to publish the List or Pivot Table Excel Report to an Excel or Office Data Connection File or to publish them to a SharePoint site.

Most of the buttons at the top of the Excel Report Builder window are used to access unique Excel Report Builder functions; yet, the actual work of creating Excel Reports occurs in the fields and panes below these buttons. We will explore the use of these fields and panes in the next section as we create a sample Excel Report.

Creating a new Excel Report via Excel Reports Builder

We have put together a real life scenario that we have come across at multiple companies to demonstrate how easy it is to create these Excel Reports.

Let's take for example an Accounts Payable Department that often needs to answer questions from Vendors on what check number actually paid a particular invoice. This can be accomplished in GP by using the inquiry windows by finding the check number and drilling in to find what document it was applied against. This works well if we just need to find a small number of these transactions, but the question from the end user is almost inevitably asked: "Is it possible for me to get a list of all my invoices and the check numbers that paid those invoices for the month, and while we are at it, can we have it refresh every month with new data and be exported to Excel?" Our initial response might be to just use SmartList, but as we have learned, SmartList doesn't always allow us to get the exact information we need. In this scenario, because both the Invoice transactions and the Payment transactions are all included in the same SmartList Object, we have no way to join them together. Our next response might be to consider using SmartList Builder to join the tables we need and build this report. This might work, but remember our company wants this data refreshed every month and exported out to Excel. If we fulfil this request using SmartList Builder, our end users would need to open SmartList each month and export an updated list. So, what is the solution? We can use Excel Reports builder to build a custom Excel Report, so all our end users need to do is open the appropriate spreadsheet every month, click refresh, and have a completed report, all without even touching Dynamics GP.

So, what do we need to do to create this Excel Report? In this example, we will be using a SQL View `vw_PaidInvoices` as our data source, which we have included.

Step by step:

1. Open the `Create_vw_PaidInvoices` text file (Provided) in SQL Management Studio and run against the TWO database to create the view.

2. Before the Builder can "see" the view, we must grant access to the view via Excel Report Builder security:

   ° From the Microsoft Dynamics GP Menu, browse to **Tools | SmartList Builder | Security | SQL Table Security.**

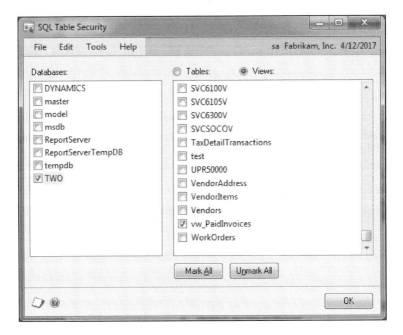

   ° Select the Database **TWO** from the Database List.
   ° Select the **Views** radio button.
   ° Select **vw_PaidInvoices**.
   ° Click **OK.**

3. Open Excel Report Builder from the Microsoft Dynamics GP Menu by browsing to **Tools | SmartList Builder | Excel Report Builder | Excel Report Builder.**

4. Assign **PAID INVOICES** as the **Report ID**.

5. Name the Excel Report **Paid Invoices**.

6. Choose **List** as the Report Type.

7. Add the SQL View.

   ° Click the **Add Table**button (plus sign next to **Tables**) in the lower left pane.

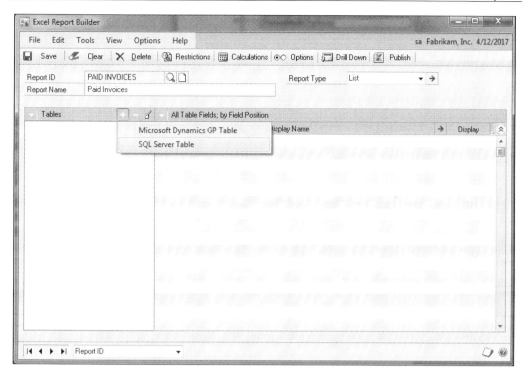

- ° Select **SQL Server Table** to open the **Add SQL Table** window. Highlight the TWO database, select the **Views** radio button, and highlight the **vw_PaidInvoices** view.

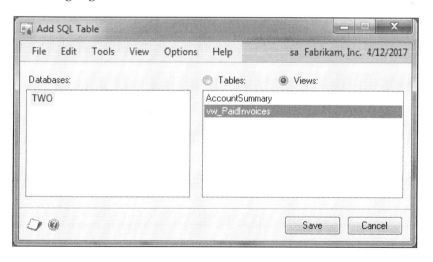

- ° Click **Save**.

8. Put a checkmark in the **Display** column for all six fields.

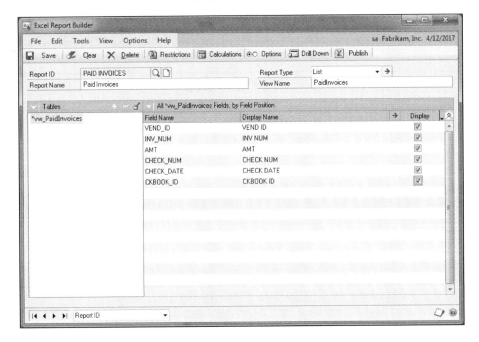

9. Make necessary changes to the column display formats:

  ○ Highlight the **AMT** field and click the blue arrow on the display column to open the **Set Field Options** window.

- ° On the **Negative Values** tab, mark the checkbox for **Display** as negative based on field.
- ° Click **Save**.

10. Save the **Excel Report**.

11. Publish the Excel Report.
    - ° Click the **Publish** button to open the Publish Report Window.

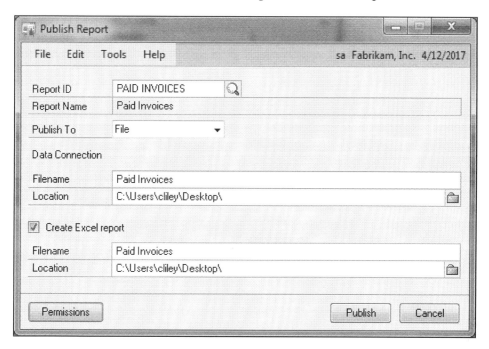

- ° Select **File** as the **Publish To** and set both the Data Connection and the Excel Report locations to your desktop.
- ° Click **Publish**.

12. Browse to your desktop and open the TWO Paid Invoices.xlsx file.

If data connections have been disabled, click **Enable Content**.

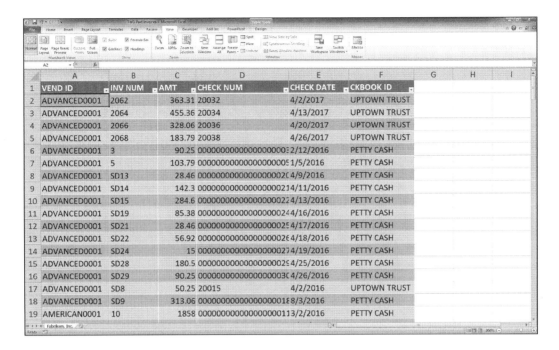

Now, we have our refreshable Excel Report, as can be seen above, that we can deliver to our user and they can simply open the spreadsheet every month and refresh the data without ever touching the Dynamics GP application.

Hopefully, this real life example has demonstrated how easy it is to utilize the power and flexibility of SQL server views and Excel Report Builder.

Additional tips and tricks for using the Builders

Although we've covered the basics of creating new SmartLists and Excel Reports via SmartList Builder and Excel Reports Builder, respectively, numerous tips and "things to watch out for" exist that can improve the functionality and usefulness of these tools even further. Although we could talk about advanced tips and techniques such as GoTos, Drillthroughs, and Importing and Exporting customized reports, we like to think you're just as excited to move on to a new chapter and a new reporting tool as we are! After you have become more experienced with the basics of each reporting tool, don't forget to take a look at their respective User Guides to learn a bit more about extending the functionality of these tools!

Summary

In this chapter, we introduced the first four tools in our Reporting Toolbox; SmartList for easy on demand ad-hoc reporting, SmartList Builder for times when the default SmartLists just don't cut it, and we need to build our own SmartList Objects; Excel Reports for viewing SmartList like data in Excel; and Excel Report Builder for when we want to extend the concept of SmartList Builder into Excel and build our own refreshable Excel Reports and/or Office Data Connections.

We began with the basic structure of each tool and what it does and ended with some real life step-by-step examples of how to use the builder tools. Finally, we looked at some tips and tricks when using the SmartList Builder and Excel Report Builder tools.

In the next chapter, we will dive into Report Writer, which has been the backbone of reporting in Dynamics GP for many years. We'll begin with understanding what Report Writer is before looking at using the tool to customize reports. We will then explore the Word Template feature that is new in Dynamics GP 2010.

4
Report Writer

In the previous chapter, we explored our first four reporting tools. These tools were mainly used for mining Dynamics GP data and providing us with lists of data. After starting with the structure of each tool and describing how to use them, we gave some real life examples to hone in on how each tool could be used to complete the example.

In this chapter, we move on to the Report Writer tool. Report Writer has been the underlying basis for reporting in Dynamics GP for many years. Every module in Dynamics GP has standard reports that originate from Report Writer. Many of these are posting journals that print when transactions are posted in the system. There are also reports such as activity reports, trial balances, modules setups, and so on. Any of these standard reports can be modified with the Report Writer tool.

Some examples of situations where we might find the need to modify these standard Dynamics GP reports could be adding aging buckets to the Receivables or Payables trial balances, customizing label fields on a report, or removing fields that are unnecessary on a particular report. Many other reasons for modifying a standard report exist.

This chapter will see us delve into the following areas within Dynamics GP Report Writer:

- Understanding the reports dictionaries and how Dynamics GP treats original reports versus modified reports
- Opening and Navigating the Report Writer windows
- Using Global Modifications to modify all reports in the application
- Modifying an existing Dynamics GP report
- Importing and Exporting Customized Reports
- Utilizing the new Dynamics GP 2010 Word template feature to render reports in Microsoft Word

Understanding the reports dictionaries and how Dynamics GP treats original versus modified reports

Before we begin using Report Writer, it is important that we have a basic understanding of the terminology used in the tool as well as how the reports are stored in the system. Report Writer has three types of reports:

- Original reports – These are the default reports that are provided with the accounting system.
- Modified reports – These are copies of an original report that have had changes made in Report Writer. Modified reports can be used instead of original reports in the accounting system.
- Custom reports – These are reports that are created using Report Writer. These can be started with a blank report or can be started by making a copy of an existing report. Stored procedures must be used to print custom reports in the accounting system.

Storing Report Writer reports

Report Writer for Dynamics GP 2010 stores reports in different files depending on which type of report it is. All of the original reports are stored in the main application dictionaries. Dynamics GP reports are stored in `Dynamics.dic`, Fixed Assets reports are stored in `FAM.dic`, and so on.

All changes and/or additions that are made in Report Writer are stored in the reports dictionary for the corresponding application. Not every application will have a reports dictionary; in fact, they are only created when changes are made. For example, modifications to standard Dynamics GP reports are stored in a dictionary called `Reports.dic` while Fixed Assets modified reports are stored in the `F309.dic` dictionary.

This method of storage maintains the integrity of the main application dictionary, meaning we never lose our original reports and we can always revert back to the original, if necessary. Additionally, GP allows us to choose whether or not to print the original or modified version of a report. Essentially, when we create a report or select a report to modify, the report is copied into the reports dictionary.

There are two common configurations for storing the report dictionaries when using Report Writer. One configuration is to store the reports dictionaries locally on each workstation. The other configuration is to store the dictionaries on a network share that is accessible by all client workstations.

Storing reports dictionaries locally

The advantages of storing reports dictionaries locally on each workstation are as follows:

- Each workstation can utilize a different set of reports. For example, one user/workstation may require sales invoices to be formatted one way, while another user/workstation may require it done in a different way.

- In the event of a corrupt reports dictionary on one workstation, it is more likely that a reports dictionary from another workstation will be available as a backup.

- Multiple users can access Report Writer at any given point in time.

The disadvantages of this configuration include:

- Report modifications that will be used by more than one user/workstation must be distributed to all other workstations that will require the same report modification.

- Numerous, highly specialized reports dictionaries require a greater effort and attempts to maintain back-up copies of each report dictionary.

Storing reports dictionaries on a network share

The advantages of storing the reports dictionaries on a network share are as follows:

- All users can access the same bank of new and modified reports.

- As new reports are created, or modifications are made to existing reports, all users with the appropriate security permissions will have instant access to these reports. We no longer have to go through the process of rolling out changes to each workstation.

Some of the disadvantages of using a network share to store reports dictionaries include:

- Access to Report Writer is limited to a single user at a time. This is not usually an issue in smaller organizations, but can become quite troublesome in larger organizations.

- In the event that the reports dictionary becomes corrupt, all users are affected until a restored copy of the reports dictionary is restored.

- Users are limited to the number of modified and/or new reports that can be used at any given time.

Care must be taken when deciding on which configuration to choose based on these advantages and disadvantages. Factors such as the number of reports we want to modify, whether our users will be creating or modifying their own reports, and how we plan to share the customized reports among users are all factors that play into this decision.

Accessing Report Writer reports

Once we've made our decision on how the reports dictionaries will be stored and begin modifying our first reports, we have two additional steps that must be taken when working with modified reports. These steps will allow us to access our modified reports from GP:

- Setting the Dynamics GP Launch File
- Setting Security to Custom/Modified Reports
- Now, let's see what each step entails so that we can start using our modified reports!

Setting the Dynamics GP launch file

When Dynamics GP is started, the launch file is what tells the runtime engine which dictionaries to use. In addition to providing a list of installed products for this instance, the launch file also lists the file location for the various application, form, and report dictionaries required by GP 2010. By default, these will be stored in the Data folder of the Dynamics GP installation. This file can be edited in System Setup by administrators or power users or by opening the `Dynamics.set` file in the application folder. If we have chosen a configuration that stores these dictionaries on a network share, we will need to edit the default `Reports.dic` path in the launch file to point to the new location on the network share.

We must take care that we have correctly specified the names and locations; otherwise Dynamics GP may not start up properly or users might receive dictionary-related error messages when attempting to generate reports that have been modified.

Setting security to custom/modified reports

Once we have set our launch file to the correct path for our modified reports, in order for the application to actually use these reports, we must use the **Alternate/Modified Forms and Reports** window inside Dynamics GP. To open this window, seen in the following image, choose **Microsoft Dynamics GP | Tools | Setup | System | Alternate/Modified Forms and Reports**.

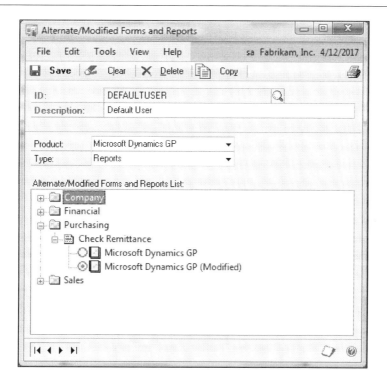

To set access, we use the following steps:

1. Specify an **ID**. This ID will be attached to specific users in User Security Setup. This can allow us to give different users access to different modified reports.

2. Select the **Product** containing the modified report. Selecting **Microsoft Dynamics GP**, for example, will show us a list of objects stored in the dictionary for the core Dynamics GP product.

3. Choose to display **Reports** in the **Type** drop down.

4. Locate the modified report by browsing through the tree view. These reports are grouped by the module in which they are used.

5. Once the modified report has been located, change the selection from the default version to the modified version (in most cases, we will see the word **Modified** to designate the customized report version).

6. Click **Save**.

After we have set the appropriate security, any users with the Alternate/Modified Forms and Report ID that we have modified will have the ability to print the modified versions of the reports in place of the original versions.

If we ever need to remove a modified version of a report, we need to be sure to set security back to use the original version of the report; otherwise Dynamics GP will not be able to properly access the reports.

Opening and navigating the Report Writer windows

As with SmartList Builder and Excel Reports Builder, the Report Writer application can be accessed from within Dynamics GP. Using the Report Writer application requires switching from the main GP 2010 windows to the Report Writer interface with its own set of buttons and menu layouts. Let's take a look at how we can open Report Writer and then explore some of the various buttons and menus that appear in this application.

Setting security permissions for using Report Writer

Before we can use the Report Writer application, we must check to ensure that we have the appropriate security permissions to do so. This, of course, is not necessary for GP logins that are assigned to the POWERUSER role, as these users, by default, have access to the Report Writer application.

Standard GP 2010 security can be used to grant access to the Report Writer application. Users must be granted access to the ADMIN_SYSTEM_008 security task in order to open Report Writer from GP. This security task should be assigned to a security role which, in turn, should be assigned to the particular user who needs access to Report Writer.

If a wide variety of users on the same system will be accessing Report Writer, we recommend setting up a new security role for Report Writer. Assign the ADMIN_ SYSTEM_008 task to this role. This new role can then be assigned to all of the users who require access to Report Writer. This is much easier to remember rather than assigning the task to a wide variety of roles!

Opening Report Writer

The Report Writer application can be opened in one of several ways. Users can open Report Writer and select a report to modify, or users can run a report in GP and, from the screen output, select to modify the report. This will open Report Writer with the selected report already on display in the application.

To open Report Writer without first selecting a report, do the following:

1. Open the **Microsoft Dynamics GP** menu.

2. Select **Tools | Customize | Report Writer.** Alternatively, users can select *Alt + F9* to perform this same action. The path to Report Writer is shown in the following image:

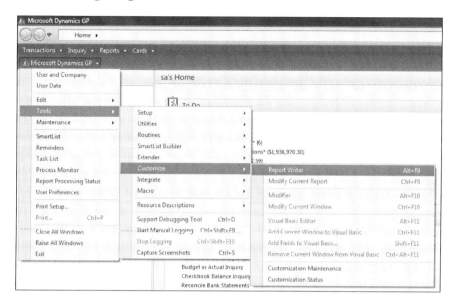

3. A pop-up window will appear, asking users to select the **Product**. Select **Microsoft Dynamics GP** to open Report Writer with a connection to the main product dictionary. This will allow us to modify reports stored in this dictionary. To modify reports in other dictionaries, such as Manufacturing, we can select that **Product** at this time.

4. Select **OK** after selecting a **Product** to allow Microsoft Dynamics GP to switch to the Report Writer application.

5. Users must then select the **Reports** button to choose from a list of reports in this product dictionary that can be modified.

Rather than opening the Report Writer application and selecting a report from a list, users can also open Report Writer with a report already selected for editing. This can be done using the Summary Trial Balance report from the Financials module:

1. Select **Reports | Financial | Trial Balance** to open the **Trial Balance Report** window.

2. Select **Summary** in the **Reports:** drop-down box.

3. Select an existing Report Option and select **Insert** to add this report to the **Print List**. The selected report should print to the screen.

4. Select **Print** to print the report to screen.

5. When the Screen Output window for the selected report appears, note the name of the report as it appears in the blue bar at the top of the output window. This is the name of the report as it will appear in Report Writer.

6. Select the **Modify** button at the top of the window (highlighted in the image below) to open Report Writer for this report. Alternatively, this same action can be completed by pressing *Ctrl + F9* on the keyboard:

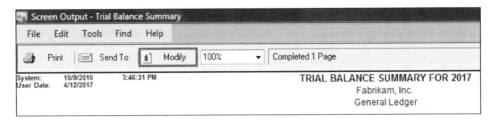

7. Report Writer will open with the **Trial Balance – Summary** report available for editing.

Report Writer Resource windows

Numerous windows can be accessed from within Report Writer that can provide users with more information about the resources that can be used in the application. Many of these windows are accessible from the **Resources** menu found in the Report Writer menu bar. Since one of the most basic resources in Report Writer is the field, we'll begin with that window.

Fields

Selecting **Resources | Fields** opens the Fields window. Alternatively, users can select the **Fields** button from the toolbar. The window that appears displays a list of global fields that can be used in the Report Writer application.

Double-click a field name to open the **Field Definition** window for that global field. This window provides users with the physical name of the field as well as the data type referenced by the selected field.

These windows are seen in the following image:

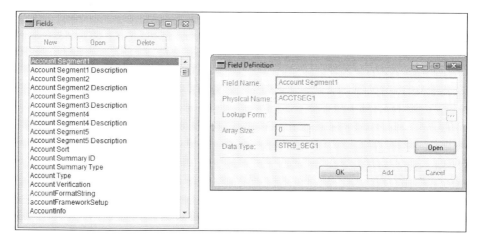

Selecting the **Open** button from the **Field Definition** window takes us to the **Data TypesDefinition** window.

Data types

To open the **Data Types** window, select **Resources | Data Types** from the menu bar. Additionally, users can select the **Data Types** button from the toolbar.

The Data Types window displays a list of the data types used by the various fields found in Report Writer. As we saw previously, each global field in Report Writer is assigned a corresponding data type.

With a data type selected in the lookup list, click the **Open** button to open the **Data Type Definition** window and see more information about the selected data type.

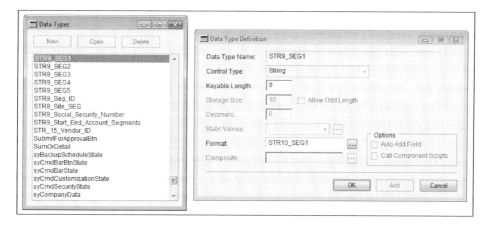

We can use data types to control the Keyable Length of a field as well as the formatting for a field. Don't forget, it can be tempting to change the Keyable Length or Format values for a particular data type with a specific field in mind; however, a single data type can be assigned to multiple fields! Changing attributes such as the selected format for a single data type will change those attributes for all fields assigned to that data type!

To change the format type assigned to a particular data type, select the ellipses button next to the **Format:** field to open the **Format Lookup** window with the specified format already selected. Double-click a format value in the **Format Lookup** window to apply that formatting type to the selected data type.

Formats

The **Formats** window returns a list of formats that are available for this report dictionary. As we might expect, the formats listed in this window govern how data types and, in turn, fields, will appear on Report Writer-based reports. To see the list of formats that already exist in Report Writer, users can select **Resources | Formats** from the menu bar.

To learn more about an existing format, users can select the **Open** button to open the **Format Definition** window. If this window has not been opened from the **Data Types Definition** window (as we described earlier in this section), double-clicking a format name will also open the **Format Definition** window. From here, we can view a list of attributes controlling how this format will be visible to the user. Depending on the value selected in the Format Type window, certain areas of this window may be greyed out or unavailable for selection.

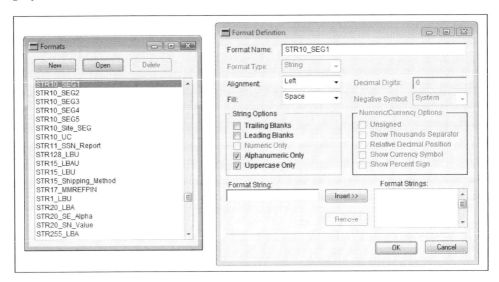

The **Formats** window is unique to the windows we have covered thus far, as it allows users to create new resources for use in Report Writer. Selecting the **New** button opens the **Format Definition** window with blank fields. Users can enter a new **Format Name** and choose from several settings to create a new format definition for use in Report Writer. This format definition can then be assigned to different data types.

Pictures

Clicking **Resources | Pictures** opens the Pictures Library list. In this list, users can see all of the pictures that are available for selection in the Report Writer application. After a picture is added to the Picture Library, it can be used on multiple graphical reports.

Users can select a picture from the list and click the **Open** button or double-click the picture to open the **Picture Definition** window. This window displays the selected picture such as the warning icon seen in the following image:

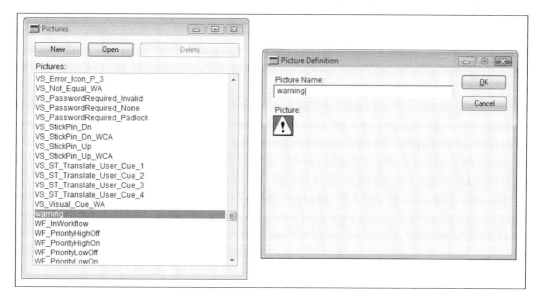

Strings

The **Strings** window can be opened by clicking **Resources | Strings** from the menu bar. String values are used throughout Report Writer and Dynamics GP as text fields. The resulting list shows us the various string values that exist in the current dictionary:

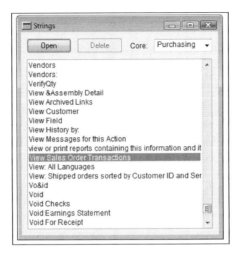

To see the strings broken down by series, change the value in the drop-down box at the upper right-hand corner of this window.

Selecting the **Tables** button and the **Tables** option from the menu bar opens the **Tables** lookup. From here, we can see a list of tables that exist for the selected dictionary. Selecting a table and clicking **Open** or double-clicking the table name opens the **Table Definition** window:

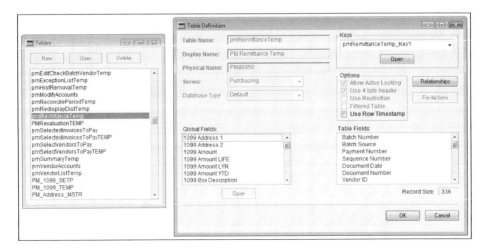

From the **Table Definition** window, we can see a list of fields that exist in this table. We can also click the **Relationships** button to create relationships to other tables with similar fields. These relationships can be used in the report modification process to add additional fields to existing reports.

Also, notice that selecting **Tables | Virtual Tables** from the menu bar opens a list of virtual tables in the current dictionary. Selecting a virtual table and clicking **Open** or double-clicking the table name opens the **Virtual Table Definition** window, as seen in the following image with the **CM_Checkbook_List_View** virtual table selected:

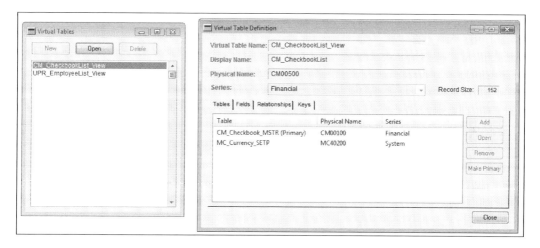

Virtual tables are used as a way to combine data from multiple tables, similar to how a view might be used in SQL. Unfortunately, virtual tables can only be created by an application developer, so most of us will stick to creating table relationships via the **Table Definitions** window!

Report Modification windows

Earlier in this section, we discussed some of the windows accessible from the Resources menu as well as the Report Writer toolbar. Now, let's take a look at what the Report Writer layout looks like when we're actually modifying a report.

Report Definition

The **Report Definition** window is the first window that appears after a report is selected from the Reports list. From this table, we can gain access to other windows, such as the **Report Layout** window, that we will need in order to make modifications to a report.

The following image shows the Report Definition window for the Check Remittance report that we will use later on in this chapter in the section on Word Template modifications:

The very important **Using Key** drop-down value allows us to control how data will be sorted on our report. If an appropriate key for sorting does not exist, we will have to create a sorting definition in the **Sorting Definition** window.

Also, from this window, we can control several important settings for the selected report. For example, we can choose the page orientation, whether or not a page header will print on the first page or if a page footer should print on the last page, as well as select from a list of formatting options.

Report Table Relationships

Selecting **Tables** on the **Report Definition** window opens the Report Table Relationships window. We can use this window to add new source tables that should be used in the selected report.

The following image shows a list of the table relationships for the Check Remittance report:

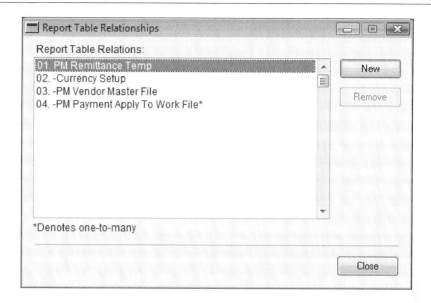

Before a table can be added via the **Report Table Relationships** window, a valid relationship must exist between the new table and one of the existing tables in the window. Use the **Table Definition** window described earlier in this chapter to create these relationships.

Sorting Definition

As we might expect, selecting the Sort button on the **Report Definition** window opens the **Sorting Definition** window. In the next image, we see a list of fields that we can select for sorting within the **Check Remittance** report:

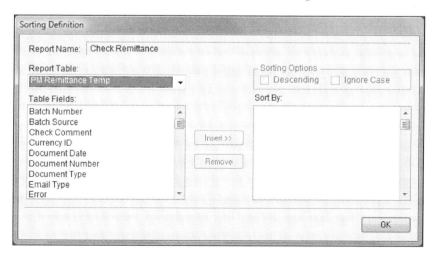

The **Sorting Definition** window allows us to control the order in which data will be printed on our report. For most reports, an appropriate key for sorting will be defined on the **Report Definition** window, so this window will be unnecessary. In cases where a valid key cannot be used for sorting, we can use the **Sorting Definition** window to identify our own sorting requirements. This method is, however, less efficient than using the key value on the **Report Definition** window for sorting.

Report Restrictions

Selecting Restrictions from the **Report Definition** window opens a list of restrictions that have been created for this report. This window can be used to add new restrictions to the report, or we can select an existing restriction to view the **Report Restriction Definition** window.

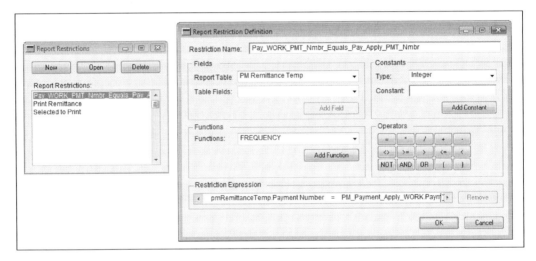

Report restrictions can be added to a report to control the output that appears when the report is actually printed.

Layout

Clicking the **Layout** button on the **Report Definition** window opens the Report Layout window for the selected report. This is where the bulk of the work in Report Writer occurs, as it displays the various sections of the report and the various fields that are contained in each section appear in this window, as well.

Accompanying the Report Layout window are two smaller windows that change depending on what fields are selected in the Report Layout.

Properties

When a field is selected in the report layout, the Properties window displays information about that field. The **Object** tab identifies what kind of data the selected field represents. Switching to the **Visual** tab allows users to see how the field is formatted for this particular report. Here, in the following image, we see the Properties window for the **Document Date** field in the Remittance Header section of the Check Remittance report:

Toolbox

The **Toolbox** window is where users can select fields to be added to the report layout. A drop-down box allows users to switch between tables that have been defined for this report. Selecting a different table or value in this drop down will change the fields available for selection.

In addition to using the **Toolbox** to select fields, other objects can be selected for addition on the report layout. These objects range from shapes to text boxes to pictures. We can also click the **Arrange** tab to display a list of options for arranging data in a selected cell.

Now that we've explored some of the windows that we will be using in Report Writer, let's move on to actually working with this tool!

Modifying all reports in the application by using global modifications

Although the most common use for Report Writer is to make modifications to individual reports, Dynamics GP Report Writer does allow for changes that affect all of the reports in a particular application. In this section, we will cover each of these global resources that can be modified in detail.

Data types

In addition to being able to adjust the keyable length as we discussed earlier, certain control types allow us to specify static values for the data type. An example of this would be the text on a push button or items included in a list box. Static text can be used in the following control types:

- Drop-down list – Indicates the selections in the drop-down
- List box – Indicates the selections in the list
- Visual switch – Displays two or more text values that will be displayed based on user clicks

To view/modify static text, do the following from within Dynamics Report Writer:

1. Select **Resources | Data Types**.
2. Select a **Data Type, 1099_Type** for instance.
3. Click **Open**.
4. Click the ellipses button next to the Static Text field.

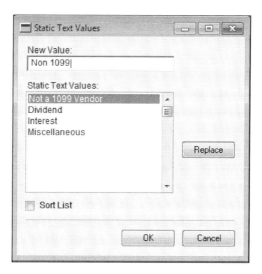

5. Highlight **Not a 1099 Vendor**.
6. Type **Non 1099** in the New Value field.
7. Click **Replace**.
8. Click OK.

Formats

Formats are the extra characters, spacing, and attributes that can be applied to a data type to format data when it is displayed or printed on reports. The easiest way to understand what formats are is to think of them as "masks" that just change the look of the information for a field without changing the data.

There are several formatting options available to change how data will appear:

- Data alignment
- String and composite formats
- Currency format
- Numeric format

These options are described in detailed tables in Chapter 18 of the Report Writer User Guide.

To view/modify formats, do the following from within Dynamics Report Writer:

1. Select **Resources | Formats**.
2. Select a **Format**, **Phone_Number** for example.
3. Click **Open**.
4. Select any of the options on the window and modify the Format String as necessary.
5. Click OK.

One thing to keep in mind is that not all composites use a format string. Some are defined through the program code.

Pictures

Although Report Writer is not well known for exceptional graphics capabilities, we can still add logos and pictures to our modified reports. Before we can use these pictures, however, we must add them to the Report Writer picture library. Report Writer limits the file size of pictures to 32 KB. For larger logos and pictures, we can use a photo editor to resize the image, or we can crop the image into several smaller parts. These smaller images can then be combined together in the Report Writer layout.

To add a new picture, do the following from within Dynamics Report Writer:

1. Select **Resources | Pictures**.
2. Click **New**.
3. Type a name in the **Picture Name** field.

4. With the picture in our clipboard, we choose Paste from the Edit menu or click *CTRL+ V* to paste the picture.

5. Click **OK** to add the picture to the library.

This functionality is extremely useful for adding company logos to our customer-facing reports!

Strings

We can use the strings resource to update all occurrences of a string in one step instead of changing the string everywhere it occurs. An example of this would be changing the words **Vendor Name** to **Supplier Name**. By changing the string, we don't have to change every individual text value for that field.

To modify a string, do the following from within Dynamics Report Writer:

1. Select **Resources | Strings**.

2. Select the dictionary **Core** or series, **Purchasing** for example.

3. Highlight **Vendor Name**.

4. Click **Open**.

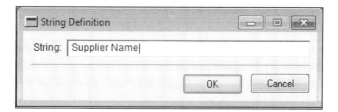

5. Type in the new value for the **string** name, **Supplier Name** in our example.

6. Click **OK**.

Modifying an existing Dynamics GP report

Though Dynamics GP Report Writer allows for not only modifying original reports, but also creating new reports, the focus of this book is on modifying existing reports. With the ever expanding amount of reporting tools available, there are usually better options for creating reports from scratch than using Report Writer. Let's take a look at some of the common modifications made to reports, before diving into a step-by-step example.

Common modifications

Modifying existing reports is the most common task performed with Dynamics Report Writer. The Report Writer User's Guide that is included with the GP 2010 installation lists some of the more common modifications:

- Modifying the layout – This category includes any of the basic layout changes that may be required due to a particular user's preference, a desire to standardize customer-facing reports to an organization's marketing standards, modify a check format to fit on pre-printed check stock, and so on. Fortunately, most of these changes do not require use of the advanced Report Writer tools, and users are capable of making these changes within the Report Layout window.

- Changing the page orientation – Although many reports are designed to print in landscape format, some users may prefer to view the report in portrait orientation. Although this allows more records to fit on a single page, it may require sacrificing space between fields removing unnecessary fields entirely. Setting a report's page orientation in Report Writer also allows us to override a user's print settings and always print the report in the specified orientation.

- Adding or removing fields – Although many of the default Report Writer reports come preloaded with the relevant fields required for a particular report, we will often find a need to add a new field to a report. For example, if the multi-bin functionality in Inventory Control module is enabled, we may want to add bin location fields to our inventory-related reports. On the other hand, we may find that the default reports include too much information; therefore, we can use Report Writer to remove these fields.

- Using VBA with reports–If we have Modifier with VBA installed in our environment, we can use VBA code to customize our reports beyond the capabilities offered through standard Report Writer.

Modifying a report: Adding aging buckets to Payables Trial Balance Report

Dynamics GP allows for up to seven aging buckets in Accounts Payable. By default, the Historical Aged Trial balance summary report only prints the first four. In this step by step example, we will modify this aging report to include two additional aging buckets:

1. In Dynamics GP, browse to **Reports | Purchasing | Trial Balance**.

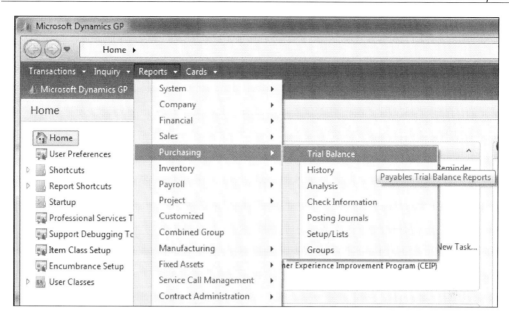

2. This will open the **Payables Trial Balance Reports** window:

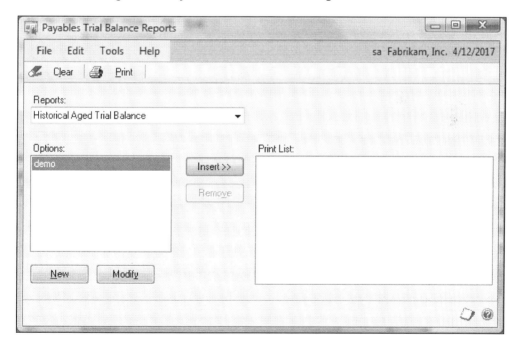

3. Choose **Historical Aged Trial Balance** from the **Reports:** drop down and highlight the **demo** Option and click **Modify**.

4. This will open the **Payables Trial Balance Report Options** window:

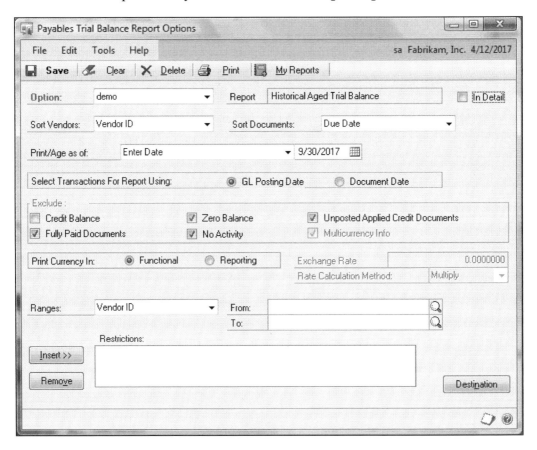

5. On the report options window, set your parameters by changing the necessary fields. For our example, set the following fields:

   ° Uncheck the **In Detail** checkbox.

   ° Set **Print/Age as of** to enter date and enter a period end date (You can use the drop down to select Current Date, End of Month, End of Period, and so on. We are using 2017 for our year because of our sample data).

   ° Accept the rest of the defaults or add any range filters necessary.

6. Click **Destination**.

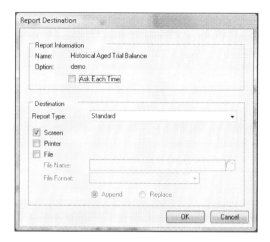

7. As seen in the previous image, on the **Report Destination** window, accept the default Report Type of **Standard** (Template will be covered later in this chapter with Word Templates) and select the **Screen** checkbox. Click **OK**.

8. On our **Payables Trial Balance Report options** window, click the **Print** button.

9. This will print our **Summary Historical Aged Trial Balance report** to the screen. We can verify from here that we only have the first four aging buckets.

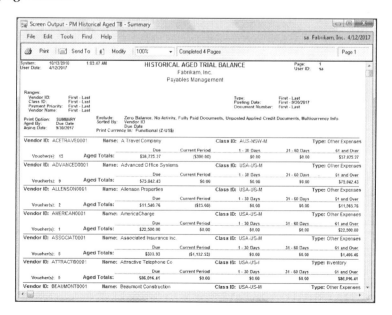

10. Click **Modify** (Note, we will only have access to modify if our user has the security role discussed in the Accessing Report Writer section of this chapter).

11. When asked to save changes to the report option demo, answer **Save**.

12. After selecting Save, we will automatically be taken to the **Report Layout** for our report in Report Writer. (Depending on your screen resolution, you will probably also see the **Toolbox, Report Definition** and **Properties** windows).

13. Close the **Report Layout** and on the **Report Definition** window, change the **Page Orientation** to **Landscape**.

14. Click the **Layout** button to return to the **Report Layout** window:

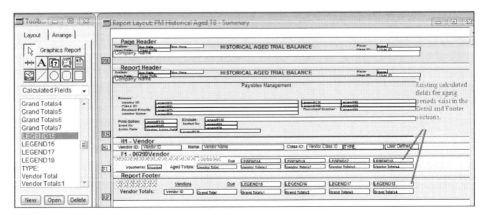

15. From the **Toolbox**, we select **Calculated Fields** from the drop down list. Scroll down until we find the **LEGEND** fields. We will find that Report Writer only has predefined calculated fields for the four default aging buckets.

16. On the **toolbox** window, click **New** to create a new LEGEND field for the 5th and 6th aging buckets we are adding.

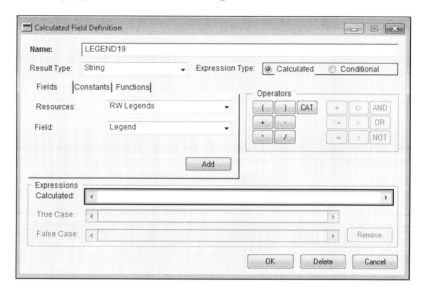

17. On the **Calculated Field Definition** window, set the following fields:
    ○ **Name**: Set name to **LEGEND19**
    ○ **Result Type**: Set to **String**
    ○ **Expression Type**: Accept default value of **Calculated**
    ○ On the **Fields** tab, **Resources**: Choose **RW Legends** from the drop down
    ○ On the **Fields** tab, **Field**: Choose **Legend** from the drop down

18. Click **Add** on the Fields tab and enter **19** as the **array index**.

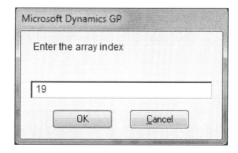

19. Our completed calculated field should look like the following:

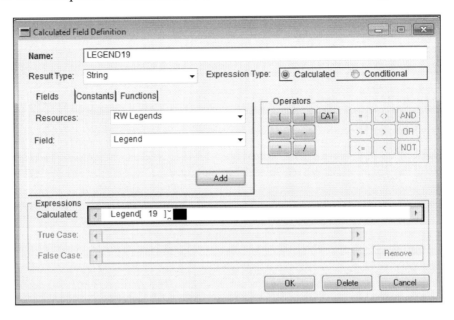

20. Repeat the steps for LEGEND20.

21. Once the calculated fields are added, we can drag them on the report layout from the toolbox. Once on the layout, we can set the same properties on our fields as the other legend fields in that section.

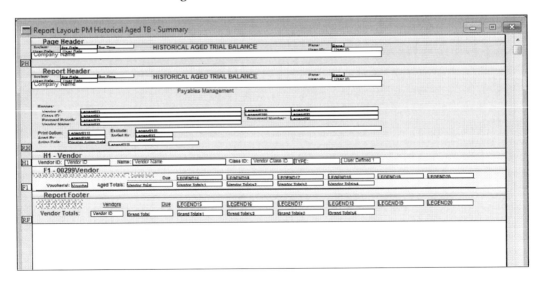

22. Now that our column headings have been added, we need to add our Vendor Totals and Grand Totals for our 5th and 6th aging buckets.

23 Dynamics Report Writer has the necessary calculated fields for the Vendor Totals and Grand Totals already created, we just need to add them to the report.

24. From the **Toolbox**, choose **Calculated Fields** from the drop down and scroll through the list until locating the **Vendor Totals5**, **Vendor Totals6**, **Grand Totals5**, and **Grand Totals6**. Drag and drop them onto the report layout in the same manner as we did with our LEGEND fields. Set field properties as necessary by comparing the other fields currently on the report.

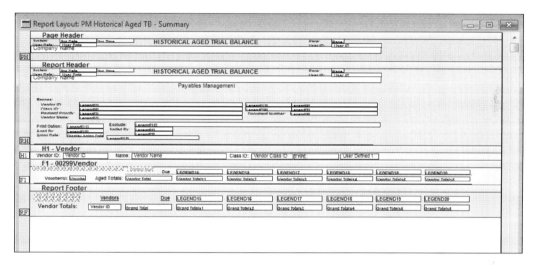

25. Now, we can see that we have the column headings, the vendor totals and the grand totals for our 5th and 6th aging buckets.

26. Close **the Report Layout** and click **Save** when prompted to save the Layout.

27. On the menu bar, click **File | Microsoft Dynamics GP** to return to Dynamics.

28. Click **Save** to save changes to the report when prompted.

29. Remember, before we can print our modified version of the Aging report, we need to set security to the modified version as described earlier in the chapter in the Setting Security to Modified Reports section. The following is what our alternate/modified report window should look like:

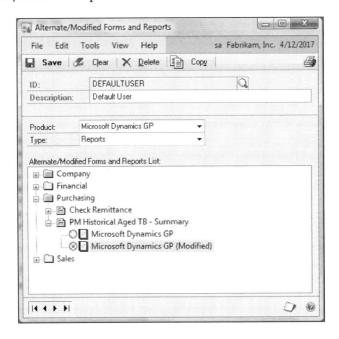

30. Repeat steps 1 – 9 of this exercise to print our modified version of the report.

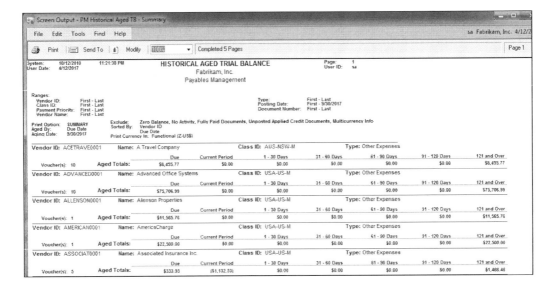

31. From the previous image, we can now see that our 5th and 6th aging buckets are now printing on our Summary Historical Aged Trial Balance Report.

With this step-by-step guide, we should now have more confidence in using the Dynamics Report Writer to make modifications to the existing Dynamics GP Reports!

Importing and exporting customized reports

Reports that are modified via Report Writer are portable, meaning we can make a modification to a report and transfer it to other workstations or GP instances. Now that we've explored how to customize our own reports, we may want to utilize the Import and Export functionality to transfer the modified report to another local reports dictionary. This can be used in cases such as the one we discussed earlier in this chapter where individual workstations on the same system are accessing separate report dictionaries. It can also be used to transfer customized reports from one company database to another or even from one system to another.

The ability to import and export customized reports means the developers and consultants can create custom reports on a test database, test them, and solicit user feedback and approval—without ever impacting the production environment! Once a report customized on a test database has been approved by the user, the customized report can be wrapped in package file and imported into the production database.

The Import and Export functionality for customizations is also an invaluable tool in saving prior versions of reports. For any given report on a GP workstation, only the default report and one modified report can be used. Before making additional changes to the modified version of the report, it may be worth exporting a package file for the customized report that is being modified. In this way, prior versions of a single report can be maintained, and if any issues arise from the modified report, a previous version can be imported to prevent interruptions to the reporting process.

Exporting customized reports

Before a customized report can be transferred to another environment, the report must be converted to a package file. This can be done from within GP 2010:

1. Open the **Microsoft Dynamics GP** menu.
2. Select **Tools | Customize | Customization Maintenance** to open the **Customization Maintenance** window.

The **Customization Maintenance** window (seen in the following image) contains a list of the various customizations that exist in the current GP installation. This includes forms of customizations beyond just reports modified by Report Writer; other customizations, such as those originating from Modifier or VBA will appear in this window, as well. To help us understand the customizations, GP lists each customization, followed by the **Type** of customization and the **Product** in which the customization resides. Customized reports related to **Fixed Assets** will most likely appear in the **Fixed Assets Product** whereas basic reports, such as the Trial Balance Summary, will appear as part of the standard **Microsoft Dynamics GP Product**.

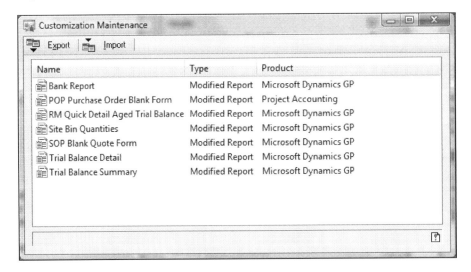

1. Select the customized reports that should be exported to the package file. By selecting the *Ctrl* key, users can select multiple components. Holding down the *Shift* key while selecting two non-adjacent components will allow users to select the entire range of components between the two selected components.

2. Select the **Export** button to open the Windows Explorer window for saving the package file.

3. Select a location on the network or local computer in which the package file can be saved. Package files will be denoted with a `*.package` suffix. If desired, rename the first portion of the file name to a more descriptive term for easier identification. In the **Save as Type** drop-down box, **Customization Package (*.package)** should be displayed.

4. Click **Save** to save the package file to the selected location. This file can now be used for importing these customizations to another GP install accessing a separate reports dictionary.

Importing customized reports

Once we've exported a package file from another GP install, we can use that package file as the source file for a customization import. This will apply the customizations to the new installation, and users can then choose whether or not the modified or default reports should be visible to the users. Be careful! When importing a package file containing a customized report to another GP workstation on which the same report has also been customized, the existing report will be overwritten! Before going through with the import, make absolutely certain that the report(s) should be overwritten!

Prior to importing a customization, we should have our package file ready to go. For tips on creating such a package file, refer to the previous section on exporting customized reports from GP. If necessary, it may be worth completing a test import using a test database to ensure that our import will bring in the correct customizations. Better safe than sorry!

Once we are ready to go through with the import, the process is fairly easy. In the following example, we'll use the `TrialBalanceModified.package` file to import two modified reports: the Trial Balance Summary and the Trial Balance Detail.

1. Open the **Microsoft Dynamics GP** menu.

2. Select **Tools | Customize | Customization Maintenance** to open the **Customization Maintenance** window. This is the same window we used in the previous section to export our customized reports.

3. Select the **Import** button to open the **Import Package File** window.

4. Select the **Browse** button to open the Windows Explorer window for selecting an existing `*.package` file. In this case, we will select the `TrialBalanceModified.package` file. A list of the reports found in the selected package file is displayed in the **Import Package File** window. Reports in this package file for which a customized version already exists on the target database will display an **X** in the **Overwrite** column.

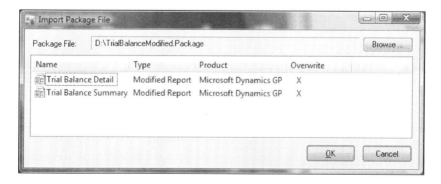

5. Assuming we wish to import this package file, we can select the **OK** button. Microsoft Dynamics GP will offer a helpful warning message that existing items will be overwritten by the import. Assuming that this is desired behavior, we can select the **OK** button to complete the import.

6. The **Import Package File** window will close, and we are returned to the **Customization Maintenance** window. If the import was successful, a message to this effect appears at the bottom left-hand corner of the window. Otherwise, we can click the **Errors** button at the bottom right-hand corner of the window to see and print a list of errors from the import process.

Completing the import process adds the customized reports to the customized reports dictionary referenced by the current GP client. If this is the first time the customized report is being used in this environment, use the Alternate/Modified Forms and Reports window to select the modified report(s) for use in this new environment. Details on how to do this can be found earlier in this chapter!

We have now successfully exported and imported our own package file of customized reports. This functionality can be quite the time-saver for developers and consultants who work in multiple company databases and systems!

Using modified reports from the Reports Library

For those of us who have access to Microsoft's CustomerSource or PartnerSource portals, a handy list of previously modified reports can be found in the Reports Library. The Reports Library contains a list of some of the most commonly modified reports broken down by version number and module. For example, numerous reports in the Reports Library are customized to print in portrait orientation rather than the more traditional landscape orientation. While many developers and consultants may be capable of making these kinds of modifications themselves, it's still helpful to have this list of reports available to save time and effort!

Rather than recreate these customizations ourselves, we can download these customized reports in package file format and then import them into GP installations using the Import and Export functionality that we just covered. Before customizing a particular report, it may be helpful to check the Reports Library to see if the modification has already been made or, at the very least, if a similar modification exists to which we can add our own customizations.

For CustomerSource, the Reports Library is located at:

```
https://mbs.microsoft.com/customersource/support/downloads/
reportslibrary/
```

For PartnerSource, the Reports Library is located at:

```
https://mbs.microsoft.com/partnersource/deployment/resources/
reportslibrary/
```

Rendering reports in Microsoft Word by utilizing the new Dynamics GP 2010 Word template feature

Users who are familiar with versions prior to GP 2010 may be surprised to see a new feature when printing certain reports in GP 2010. As seen in the **Report Destination** window image below, users are now given a choice of selecting a **Report Type** of **Standard** or **Template**.

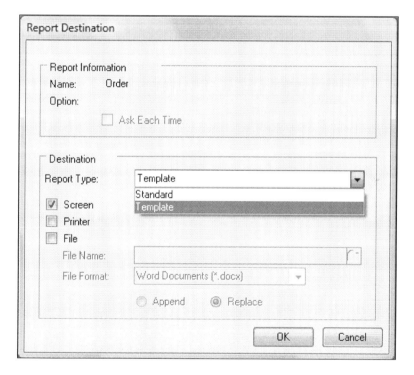

The Template option is a new feature for GP 2010 that allows users to print certain standard GP reports in Word template format! Once a report is printed to Word template, the contents of the report can be reformatted, the report can be saved to a file directory location for later reference, or it can also be included as an email attachment. In short, this option brings a fresh, new look to the report generation process in GP 2010!

Before a report can be printed in Word template form, however, it must be template-enabled, a process which requires use of Microsoft Dexterity. While this is beyond the technical level of this book, we are happy to point out that 23 reports are already Word template-enabled and ready for modification in GP 2010! These reports are primarily customer and vendor facing reports, which is great news as the Word template functionality gives us greater control over visual aspects of the report such as formatting, logos, and more!

First, let's take a look at the steps required to enable these templates for use in GP 2010, then we'll explore the process of making some basic modifications to existing Word templates.

Enabling Word templates

The **Template Configuration Manager** window should be the first stop for anyone seeking to work with Word templates in GP 2010. This window controls the ability, among other things, to turn the Word template feature on and off in a company database, to assign a company logo to all reports with an associated Word template, and to determine which individual reports should be made available in Word template format. As we've mentioned earlier, 23 reports in GP 2010 have associated Word templates, so we can use this window to perform these functions during our initial setups of GP 2010.

The **Template Configuration Manager** window can be accessed from GP 2010 by clicking **Reports | Template Configuration Manager**. We can expand the various nodes to see an image similar to the following:

In this window, we can select the default templates that should be enabled on a company by company basis. Modified templates will not display in this view. Expanding the **Enable all templates for all companies** node displays a list of company databases. Underneath each company database node, we see a list of series that contain Word templates that can be assigned for that company. By default, only the Sales and Purchasing series contain predefined Word templates that can be assigned or unassigned from the company databases.

If we don't want a particular report available for printing in its Word template format, we can deselect that report from this list. **Template** will no longer display as an option in the Report Options window when printing this report.

To completely disable Word templates users can either deselect the **Enable all templates for all companies** option, or, in the more preferred manner, deselect the option to **Enable Report Templates** that can be found at the bottom of this window. Either way, these options will quickly remove the Word template options from the **Report Options** window for available reports.

From this window, we can also decide if the standard report formats should be made available for printing along with the templates for Word template-enabled reports. If we want to force users to use the Word templates wherever possible, we can deselect the option to **Allow printing of standard report when template is available** option at the bottom of this window.

Installing the Dynamics GP add-in for Microsoft Word

Word templates can also be modified! Before modifying or creating new templates from scratch with the new Word template functionality, a special add-in must be installed for Microsoft Word. This add-in is available as an additional product that comes with the install media of GP 2010. Run the setup.exe file from the install media and select **Microsoft Dynamics GP Add-In for Microsoft Dynamics** to begin the install. The following image shows an example of some of the other additional products that can be installed from this window:

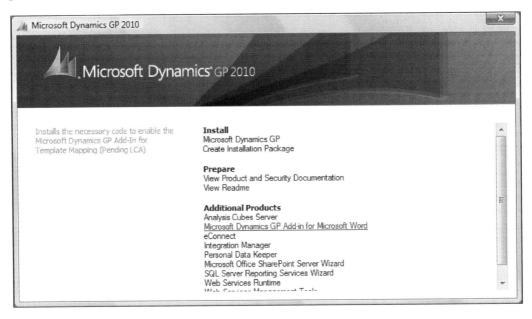

This tool only needs to be installed on workstations where modifications will be made to the Word templates. It is not necessary to install this tool in order to generate Word template reports from GP 2010!

Once this add-in has been installed, a new section is added to the Developer tab in the Ribbon in Microsoft Word. If the Developer tab is not enabled for the Ribbon, enable it with the following steps:

1. Open Microsoft Word.
2. Click **File** (or the **Office** button on earlier versions of Word) in the upper left-hand corner of the application.

3. Click **Options** (or **Word Options** on earlier versions of Word) to open the **Word Options** window.

4. In Word 2010, click the **Customize Ribbon** tab and confirm that the **Developer** tab is checked in the right-hand pane. In earlier versions of Word, click the **Popular** category and select the **Show Developer Tab in Ribbon** option.

5. Click **OK** to close the Word Options window.

The **Developer** tab should now appear at the top of the window. A new section seen in the following image by the name of **Microsoft Dynamics GP Templates** should now appear in the **Developer** tab:

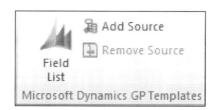

We will use this section for adding new fields once we begin modifying Word templates.

Understanding the Word template modification process

When a template-enabled report is printed, a combination of the standard report definition, a custom XML file containing the report definition and data, and the Word template file are all merged in a Template Processing Engine to create the final report. Fortunately, we don't have to be experts in the underlying technical details to be able to make modifications to the Word templates!

One of the most common misconceptions when beginning work with the new Word template feature is that only the Word template itself must be modified. While this is true in certain cases such as changing the font and colour of a particular field or adding a watermark to a document, other Word template changes require modifications to the underlying report definition in Report Writer. As a general rule of thumb, we should remember that if we are going to add new data to a Word template, we must first add the tables and fields to support that new data to the accompanying report definition in Report Writer.

If one of the template-enabled reports is modified in Report Writer and is then selected as the default report for use in the GP application, a new Word template must be created to use with the modified report. Until this new Word template is created, users will not be able to select the Template option when printing the report, even if the Word template for the original report is enabled!

Modifying the presentation of a default Word template

Now that we've discussed how the Word template modification process works, let's start making some changes to our existing Word templates! Since the process for making minor formatting changes to an existing template differs from the process for adding and removing fields, we have split this into two separate sections.

Applying simple formatting changes to an existing template

For our first modification, we'll modify the default SOP Blank Invoice Form Template by changing the **Total** field to a red font colour so that customers will easily see how much they owe. Additionally, we'll make the **Comment** fields larger and italicized to draw the customer's focus to important comments that may exist on the invoice. In the end, our modifications should improve the visual appeal of this report for customers who will receive these invoices.

Let's begin:

1. Open the **Report Template Maintenance** window by selecting **Reports | Template Maintenance**.
2. Click the **Report Name** field in the area that says **(Click here to select a report.)**.
3. Select **More Reports** to open the **Reports** window.
4. In the **Product** field, select **Microsoft Dynamics GP**.
5. In the **Series** field, select **Sales**.
6. In the **Status** field, select **Original**.
7. Scroll down to find and select the **SOP Blank Invoice Form**.

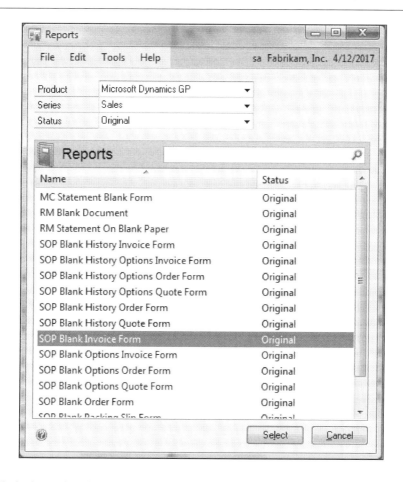

8. Click the **Select** button to return to the **Report Template Maintenance** window.

9. Since we cannot modify the Default template, we must create a copy of the template. To do this, select the default report in the **Template Name** pane. Click the **New** button at the top of the window to open the **New Template** window.

10. In the **New Template** window, select **From Existing Template**.

11. Enter the value **SOP Blank Invoice Form Template – Formatted** in the **Template Name** field.

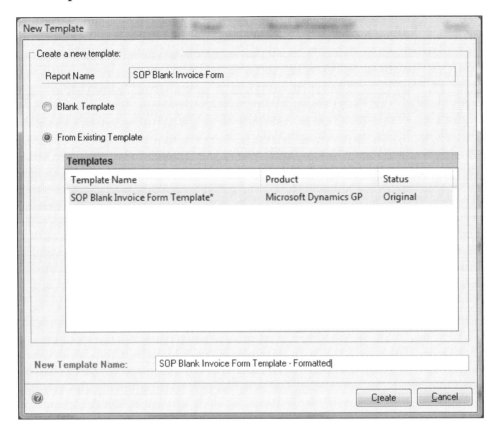

12. Click the **Create** button to create this new template and return to the **Report Template Maintenance** window.

13. Select the newly added report template from the **Template Name** pane and click the **Modify** button to open the report for modification in Word.

14. Towards the bottom right-hand corner of the report, find the **Total** field. Select the string of **X** values next to this field. A small screen tip will appear above the **X** values identifying this as the **F/O Document Amount** field.

15. On the **Home** tab in the ribbon, select the **Font Color** button and change the font colour of this field to red.

16. Now, find and select the first row of comment fields on the bottom left-hand corner of this template. This screen tip is identified as **sopUsrDefWorkHist**.

17. On the **Home** tab in the ribbon, select the **Italics** button to italicize comment text. Additionally, adjust the size of the text in this field to **10**. Because the comment text fields share a table with the total values on the right-hand side of the report, we want to make sure we don't make the comment text fields too large, as this may cause the total fields to spread out too far from each other.

18. Repeat the previous step for the additional comment lines.

19. With all modifications made to the report, click **File | Save As**.

20. Save the template to a file directory location that can be accessed in a later step. If an option exists in the file directory to **Maintain compatibility with previous versions**, select this option! Once the template is saved, close the Word document.

21. Return to the **Report Template Maintenance** window. In the **Template Name** pane, select the report template that was just renamed and modified.

22. Click the green plus sign at the top right-hand corner of the **Template Name** pane.

23. In the file directory, browse out to the location in which the modified template was saved. Select that template and click **Open**. When the override warning message appears, select **Yes** to replace the template.

Setting the default Word template for a company database

Now that we've modified our first Word template, we have a few steps remaining to assign the Word template as the default template for use in GP. Within a single GP company database, only one template version for each report can be selected as the default template. This template is the one that will print anytime the report is printed to the Template Report Type.

At least one report template must be set as the default template for the company database. Additionally, depending on the type of Word template we are working with, we have the ability to assign a modified template to a range of customers or customer classes (if we are working with Sales reports) or vendors or vendor classes (if we are working with Purchasing reports).

In this example, we'll set this report as the default report for the current company database:

1. Return to the **Report Template Maintenance** window and select the modified template in the **Template Name** pane.

2. Click the **Assign** button and select **Company** to open the **Company Assignment** window.

3. Select the checkbox next to the current company database:

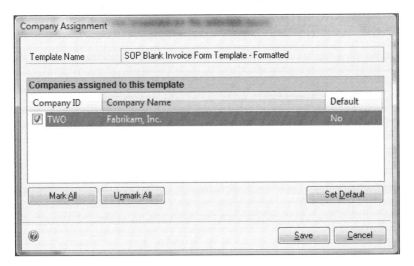

4. Click the **Set Default** button to open the **Default Assignment** window. Note the **Company Name** drop-down field in this window. If we had other company databases installed, we could select those databases to assign different default templates to each database.

5. Select the report that should be assigned as the default template. In this case, we will select the **SOP Blank Invoice Form Template – Formatted** report.

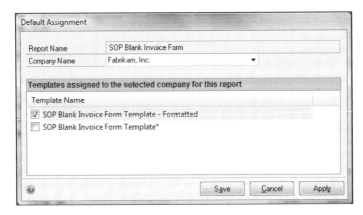

6. Click **Save** to close this window and save the selected report as the default report for this company database. Click **Save** on the **Company Assignment** window, as well.

To see the effects of our Word template modifications, let's print a Sales Invoice to screen using the **Blank Paper** format and **Template** as the **Report Type**!

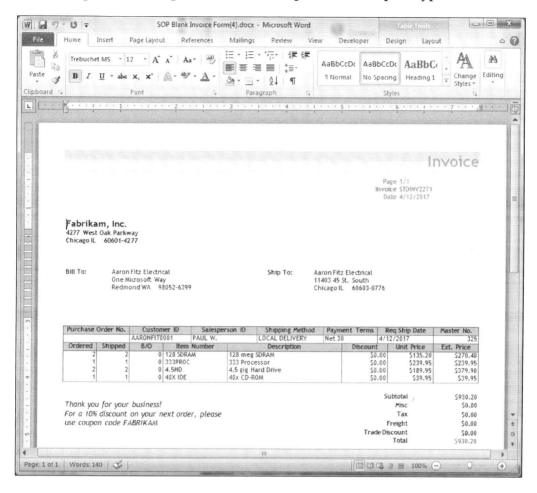

Congratulations, you've now modified your first Word template!

Adding fields to an existing Word template

Now that we've explored making formatting changes to Word templates, let's dig a little deeper and take a look at what is required to add new information to an existing Word template. In this example, we'll modify the Check Remittance report by adding the Vendor Contact name to the Remittance Header section.

Adding new fields to the Check Remittance template

Remember, as we said earlier, adding new fields to a Word template requires that we first make this change in the underlying report definition. To do this, we'll need to use Report Writer. Since we've already covered some basic modifications using Report Writer, we won't need to go into as much detail with this section as we will with making the change to the actual Word template:

1. Open Report Writer by selecting **Microsoft Dynamics GP | Tools | Customize | Report Writer**.

Before we go any further, we should note that the Vendor Contact field is found in the PM Vendor Master File table. This table is not included in the default report definition for the Check Remittance, nor does a pre-existing relationship exist between this table and any of the existing tables in the report definition. We must first create a table relationship between the PM Remittance Temp table and the PM Vendor Master File. Click the **Tables** button to find the **pmRemittance Temp** table and begin creating a relationship between that table and the **PM Vendor Master File** table.

Once the relationship is made, we can open our report to make the necessary modifications.

2. Click the **Reports** button to open the list of reports. Find and select the **Check Remittance** report and click the **Insert** button to add it to the list of **Modified Reports**.

3. With **Check Remittance** selected in the **Modified Reports** pane, select **Open** to open the **Report Definition** for the Check Remittance. Select the **Layout** button to open the Report Layout, as well.

4. In the **Toolbox** window that opens alongside the report layout, select **PM Vendor Master File** in the drop down.

5. Find and select the **Vendor Contact** field. Click and drag this field into the **H1 – Remittance Header** section of the report layout. Move the existing fields around to make room for the newly added field. Use the **Properties** window to modify the formatting of the new field to match the formatting of the existing fields in the same section. Additionally, add a text string to display the words **Vendor Contact** over the newly added field. When all modifications are made, our report should look similar to the following:

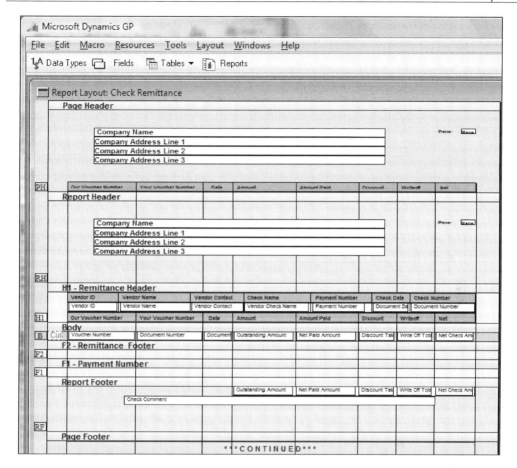

6. With all changes made, save and close the report layout and report definition.

7. Click **File | Microsoft Dynamics GP** to return to the GP 2010 application.

With the changes made to the underlying report definition, our focus now turns to modifying the Word template to reflect these changes. We return to the Report Template Maintenance window to make these changes:

8. Select **Reports | Template Maintenance** to open the **Report Template Maintenance** window.

9. Click the **Report Name** field in the area that says: **Click here to select a report**.

10. Select **More Reports** to open the **Reports** window.

11. In the **Product** field, select **Microsoft Dynamics GP**.

12. In the **Series** field, select **Purchasing**.

13. In the **Status** field, select **Modified**.

14. Scroll down to find and select the **Check Remittance** report.

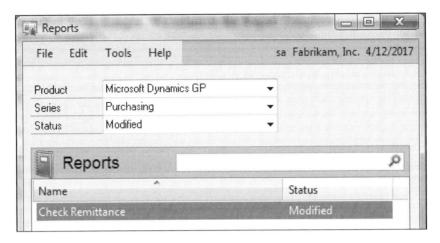

15. Click the **Select** button to return to the **Report Template Maintenance** window.

16. Click the **New** button to open the **New Template** window.

17. Select **From Existing Template.**

18. Enter the value **Check Remittance Template – Vendor Contact** in the **Template Name** field and click **Create** to return to the **Report Template Maintenance** window.

19. Select the template in the **Template Name** pane and click **Modify** to open the newly created template in Word for modification.

20. With Word open, select the **Developer** tab on the ribbon. Select the **Field List** icon in the **Microsoft Dynamics GP Templates** section of this tab. If you do not see the **Developer** tab or the **Microsoft Dynamics GP Templates** section, refer to the earlier section on Installing the Microsoft Dynamics GP add-in for Word.

21. In the newly opened Field List, select the drop-down under **XML Resource** and select **Check Remittance**. We are now shown a list of the sections in this report. Selecting a section displays a list of the fields that are available for use in that section. This is why it is so important that we modify the underlying report definition in Report Writer first; if we had not added the Vendor Contact field to the report in Report Writer, we would not be able to select that field in the Word template.

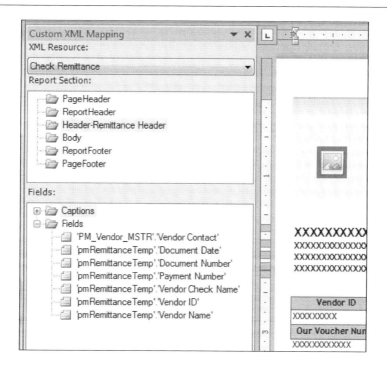

22. In the Word document, find the cell containing the words **Payment Number**. Select this cell and the one below it. Right-click and select **Insert | Insert Cells**. When prompted, select to **Shift Cells Right**. This creates a new set of cells where we can add our Vendor Contact caption and Vendor Contact field.

Check Name			Payment Number	
XXXXXX			XXXXXXXXXX	
	Amount	Amount Paid	Discount	Writeoff
	XXXXXXXXXXX	XXXXXXXXXXX	XXXXXX	XXXXXX

23. In the **Report Section** of the **Field List**, select **Header – Remittance Header**. In the **Fields** section, under the **Captions** folder, select **Vendor Contact**.

24. Click and drag the **Vendor Contact** caption to the upper-most cell that was just added to the template. At this point, it may be tempting to just type the words in this cell, but this is not recommended! In fact, although these words will appear in the template, when printing this template, the words will no longer appear. We must use the captions and fields from the **Field List** to generate and display data we want to see in the template!

25. Return to the **Field List** and select **PM_Vendor_MSTR.Vendor Contact** under the **Fields** folder.

26. Click and drag the **PM_Vendor_MSTR.Vendor Contact** field to the upper-most cell that was just added to the template.

27. Compare the newly added caption and field to surrounding cells to ensure that they are formatted and aligned in similar fashion. Use the **Home** and **Table Tools | Layout** tabs on the Ribbon to make these changes. At the end, your report template should look similar to this:

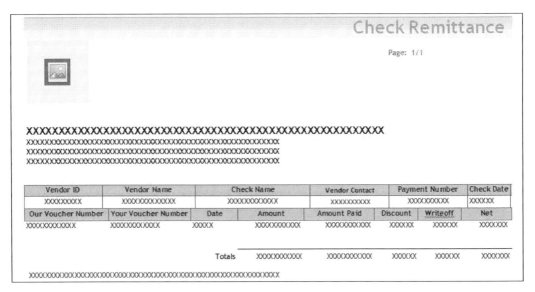

28. With all modifications made to the report, click **File | Save As**.

29. Save the template to a file directory location that can be accessed in a later step. If an option exists in the file directory to **Maintain compatibility with previous versions**, select this option! Once the template is saved, close the Word document.

30. Return to the **Report Template Maintenance** window. In the **Template Name** pane, select the report template that was just renamed and modified.

31. Click the green plus sign at the top right-hand corner of the **Template Name** pane.

32 In the file directory, browse out to the location in which the modified template was saved. Select that template and click **Open**. When the override warning message appears, select **Yes** to replace the template.

At this point, we must now choose to assign this report as the default for this company. Steps on how to do this were included at the end of the earlier section on changing formats in Word templates. Refer to these instructions to set the newly modified template as the default template when the **Template** option is selected for the Check Remittance report.

Once we've set this template as the default, let's print a Check Remittance to see what our efforts have created!

We have barely scratched the surface of what can be achieved with Word template functionality. We hope you'll expand on this information to extend the capabilities of the Word template functionality to create even more useful and aesthetically pleasing customer and vendor-facing documents!

Summary

In this chapter, we covered the Report Writer tool in GP 2010. As one of the oldest report writing tools associated with Dynamics GP, numerous reports in the current versions of GP originated and are still maintained with Report Writer. Although newer, easier to use reporting tools continue to be developed, developers and consultants will still find themselves needing a bit of Report Writer "know-how" in order to make modifications to the standard GP 2010 reports!

Just as we covered one of the oldest reporting tools in the Dynamics GP space, we also took a look at one of the newest tools in the same arena. In an effort to provide us with more user-friendly, portable reports, Microsoft has added the Word template functionality to the latest version of Dynamics GP. Rather than print clunky Report Writer reports to screen, numerous reports can now be printed to a Microsoft Word document. This Word document can then be formatted, saved, and even attached to an email document. We think GP users are only just beginning to learn about this great new functionality, and hopefully this chapter has provided just enough information to give us a leg-up on this great tool!

In the next chapter, we'll explore the SSRS Reports Library and the reports that comprise this toolset. The SSRS Reports Library offers us a predefined set of reports that can be deployed to an SSRS environment, but we'll also explore the basics of creating a simple SSRS report from scratch.

5
SSRS Report Library

Of the reporting tools covered in this book, Microsoft SQL Server Reporting Services, or SSRS for short, is perhaps the most well-known and widely used tool of all. As one of the components of SQL Server, SSRS can be used for reporting across a wide range of data sources. SSRS provides a mechanism for designing and creating reports, publishing reports to a Report Server, managing access to these reports through role-based security, and viewing these reports through a web-based connection. In short, SSRS is capable of managing the entire reporting process from beginning to end.

Because of its versatility and sophistication, however, SSRS can be a challenging tool to learn in the context of being used with a single application such as Dynamics GP 2010. In years past, report development via SSRS has often been considered the domain of the technical experts on staff. But this is changing! With recent versions of GP, even the less technically adept developers and consultants are now able to add SSRS as an important instrument in their reporting toolset. Dynamics GP 10.0 introduced a series of pre-defined SQL Server Reporting Services-based reports that cover a wide range of modules and can easily be deployed in an environment in which SSRS is installed and configured properly. These SSRS reports are accessible just as any other SSRS report with one exception: we can also modify GP to allow us to access these SSRS reports directly from GP!

Dynamics GP 2010 took the pre-defined SSRS report concept a step farther and introduced us to SSRS-based Charts and Key Performance Indicators (KPIs). Although charts and KPIs have been available in earlier versions of GP, they were not SSRS based and could not be easily modified. Now, with GP 2010, developers and consultants can deploy a series of pre-defined charts and KPIs and they can also create their own metrics that can be displayed on the GP Homepage!

Obviously, a lot can be achieved with SSRS. Our goal with this chapter is not to provide a step-by-step guide to using SSRS in order to create reports from scratch. That would require far more than just a single chapter, and, to be quite honest, numerous resources already exist that describe SQL Server Reporting Services in far greater depth than we can here! For readers who are interested in learning how to use SSRS to its fullest capabilities, we strongly suggest that you take the time to discover and read through those resources.

What we will cover in this chapter, however, is how the predefined SSRS reports and charts can be used to jumpstart our use of SSRS as a valuable tool for our organization. Using these reports will allow us to form a base from which far more effective and useful reports can be developed. In this chapter, we'll cover the following topics:

- Installing and configuring reporting services
- Deploying the predefined SSRS reports and metrics to the report server
- Exposing the predefined reports and metrics in Dynamics GP 2010
- Managing security for these reports
- Using Visual Studio to modify a predefined SSRS report
- Using Report Builder to create a new metric

Getting started with SQL Server Reporting Services

Before we can deploy and utilize the SQL Reporting Services Reports available for Dynamics GP we must have an SSRS Report Manager site available to us. Installing and configuring this is actually a very easy task. Dynamics GP supports both Windows Server 2003 and 2008 and SQL Server versions 2005 and 2008. We will discuss the configuration for both of these.

Deployment configurations

Reporting Services can be deployed in several ways. Our first step is to determine which deployment model we will use. The two models we will be discussing are:

- Standard deployment model
- Scale-out deployment model

Let's take a look at the two models in detail.

Standard model

The standard model is made up of a single reporting server instance that will use either a local or a remote SQL server to host the reporting services database. A major consideration here is processing resources, as both the report server and the database engine compete for CPU time, memory, and disk access. The report server will attempt to use all available memory for rendering reports. We must also consider disk space, as the disk space needed can grow pretty significantly at run time depending on how many users require access to the reporting server and how much data will be retrieved.

The standard model of deployment consists of two further options:

- Single-server configuration – This is where the report server database is installed locally so that all components are on the same server
- Separate server configuration – This is where the report server is on its own IIS Web Server that connects to a separate SQL server for the Reporting Services Database

Scale-out model

The scale-out model is made up of multiple reporting servers that share a single reporting services database. This gives us the benefit of running these servers in a server cluster. In this model, the database can be installed on a remote SQL server instance or locally on one of the report servers in the reporting server cluster.

Additional software and tools that support either virtual servers or Network Load Balancing must be used if we wish to set up a server cluster, as Reporting Services does not natively provide clustering or virtual server management.

Depending on the extent of Reporting Services usage, the Standard deployment model is usually the easiest and quickest to get deployed.

[141]

Prerequisites for installing SQL Reporting Services

In order to use Reporting Services, there are quite a few components that must be installed before we can install SQL Server Reporting Services for use with Dynamics GP. The following chart from Microsoft lists the necessary Operating System, Database, Web Server, and Web Browser requirements:

Item	Requirements
Operating system 32 bit and 64 bit supported	**Server** Windows Server® 2003 with latest service pack Windows Server 2008 with latest service pack **Client** Windows XP with latest service pack Windows Vista® with latest service pack Windows 7 with latest service pack
Database	Microsoft SQL Server 2005 with service pack 2 or later Microsoft SQL Server 2008 with service pack 1 or later
Web server for Reporting Services 2005	Internet Information Services (IIS) 6.0 IIS 7.0 on Windows Server 2008
Web browser	Internet Explorer 8 Internet Explorer 7
Microsoft Dynamics GP	Microsoft Dynamics GP 2010

Configuring IIS for Reporting Services

Internet Information Services (IIS) must be installed before Reporting Services can be installed, as both a website and a web service are created during the installation. IIS is the technology that hosts both of these.

Configuring IIS for Windows Server 2003

1. Open Add/Remove Programs. **Start | Control Panel | Add/Remove Programs**.

2. Click **Add/Remove Windows Components** to open the Windows Components Wizard.

3. Select **Applications Server** in the list and click the **Details** button.

4. Mark the following Application Server subcomponents:
   - ○ ASP.Net
   - ○ Enable network COM + access
   - ○ Enable network DTC access
   - ○ Internet Information Services (IIS)

5. Click the **Details** button on **Internet Information Services (IIS)**.

6. Mark the following IIS subcomponents:
   - ○ Common Files
   - ○ Internet Information Services Manager

7. Click OK.

 Adding these components may require that the Windows Server 2003 product CD be inserted, so be sure to have it available. A reboot might also be required so be sure to plan ahead in the event that this is necessary.

Configuring IIS for Windows Server 2008

1. Open the Server Manager. **Start | Administrative Tools | Server Manager**.

2. Select the **Roles** node.

3. Choose **Add Roles** from the **Action Menu**. The **Add Roles Wizard** will appear. Click **Next** to continue.

4. Select **Web Server (IIS)** role from the list of available roles.

5. Click **Next** to continue.

6. Review the information regarding the web server role and click **Next** to continue.

7. In the Select Role Services window, select the following subcomponents for the web server role services:
   - ○ Common HTTP Features
   - ○ Static Content
   - ○ Default Document
   - ○ Directory Browsing
   - ○ HTTP Errors

- ○ HTTP Redirection
- ○ Application Development
- ○ ASP.Net
- ○ .Net Extensibility
- ○ ISAPI Extensions
- ○ ISAPI Filters
- ○ Security
- ○ Windows Authorization
- ○ Request Filtering

8. In the **Select Role Services** window, select the following components for the Management Tools role services:

  - ○ IIS Management Console
  - ○ IIS 6 Management Compatibility

9. Click **Next**.

10. Review installation messages and click **Install**.

Installing and configuring Reporting Services

Once we have Internet Information Services configured for Reporting Services, we can install and configure Reporting Services. The version of Reporting Services we will install is dependent on which version of SQL Server we are running. For SQL Server 2005, we will install Reporting Services 2005 and for SQL Server 2008, we will install Reporting Services 2008.

The following instructions will guide you through installing SQL Server Reporting Services 2008. For detailed instructions on installing Reporting Services 2005, please see the SQL Server Reporting Services guide that comes with Dynamics GP 2010. These instructions assume that SQL Server 2008 is already installed and that Reporting Services is being installed in a single-server configuration. When running the installation, we must be logged in as a member of the local system administrators group and the SQL Server login we are using must have administrative privileges in SQL Server in order to create logins, roles and databases, and to assign roles to logins.

Installing Reporting Services

1. Insert the SQL Server 2008 installation disk. If the installation splash screen does not appear, we can browse the media and double-click the `setup.exe` file.

2. If the system is set up to use User Account Control, click **Yes** to allow changes, otherwise skip to step 3.

3. In the **SQL Server Installation Center**, click **Installation**.

4. Click **New SQL Server stand-alone installation** or add new features to an existing installation.

5. In the **Setup Support Rules** page, click **OK**.

6. In the **Setup Support Files** page, click **Install**.

7. The computer will be scanned for any conditions that could cause installation problems. To proceed, click **Next**.

8. In the **Installation Type** window, select **Add features** to add to an existing instance of SQL Server 2008 and click **Next**.

9. In the **Feature Selection** window, select **Reporting Services** and any other feature that needs to be installed. Click **Next**.

10. In the **Disk Requirements** window, click **Next**.

11. In the **Server Configuration** window, enter the **Account Name**. Click **Next**.

12. In the **Reporting Services Configuration** window, click **Next**.

13. In the **Error and Usage Reporting** window, click **Next**.

14. In the **Installation Rules** window, click **Next**.

15. In the **Ready to Install** window, click **Next**.

16. The **Installation Progress** window will appear, allowing us to view the status of the installation. Click **Next** after the installation has completed.

17. In the **Complete** window, click **Close** to exit the wizard.

18. Restart the computer if instructed to do so.

Configuring Reporting Services

1. Start Reporting Services Configuration Manager by browsing to **Start | All Programs | Microsoft SQL Server 2008 | Configuration Tools | Reporting Services Configuration Manager.** If set up to use User Account Control, click Yes to make changes:

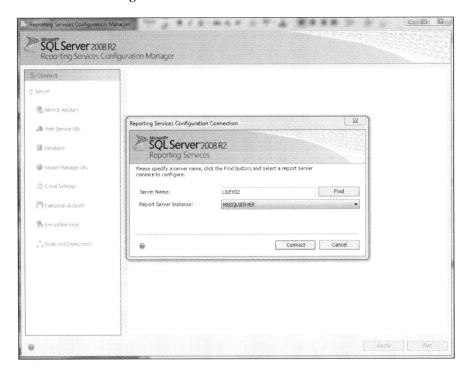

2. As the previous image depicts, enter the **Server Name** and select a **Report Server Instance** to connect to. Click **Connect**.

3. If Reporting Services isn't running, click the **Start** button in the **Report Server Status** page. Otherwise, your screen should look like the following image:

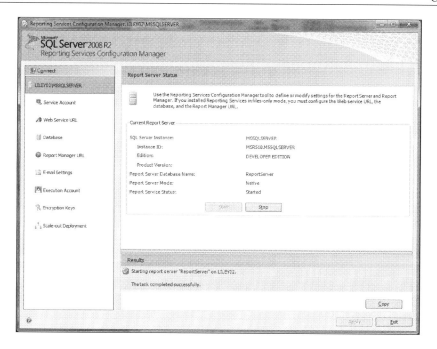

4. In the navigation pane, click **Service Account** to open the page. Be sure that the **Use the built-in account** option is selected as it is in the following image:

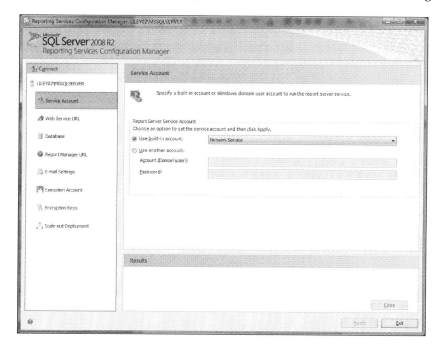

5. In the navigation pane, click **Web Service URL** to open the **Web Service URL page**. Accept **ReportServer** as the name of the virtual directory used by the Reporting Services Web service. Your screen should look similar to the following:

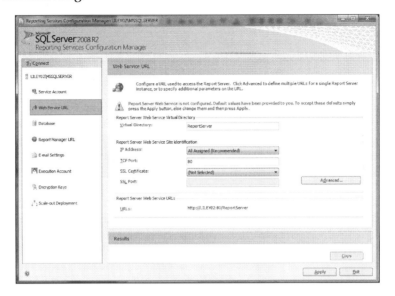

6. Click **Apply** to create the new virtual directory.

7. In the navigation pane, click **Database** to open the **Report Server Database** page seen in the following screenshot:

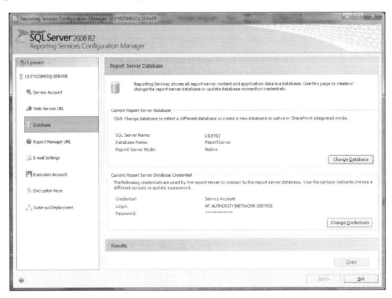

8. Click the **Change Database** button to open the **Change Database** window seen in the next image:

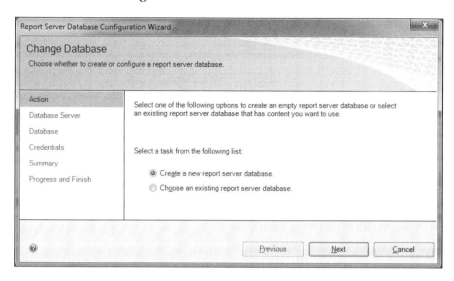

9. Select **Create a new report server database** and click **Next**. This takes us to the Database Server tab (seen in the next image), where we can identify a server name and authentication type:

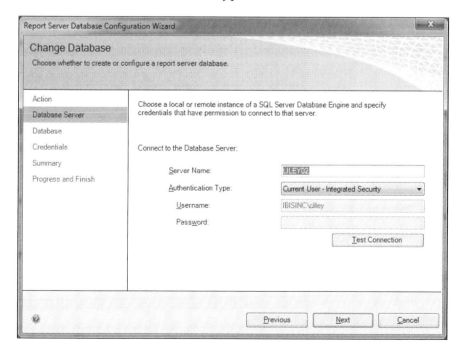

10. Select **Authentication type** and specify the username and password to connect to the Report Server Database. Click **Next**. We are taken to the **Database** tab (seen in the next image) where we can identify specifics about the new database that will be created:

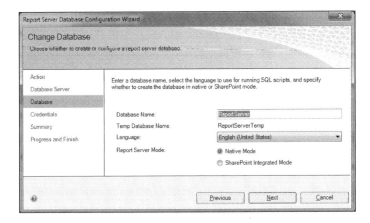

11. Specify the **database name (Report Server by default)** and specify the **Report Server mode**. Click **Next**.

12. Select **Authentication type** and specify the username and password for the appropriate credentials (if different from step 10). Click **Next**.

13. Verify the database information and click **Next**.

14. After the database is configured, click **Finish**.

15. In the navigation pane, click **Report Manager URL** to open **the Report Manager URL page** found in the following image. Click **Apply**.

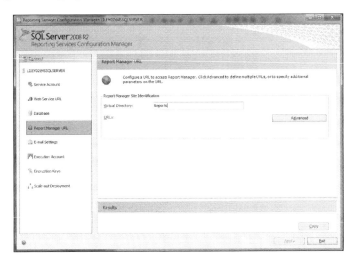

16. Click the **Advanced** button to open the **Advanced Multiple Web Site Configuration** window.

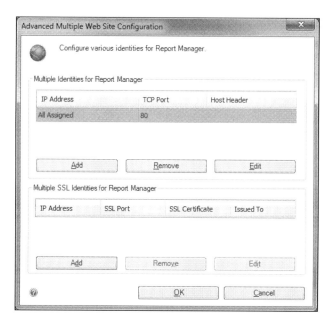

17. Under the **Multiple Identities for Report Manager** section, click the **Add** button.

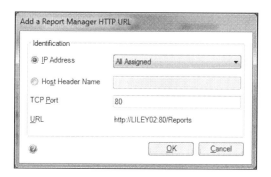

18. On the **Add a Report Manager HTTP URL** window, verify **All Assigned** is selected for **IP Address** and click **OK**.

19. Click **OK** on the **Multiple Identities for Report Manager** section.

20. Click **Exit**.

Starting Report Manager

Once installation and configuration is complete for the version of Reporting Services, verify that the Report Manager site is accessible. To do this, perform the following steps:

1. Open Microsoft Internet Explorer 7.0 or later.

2. Type the Report Manager URL in the address bar. If you used the default path, the URL will be `http://<ComputerName>/Reports`.

 If the Report Manager site is on a port other than the default site, the URL would be `http://<ComputerName>:<Port Number>/Reports`.

The Report Manager is the landing screen for the Reporting Services website. This is where users can browse the data sources, folders, and reports as well as generate the reports that have been deployed to the Report Manager site. More detail on this will be covered in the next section.

Deploying SQL Reporting Services reports and metrics

A new feature was added beginning with GP 10.0 that allows users to deploy predefined SSRS reports for use with GP data. Numerous reports span many GP modules including:

- Financials & Bank Reconciliation
- Receivables Management & Payables Management
- Sales Order Processing & Purchasing Order Processing
- Inventory
- Project Accounting
- Payroll
- Human Resources
- Contract Administration
- Manufacturing
- Returns Management

If set up properly, these reports can be accessed from within GP, meaning users will spend less time browsing out to the SSRS landing page and finding the correct report in the correct folder. Instead, they will select from the list of Custom Reports to see the reports that were deployed using the SQL Server Reporting Services Wizard for Dynamics GP.

Additionally, since the introduction of GP 2010, users are now able to deploy Charts and Metrics that are available from the Home page when logging into the application. This feature is only available for users who are running on SQL Server 2008 or later.

Let's take a look at the steps required to deploy and utilize our pre-defined SSRS reports.

Installing the SQL Server Reporting Services Wizard

Before we can deploy our predefined reports, we need to install the SQL Server Reporting Services Wizard. Once the wizard is installed, we will use it to deploy reports to various GP company databases.

1. To begin the installation of the wizard, select the **SQL Server Reporting Services Wizard** option from the GP 2010 install CD. With so many additional products, it can be easy to miss, so use the following image as a guide:

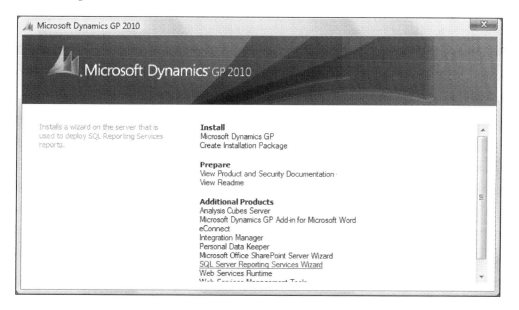

2. Read through the terms of the License Agreement and select **Next** after agreeing to the Terms and Conditions for using this wizard.

3. In the **Select Features** window seen in the following screenshot, determine which features should be installed as well as the location to which the Wizard should be installed:

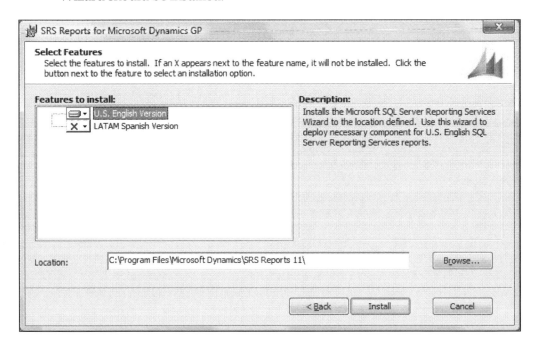

4. Click **Install** to install the wizard to your selected location. When the install is complete, select **Finish** to exit.

Deploying predefined Reporting Services Reports and metrics for Dynamics GP

Once the SQL Server Reporting Services Wizard has been installed, we can now begin deploying our reports for a single company database:

1. From the server or computer on which the SQL Server Reporting Services wizard was installed, click **Start | Programs | Microsoft Dynamics | Business Intelligence | Microsoft SQL Server Reporting Services Wizard** to open the wizard.

2. Click **Next** at the initial screen to open the **Connect to Database Server** window.

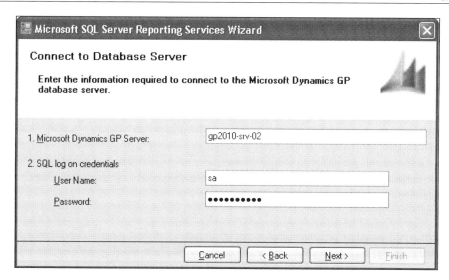

3. In the **Microsoft Dynamics GP Server** field, enter the name of the server that contains the Dynamics GP database(s).

4. Enter a **User Name** and **Password** to use for connecting to the server and database.

5. Click **Next** to open the **Select Database and Module** window.

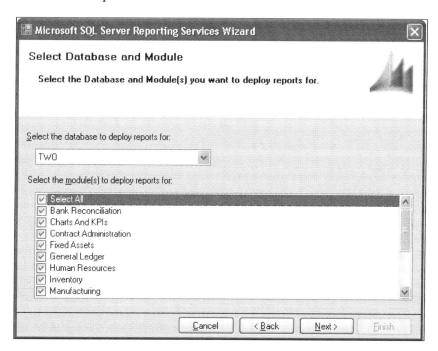

6. In the drop-down box, select the database for which reports should be deployed.

7. Select the modules for which reports should be deployed. Remember, if the deployment is occurring in a SQL Server 2005 environment, the **Charts and KPIs** option should not be selected. Otherwise, the deployment will fail with a message that the target server is not SQL Server 2008!

8. Click **Next** to open the **Define Location and Deploy Reports** window.

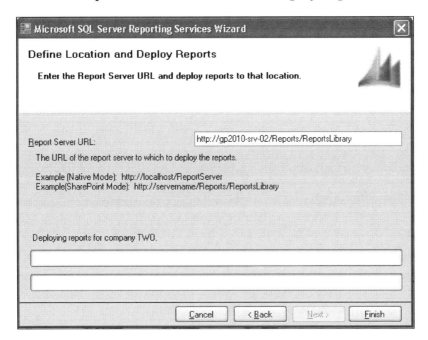

9. Depending on how SSRS is configured in your environment, enter either the file path to the Report Server or the path to the SharePoint Reports Library.

 Note that if performing this deployment for GP 10.0, only the Native Mode option can be used.

10. Click **Finish** to begin deploying the selected reports for the selected company database.

11. Once the deployment is complete, users have an option to deploy reports for another company database, or to close the wizard.

Once the reports have been deployed, they can be viewed from the Report Manager. The default URL for the Report Manager is `http://<ComputerName>/reports`. If deploying these reports to Native Mode, the Homepage for SQL Server Reporting Services will look similar to the following image:

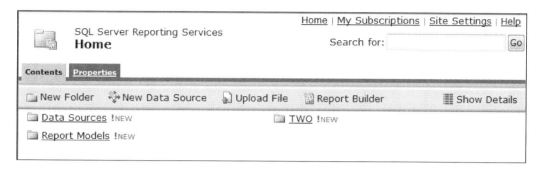

Notice that during the installation, several new folders were created. First, a Data Sources folder is created. This folder contains data sources for the DYNAMICS database as well as the GP company database selected during the install. A second folder is named after the GP company database. This folder contains the deployed reports, grouped together in folders by specific modules. Additionally, if Charts and Metrics were deployed then these charts will be found under the company database folders. Finally, we will see a Report Models folder containing all of the report models generated by this deployment.

Listing SQL Server Reporting Services reports in the Dynamics GP Report List

The next step is making the changes necessary to be able to view these reports and metrics straight out of the Dynamics GP application. Rather than switching to a browser application and logging in to the SSRS Homepage, we can connect directly to these predefined reports from within GP!

1. Open the Microsoft Dynamics GP menu.

2. Select **Tools | Setup | System | Reporting Tools Setup** to open the **Reporting Tools Setup** window. The **SQL Reporting Services** tab should be selected.

3. In the **Report Server URL** field, enter the location of the Report Server. Depending on whether it is a Native Mode installation or SharePoint installation, the syntax will vary:

   `http://localhost/ReportServer/ReportService.asmx`

OR

```
http://IISServername/reports/Pages/Folder.aspx
```

4. In the **Report Manager URL** field, enter the location of the Report Manager. Depending on whether it's a Native Mode installation or SharePoint installation, the syntax will vary:

```
http://localhost/ReportServer/ReportService.asmx
```

OR

```
http://IISServername/reports/Pages/Folder.aspx
```

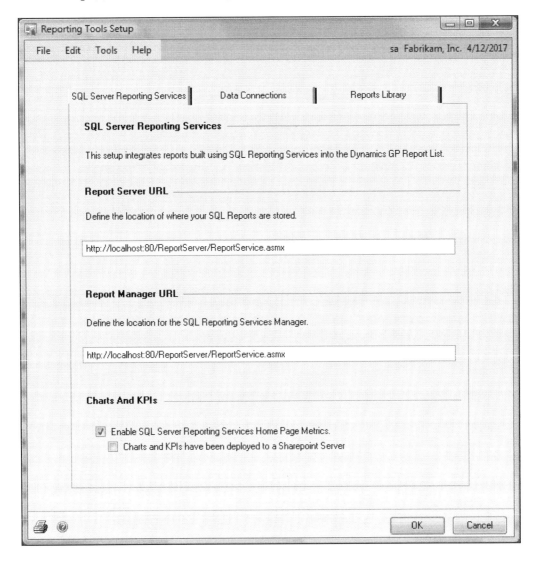

5. Finally, if Charts and KPIs were included in the deployment, mark the **Enable SQL Server Reporting Services Home Page Metrics** option near the bottom of this window. This will allow us to replace the standard, non-SSRS **Metrics** on the GP 2010 **Home** page with SSRS metrics, instead.

6. If the deployment was done to a SharePoint Server, mark the **Charts and KPIs have been deployed to a SharePoint server** option, as well.

7. Click **OK** to save these changes and close the **Reporting Tools Setup** window.

 Note that, if SSRS is using a port other than the default (80), the URLs listed in the previous steps may need to be modified to include the new port number. The URL would then look similar to the following (where 81 is the new port number):

```
http://localhost:81/ReportServer/ReportService.asmx
```

In addition to being visible from the Report Manager in a web browser, the reports are now available under the **Custom Reports** list from within GP. Selecting **Custom Reports** will open a list of the deployed SSRS reports found at the location identified in the preceding steps. To open this list, click on **Custom Reports** in the left-hand sidebar with the **Home** tab selected:

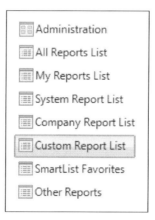

Using the predefined SSRS reports

Most of the predefined SSRS reports contain parameters that can be modified by the user in order to change the report content. Some reports have default values for parameters, enabling the report content to be viewed immediately upon opening the report. Others, however, require the user to specify values before the report content can be generated.

For example, one of the predefined reports found in the Financial module is the Trial Balance Detail. Assuming we have followed the instructions for enabling the selection of the predefined reports directly from GP, we can scroll through our list of reports in the Custom Reports window and double-click the **Trial Balance Detail**. This opens the **Trial Balance Detail** report in SSRS, as seen in the following screenshot:

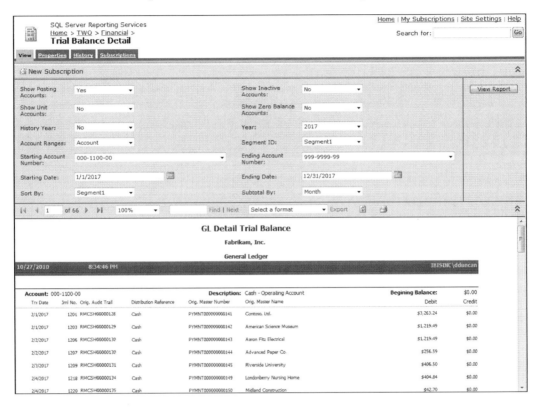

At the top of this particular report, we see 14 different parameters that can be used to control the content of the generated report! Although some parameters default, it is highly likely we will want to change some of the other parameters to control what appears in our report. Because we are using Fabrikam sample data in the displayed example, we can set our data parameters to pull transactions between 01/01/2017 and 12/31/2017 to view detailed transactions for the current year. Once we've selected or changed our parameters, we can select **View Report** to regenerate our report.

Viewing the charts and KPIs from within GP

If you'll recall, during the deployment of the pre-defined SSRS reports, we were given an option to also install Charts and KPIs. This option is only available for GP 2010 and SQL Server 2008 installations. After these Charts and KPIs are deployed, they reside under the Report Manager or Reports Library in a folder called **Charts and KPIs**, which is found under the module-level folders for each company. However, with just a few minor setups, we can expose these charts and metrics so that they are visible from each GP 2010 user's Home page as they are in the following image:

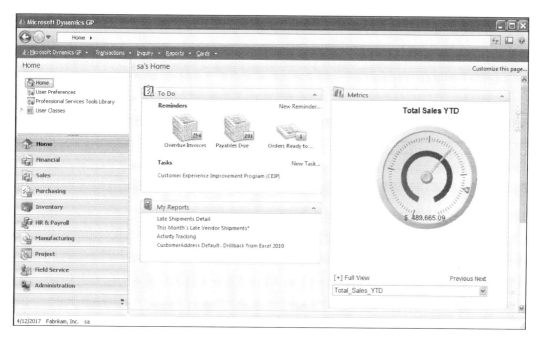

Before following this next set of instructions, confirm that Charts and KPIs have been deployed. Additionally, confirm that the Report Server and Report Manager URLs have been defined in the Reporting Tools Setup window and that the option to enable Charts and KPIs in the same window has been enabled. Instructions for completing both of these steps are listed earlier in this chapter. Now, let's take a look at the final steps required to add the metrics to a user's homepage.

1. Open Microsoft Dynamics GP. Log in with the user who will need access to the metrics.

2. On the **Home** page, click **Customize this page** to open the **Customize Home Page** window. This option is found in the upper-right hand corner of the **Home** page.

3. Mark the **Metrics** checkbox.

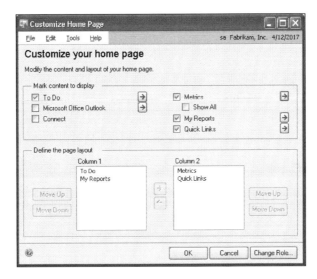

4. Click the blue expansion arrow next to **Metrics** in order to open the **Metrics Details** window. This window will generate a list of the available Charts and KPIs in the left-hand pane.

5. In the **Metrics Details** window, select from the list of available Charts and KPIs and click **Insert** to move the selected metric to the right hand column. This will cause the selected metric to be displayed on the **Home** page.

6. Repeat the process of adding options for additional metrics that should be displayed on the **Home** page. In the following image, the **Top_Customer_ Balances** and **Total_Sales_YTD** metrics have been selected for viewing:

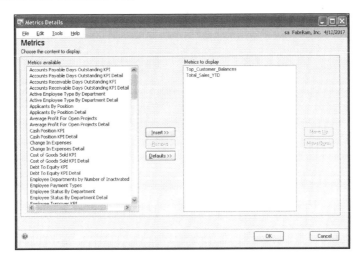

7. Once all metrics have been added, click **OK** to close the **Metrics Details** window and return to the **Customize Home Page** window.

8. Depending on the number of metrics that were selected in the previous window, it may be beneficial to click the **Show All** button under the **Metrics**option. Selecting this option will force all metrics to appear on the **Home** page at the same time. The metrics can be quite large, so this may not be prudent in cases where more than four were selected on the **Metrics Details** screen!

9. Once all options have been set properly, click **OK** to close the window.

The selected metrics will now be visible on the Homepage. It may be necessary to click away from the Homepage and then back in order to allow the page to refresh with the new settings. At some point, however, users will be able to see the selected metrics. If the **Show All** button was not selected, then users can select the drop-down menu or select the Previous/Next buttons to cycle between available metrics. Additionally, users can select the **Full View** button to open the corresponding metric in an SSRS browser.

Configuring security for Reporting Services

Once we've installed the predefined reports metrics, we need to define which users will have access to these objects. Security for SSRS reports is two-fold: first, we must grant access to the actual reports in the Report Manager, and then we must grant database access to the report so that it can actually retrieve data from the database.

Note that, after the initial deployment, only users who are members of the web server's local administrator group and the database server's local administrator group will be able to view and generate reports from the Report Manager. All other users must wait for the security policy to be modified so that they can also view and generate data for the reports.

Assigning access to the Reporting Services website

The first step to setting up security for the predefined SSRS reports is to set security for the Reporting Services website. This is done by granting access to Windows Groups or Users to Roles that have been set up in the Report Manager. Although individual Windows Users can be granted access to these SSRS Roles, we recommend setting up Windows Groups, if possible.

The process of granting access to Reporting Services can be done within the Report Manager or SQL Server Management Studio while using an account with administrative privileges on the server. In this example, we'll use the Report Manager to grant access to the Reporting Services website. In this example, we have set up a Windows Group called "GP Users". To this group, we have added users who will need access to Reporting Services website in order to view the pre-defined reports that we just deployed.

1. In this example, in which we assume a Native Mode installation, connect to the Report Manager Homepage. By default, this URL is `http://<ComputerName>/reports`.

2. Click the **Properties** tab highlighted in the following image:

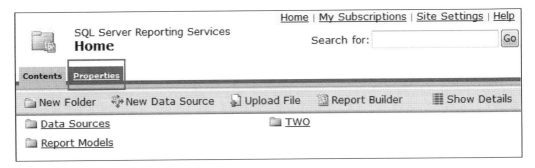

3. Click the **Security** tab so that your view looks similar to the following image.

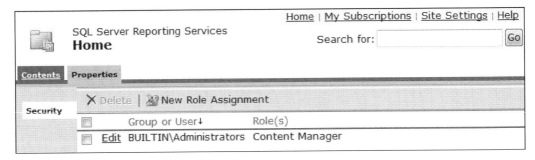

The **BUILTIN\Administrators** group should already be assigned the role of Content Manager for the Home level. SSRS security operates via inherited permissions, meaning that if we assign a group or user to an item-level role at the Home level, the permissions granted by that role will be extended to all subfolders of the Home page, including the TWO and Data Sources folders.

4. Click **New Role Assignment** to open a list of the item-level roles that have been created in SSRS.

5. In the **Group or User Name** field, we'll enter **GP Users** as the name of the group being granted permissions.

6. Select the pre-defined **Browser** role to allow users in the **GP Users** group to view folders, reports, and subscribe to reports under the Homepage. To see a list of all tasks assigned to the **Browser** role (or any other role, for that matter), click the role name. This will open the **Edit Role** window and allow us to see the tasks assigned to this role. Click the browser's **Back** button to return to the **New Role Assignment** window seen in the following image:

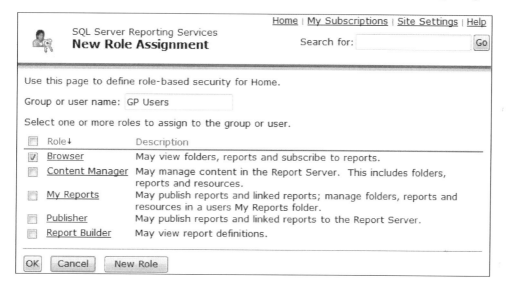

7. After confirming that the **Browser** role is selected for the **GP Users** group, click **OK** to commit this change. If an error message appears, oftentimes it means that the group or user entered in the previous window was either misspelled or has not been setup in Windows.

Otherwise, we will be returned to the **Properties** page of the Home level to see that our group has been assigned to the **Browser** role. The permissions granted by this role have now been extended to the folders below the Home level. We can confirm this by clicking into any of these folders and selecting **Properties | Security**.

In this example, we have used one of the pre-defined item-level roles to grant read-only report permissions to a Windows group. Additional roles can be set up if our company's security requirements dictate stricter security measurements. Also, in multi-company databases, a company may require that users in one group have access to reports for a single company database. This would require manipulating the inherited permissions policy that we discussed earlier in our example. To handle these specific security needs, we strongly encourage readers to refer to SQL Server Books Online or other SQL Server Reporting Services material for information on how to properly set up Reporting Services security.

Setting up database security for predefined SSRS reports

By default, the data sources that were deployed with the pre-defined SSRS reports are set up to allow connections to the database via Windows integrated security. In other words, when generating an SSRS report referencing data in a GP database, the current Windows user account will be authenticated against the database. If that individual user, or a group to which that user has been assigned, has been granted permissions to the appropriate roles in the GP and DYNAMICS databases, then the report will return data from that database.

In this step, we will create a SQL login for our newly created GP Users group. Then, we will map that SQL login to several database roles that have been set up to control database access for SQL Reporting Services users.

1. Open SQL Management Studio.
2. In the **Connect to Server** window, select **Database Engine** as the server type.
3. In the **Server Name** field, enter the name of the server that contains the GP databases.
4. In the **Authentication** field, select either **Windows Authentication** or **SQL Server Authentication**. The selected user should have administrative rights on the server.
5. Click **Connect**.
6. Expand the **Security** node.
7. Right-click the **Logins** node and click **New Login** to open the **Login – New** window.
8. In the **Login Name** field, enter the name of the Windows user or group being granted database access in the form of <domain>\<username> or <domain>\<groupname>. Click the **Search** button to look up the group or user from a list.

9. On the **Login – New** window, confirm that **Windows Authentication** is selected.

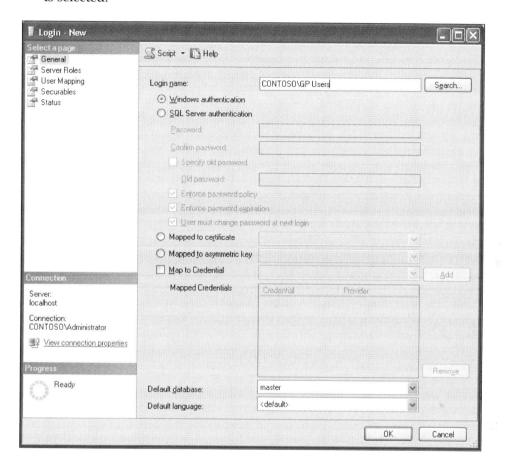

10. Click the **User Mapping** page from the left-hand pane.
11. Click the checkbox next to the **DYNAMICS** database.
12. In the **Database Role Membership** pane at the bottom of the window, click the checkbox for the **rpt_all user** role.
13. Back in the database pane, click the checkbox next to the GP database for which SSRS reports were deployed.

14. In the **Database Role Membership** pane at the bottom of the window, click the checkbox for the appropriate roles preceded by "rpt_". Refer to the link at the end of this section for more information on how to determine which roles are necessary for the group or user.

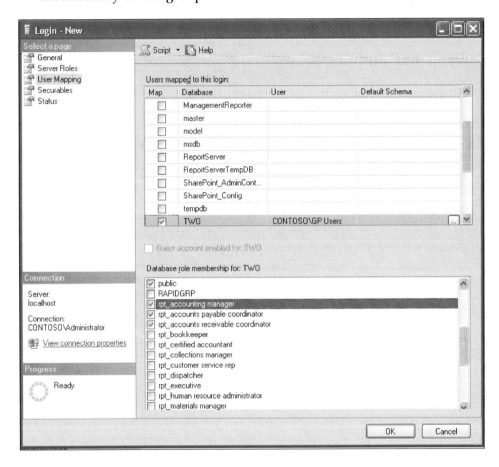

15. Repeat the mapping process for any additional GP company databases.

16. Click **OK** to add the new login to the SQL server database with the user mappings that we have just defined.

If the pre-defined Excel Reports described in Chapter 3 have also been deployed to this server, the "rpt_" database roles will have already been created on the server. These database roles will be used for both the pre-defined Excel Reports and the pre-defined SSRS reports.

For those of us with a CustomerSource or PartnerSource login, a handy document can be downloaded that details each of the SSRS reports and the corresponding database roles that are required to view that report. This document can be found at the following link:

```
https://mbs.microsoft.com/fileexchange/?fileID=80628e60-729d-4e47-
bbd5-37af74ea39c7
```

Modifying the canned reports with Visual Studio

Now that we have learned how to deploy the pre-defined Reports, access them in Dynamics GP 2010 and how to assign security to them, we will now take a look at modifying these reports with Visual Studio to curtail them too our particular organization's needs. We will look at modifying the GL Detail Trial Balance report (see the following image) to include the Transaction Source Document code. This code can be used in a number of ways, the most common being the sub ledger where the transaction originated, but also it can be used to sort transactions.

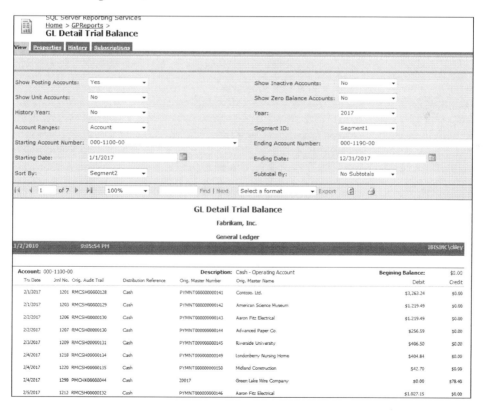

In order to begin, we need to get the report into Visual Studio so that we can work with it. There is a Visual Studio solution file provided with Dynamics GP 2010 that can be opened in Visual Studio and changes can be made there and re-deployed to the Report Server. Another way, which we will discuss here, is to copy down the report file from the Report Server and open that file in Visual Studio. One advantage of doing it this way is that we can be sure we are using the most recent copy that is in use.

Let's go ahead and take a look at the steps required to copy and make changes to our existing report file:

1. Launch the **Report Manager** by opening a web-browser and type in the **Report Manager URL** into the address bar.

2. Browse the folders on the Report Manager to the location of the GL Detail Trial Balance and click the report to open it.

3. Click the **Properties** tab to open a view similar to the following:

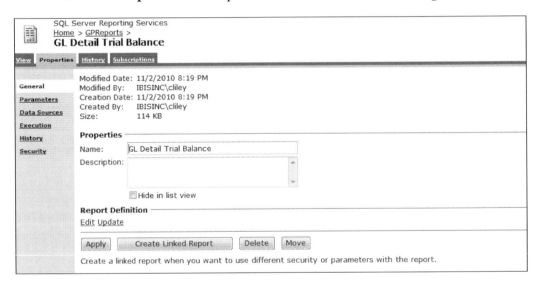

4. In the Report Definition section, select **Edit**:

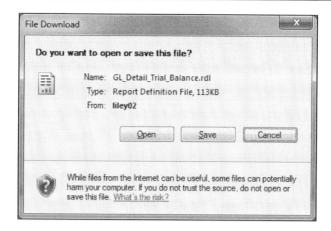

5. Save the `GL_Detail_Trial_Balance.rdl` file to a local folder or a file share.

6. Launch Visual Studio by going to **All Programs | Microsoft Visual Studio 2008 | Microsoft Visual Studio 2008**.

7. Create a new project by selecting **File | New | Project** from the menu bar.

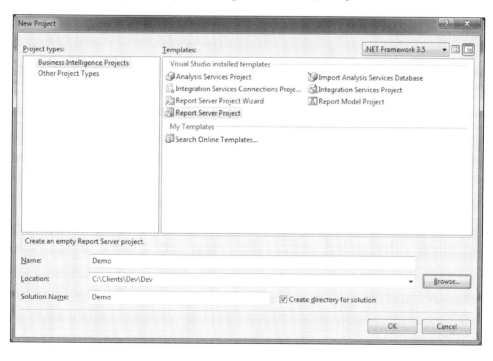

8. As seen in the previous image of the **New Project** Window, select **Report Server Project**, enter **Demo** for the name of the project, browse to a location to store the project, and enter **Demo** as the solution name.

9. Click **OK**.

10. Once the project is created, in the right-hand pane will be the Solution Explorer. We want to add our existing GL_Detail_Trial_Balance.rdl file to our project.

11. In the **Solution Explorer**, right click **Reports** then select **Add | Existing Item**.

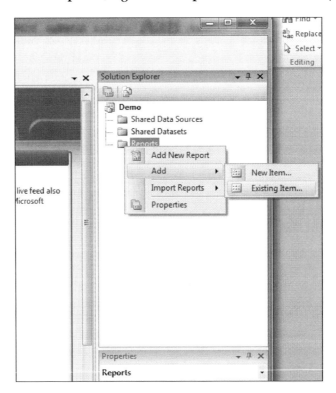

12. Browse to the location we stored the file and click **Add** to open the **Add Existing Items** window as seen in the following image:

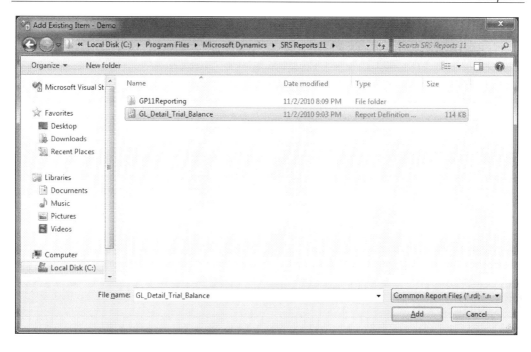

13. In the **Solution Explorer**, **GL_Detail_Trial_Balance.rdl** will now show up as a report. Double-click to open the report in design mode.

14. In the **Design** layout, we will select our **Jrnl No** column (see image below), right click, select **Insert Column | Left**:

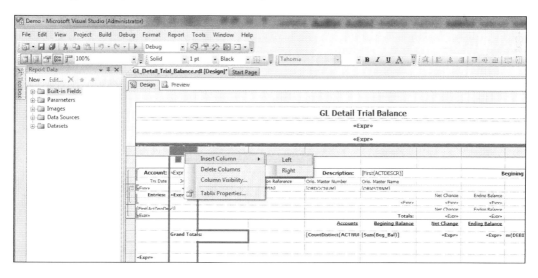

15. In our new column, we will type in a heading of **Source Doc**.

16. In the detail line, we can either expand the Datasets folder on the left pane to browse for our field or we can simply click the Dataset icon on the field itself and browse the pop up list for the field SOURCDOC.

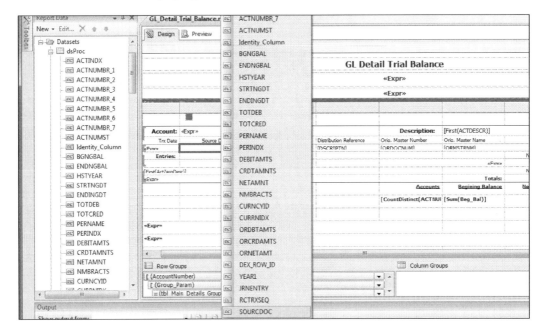

17. After we have added our SOURCDOC field, we can make any necessary font and alignment changes in the property box in the lower right pane.

18. Click **Save**.

19. Now that we have made our change to our report, we need to redeploy it to the Report Server. To do this, we need to set our project deploy options in the Solution Explorer.

20. Right Click the **Demo** project and click **Properties** to open the Property Pages window as seen in the following screenshot:

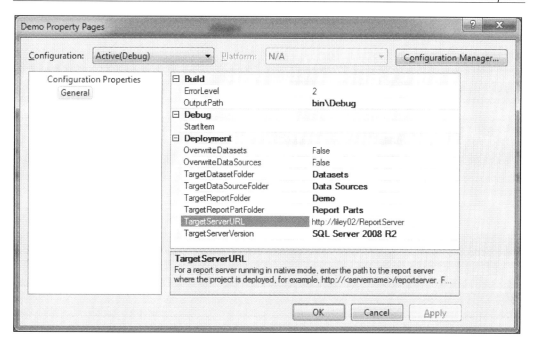

21. Set the **TargetServerURL** to be Report Server site. The default location is typically `http://<computer name>/ReportServer`.

22. Make any necessary changes to the target folders. If replacing the old report, make sure you change the folder name here to the folder where the original report is located.

23. Click **OK**.

24. Right Click the **GL_Detail_Trial_Balance.rdl** report and choose **Deploy**.

25. After the deploy finishes, you will be provided messages in the Output pane located at the bottom of the window similar to the following:

26. Browse back to the Report Manager and regenerate the report. We should now see our new column Source Doc with the values showing. Our completed report will look like the following:

This is a fairly simple example of how you can modify the pre-defined reports and customize them to an organization's particular need. Although this example was simply adding a field, we could just as easily change the layouts, report groupings, add/remove parameters, and so on. Also, this example used Visual Studio to make these modifications, but as you will learn in the next section, we can use the SSRS Report Builder to make modifications as well.

Creating a new reporting metric via Report Builder

Earlier in this chapter, we discussed the deployment of pre-defined Charts and KPIs that can then be made visible on the GP 2010 Homepage. In this section, we'll take a look at creating a metric that shows us the top ten items on un-posted sales orders by extended price. A metric of this sort can give members of our organization insight into which items are generating the most sales at the moment. As the data source for this metric, we'll use one of the SQL views that is generated in each GP company database by the predefined Excel Reports deployment that was covered in Chapter 3 of this book: dbo.SalesLineItems. Remember, SSRS metrics are only available for GP 2010 and SQL Server 2008 environments!

In the previous example, we used Visual Studio to modify a canned report. In this example, however, we are going to use the Report Builder to create a new metric from scratch. Report Builder is a component of SSRS that can be used to modify and create new reports and charts. We will use Report Builder in this example because it has a simple, easy-to-use user interface that will seem familiar to anyone who has used the Microsoft Office suite of programs!

To begin, we will open our web browser to our Reports Manager or Reports Library depending on whether or not SQL Server Reporting Services is configured in Native mode or SharePoint Integration mode. From this location, we should be able to see our GP company database folder that contains the pre-defined reports and charts.

If SSRS is configured in SharePoint mode, click **New | Report Builder Report** to open the Report Builder. If SSRS is configured in Native mode, click the button that says **Report Builder**. Either way, this will launch the Report Builder application from which we can begin creating a new report:

1. In the blank report that appears, right-click and select **Insert | Chart** to open the **Select Chart Type** window.

2. In the **Bar** chart section, select the **Bar** chart type and click **OK**.

3. In the **Dataset Properties** window, enter **TWO_Sales_Line_Items** as the name for the new Dataset that we will create.

4. Select to **Use a dataset embedded in my report**.

5. Click the **New** button in the **Data Source** field to open the **Data Source Properties** window.

6. Name the Data Source as **TWO_Sales_Line_Items**.

7. Click to **Use a connection embedded in my report**.

8. In the **Select** connection type drop-down menu, select **Microsoft SQL Server**. Notice that we can also connect to a variety of other sources, including Microsoft SQL Server Analysis Services.

9. Click Build to open the **Connection Properties** window.

10. Enter the name of the GP company database server in the **Server Name** drop-down menu.

11. Enter the GP company database name in the next drop-down menu and click **OK** twice. For this example, the selected GP database should be one for which predefined Excel Reports have been deployed.

12. In the **Dataset Properties** window, select **Text** as the **Query Type** and enter the following SQL script in the **Query** box and click **OK**:

```
SELECT TOP(10)
[Item Number] AS [Item Number],
SUM([Extended Price]) AS [Extended Price]
FROM SalesLineItems
WHERE [SOP Type] = 'Order'
AND [Document Status] = 'Unposted'
GROUP BY [Item Number], [Extended Price]
          ORDER BY [Extended Price] DESC
```

13. The window should now look like the following image:

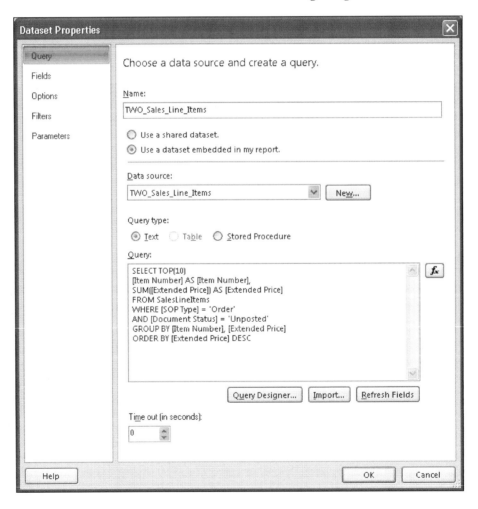

A sample view of the chart will be added to the blank template in the Report Builder pane. The chart displaying actual data will not appear until we have published the report and actually generated the chart. Before we do this, we should make several formatting changes to the chart to make it easier to read. Fortunately, Report Builder's format is fairly intuitive, especially for those of us who are familiar with the Microsoft Office suite of applications. In fact, formatting this chart will be fairly easy for anyone who has experience working with charting tools in Microsoft Excel. We will take a look at some of the formatting changes we can make to this chart, but first let's make sure we define the data labels and series values for our chart:

14. Double-click anywhere in the Chart Area. A pop-up window entitled **Chart Data** should appear. Click the green plus sign next to **Values** and select **Extended_Price** to define the series values of the chart.

15. In the Category Groups section, click the green plus sign and select **Item_Number** as seen in the following image. This will set the Item Number as the data label on the x-axis for this chart.

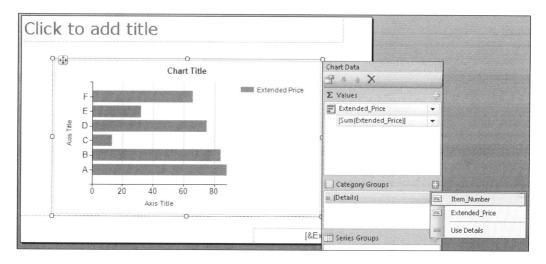

16. Once **Item_Number** is added to the **Category Groups** section, click the **Item Number** drop-down box and select **Category Group Properties**.

17. In the **Category Group Properties** window, select **Sorting**. Change the Sort By drop-down from **[Item_Number]** to **[Extended_Price]**. This will change the sorting functionality of the chart from alphabetical by item number to descending order by **Extended Price**. Click **OK** to close the window.

Now that we've defined our data for the chart, let's make some formatting changes. Feel free to experiment with additional formatting changes to find the appropriate visual effect:

18. Use the grab handles to resize the chart in the center of the template.

19. Double-click the Chart Title and rename the chart to **Top Ten Items on Unposted Sales Orders (Extended Price)**.

20. Delete both the x-axis title and the y-axis title by right-clicking them and deselecting **Show Axis Title**.

21. To ensure that all of the data labels appear on the x-axis, right-click the vertical axis values and select **Vertical Axis Properties**. On the **Axis Options** tab, in the **Axis Range and Interval** section, select the **Side Margins** drop-down box and select **Disabled**. Click **OK** to return to the chart.

22. To format the y-axis data labels, right-click the horizontal axis values and select **Horizontal Axis Properties**. Click the **Number** tab. Change the number format category to **Currency**. Select the option to **Use 1000 Separator**. Click **OK**.

Once we are done formatting the chart, we should save it to the Reports Manager or Reports Library. To ensure that the chart will be available in GP, we need to add the chart to the **Charts and KPIs** folder under one of the company-module folders that was created by the deployment of the pre-defined SSRS reports and metrics:

23. Click the Report Builder menu button and select **Save As**.

24. Browse to the Report Manager (or Reports Manager) and find the GP company database folder. Expand this folder and then expand the folder for the **Sales** module. Expand the **Charts and KPIs** folder. At this point, the file path should be similar to the following (if using SharePoint integration mode):

```
http://<computername>/reports/Reports Library/TWO/Sales
```

25. Give the file a name and select the **Save** button.

Our saved chart will now show up in the list of charts and KPIs available for selection in GP when we are defining the metrics for our GP Homepage. Our next step is to add this metric to the GP Homepage using the steps described earlier in this chapter. By default, the metric and the data within it will appear for Windows users who have administrative privileges on the report server as well as the GP database. If this is not the case, refer to the instructions on Reporting Services Security Setup in this chapter for more information on how to do this.

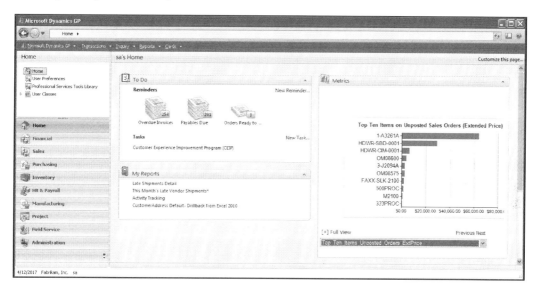

Summary

In this chapter, we explored some of the ways in which SQL Server Reporting Services can be integrated with Dynamics GP 2010. Although experienced developers and consultants have been using SSRS to develop reports for Dynamics GP for quite some time, it is only through recent versions of GP that Microsoft has begun providing pre-defined SSRS reports and metrics that can be deployed to a report server. By first installing SQL Server Reporting Services and then deploying these pre-defined reports and metrics, even developers and consultants who do not have a tremendous amount of experience with SSRS can begin taking advantage of its versatile and useful functionality. We demonstrated how this is possible by discussing how to modify one of the existing SSRS reports. We also demonstrated how users can take advantage of the new SSRS-based metrics created for GP 2010 and SQL Server 2008 by creating our own metrics. Although this chapter has only scratched the surface of what can be accomplished with SQL Server Reporting Services, we hope that it will at least set your organization down the right path towards seeing the benefit of this toolset.

In the next chapter, we will take a look at another component of SQL Server: SQL Server Analysis Services, or SSAS. This is a powerful online analytical processing (OLAP) tool that can be used to mine an organization's data and provide critical business intelligence capabilities. It is capable of aggregating large sets of data quickly and efficiently so that this data can be queried through languages such as Multidimensional Expression language (MDX).

Microsoft has developed a product called Analysis Cubes for Excel that utilizes SQL Server Analysis Services and data generated by Dynamics GP. Although the default product can be used straight out-of-the box, this is a highly customizable reporting tool. Before we cover the process of querying the data generated by Analysis Cubes, we're going to take a different approach and first demonstrate how the product can be customized to meet your organization's business intelligence requirements. We'll cover some of the basic design topics of Analysis Cubes for Excel including its various SQL server components and how they can be customized for improved end-user experience.

6

Designing Your Analysis Cubes for Excel Environment

Business Intelligence—Every organization wants it; but can every organization actually afford it? If our organization is thinking of a business intelligence environment that is architected specifically for a single company with highly visual and fancy team and individual-based dashboards and KPIs, then the answer is probably "No, we can't afford it!" The time and effort required to build such a custom solution is not cheap, and without clear focus and vision from the get-go, these kinds of projects can quickly get bogged down. For the majority of us, we need something cheaper and less expensive to maintain.

Let's not lose sight of what we're really after when we say our organization needs BI capabilities. Simply put, we need improved tools for finding, analyzing, and making sense of the mountain of data that we are storing on our servers and databases. Let's face it—as we improve our ability to store this data in Enterprise Resource Planning systems, it's only going to get harder to find and make sense of this data. This data is unique to our organization; no other organization has access to the same data that we do. If we want to be successful in an increasingly competitive business environment, our company has to be able to find trends in its data and to act on those trends before anyone else can. We need BI tools to help us do this.

Fortunately, for those of us who work in the Microsoft Dynamics GP space, we have a readily available BI tool available at our disposal: Analysis Cubes for Excel. With this product, we can quickly and easily implement an out-of-the-box BI environment that, with just a few extra tweaks and modifications, can provide users in our organization with the ability to interact with data in ways that, until now, they could only dream! The real beauty of this tool doesn't lie in the fact that it's relatively easy and inexpensive to implement as BI solutions go (although this is a major plus!); instead, the beauty is found in providing our organization with a straightforward BI platform that will enable our users to think outside the box even more when it comes to how they analyze their data. Our users will actually have the control and ability they crave in creating their own reports and metrics, and this can free us up for more important, worthwhile pursuits!

The components of the Analysis Cubes for Excel product are also highly customizable. So, even though many companies are perfectly happy to implement the cubes, make a few minor tweaks to the database, and then turn their users loose, many other companies are choosing to extend their Analysis Cubes environment even further and design it to be even more relevant to their organization's needs. There's no right way to do this. It really boils down to what works best for our organization.

In the next two chapters, we're going to take a look at how we can implement and design Analysis Cubes for Excel in our own organization. This chapter will explore the back-end topics of the Analysis Cubes product such as:

- Understanding how the components of Analysis Cubes environment interact
- Providing a step-by-step guide for installing the product
- Reviewing simple modifications that can customize our new business intelligence solution for our organization

The next chapter will focus on the actual building and designing of reports against the databases created and modified in this chapter.

Understanding the components of the Analysis Cubes environment

The Analysis Cubes product offering is composed of several different components, each of which can be modified and customized to fit the needs of our organization. Although each of these components plays a critical role in the overall end-product, understanding how each component works in relation to the others can be challenging. Fortunately for us, the components that make up the cubes are fairly well-known as they are spread across the Microsoft SQL Server stack.

Let's take a look at the various components that comprise the Analysis Cubes environment. Our next image shows an overview of an Analysis Cubes solution deployed in an environment containing three separate GP company databases:

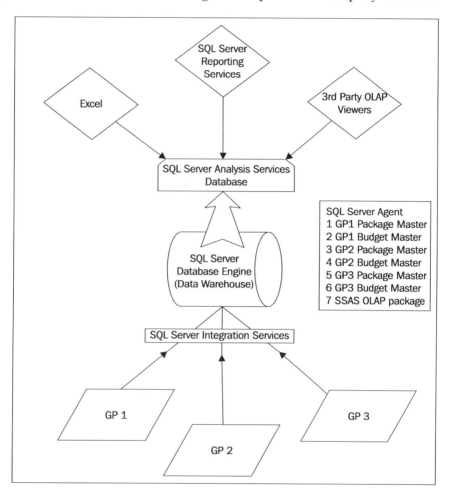

From this image, we can see the various components and their connections to each other. Notice how the users are connecting to the SQL Server Analysis Services database via viewers such as Microsoft Excel, SQL Server Reporting Services, or any one of a number of viewers designed to read data from an Analysis Services database. As we'll learn later, this is where our data eventually ends up, and all of our reporting will be done against this database.

Aside from the GP company databases and the OLAP viewers, which we'll discuss in the next chapter, we can see that Analysis Cubes is comprised of four different elements, all of which coincide with a different component of SQL Server:

1. A data warehouse, maintained within the SQL Server Database Engine

2. A SQL Server Analysis Services database

3. Several integration packages found within SQL Server Integration Services

4. A cube load and data processing job scheduled via SQL Server Agent

SQL Server Database Engine (data warehouse)

The centrepiece of the Analysis Cubes environment is the data warehouse. This collection of approximately 50 tables serves as a repository for data that will eventually be processed by the Analysis Services database. Regardless of the number of company databases that are included in the installation of the cubes, only a single data warehouse must be maintained, making it far easier to manage in cases where we might have multiple GP company databases!

Connecting to the data warehouse

To add or remove tables, view data stored in these tables, or make other modifications to the data warehouse, open SQL Server Management Studio and connect to the **Database Engine** component of SQL Server. In the list of databases that appears under the **Databases** node, we will see the DynamicsGP Warehouse, which is the default name for the data warehouse created by the installation.

Understanding the tables in the data warehouse

With over 50 tables to choose from, it can often be a challenge identifying the right table to work within the data warehouse. Fortunately, our search can be made easier by thinking of the data warehouse as an extraordinarily simplified version of the GP company databases. Back in Chapter 2, we were forced to review the often confusing naming and numbering schema associated with tables in GP company databases. With Analysis Cubes, however, the data warehouse tables and their associated fields are much easier to understand! For example, instead of having to recall that the Customer Master table in GP 2010 is the **RM00101** table, we see a table in the DynamicsGP Warehouse actually called **Customers**. It doesn't get much easier than this!

Additionally, as in GP, we can logically group the tables in the data warehouse by their function. In the data warehouse, we have the following kinds of tables:

- Setup & Maintenance tables: The contents of these tables, such as **SystemVersion** and **LastUpdated** should never be deleted. Tables such as the **SystemVersion** identify settings selected during the installation. Other tables, such as the **LastUpdated** table may need to be modified as part of regular maintenance and updates required for the data warehouse.

- Master tables: Just like the Master tables in the GP company databases (remember reading about these in Chapter 2?), these tables contain data specific to individual records maintained in GP. For example, the **Vendors** and **Customers** tables contain a single record for each vendor and customer, respectively. As we will see later, data found in these tables are used as attributes in the dimensions of the Analysis Services database.

- Transaction tables: Several tables in the data warehouse, such as **GLTransactions** and **SalesDetail** contain transaction-related data. Depending on the module, the table may include distribution information, so we can see amounts that have been posted to various GL accounts. Again, as with the master tables we just mentioned, the transaction tables provide a fairly simplified version of the tables and data we might find in the GP company databases. Although some of the data found in the transaction tables is used by the dimensions in the Analysis Services database, the primary purpose of the records in these tables is to provide the "numbers" for the cubes. As we'll soon see, these numbers display as measures in the Analysis Services database.

Remember, only a single data warehouse is created during the install regardless of the number of GP company databases included during the installation. If we take a look at the master and transaction tables, we can see that each record has an associated Company ID field. This allows us to combine data from multiple company databases into a single database, without losing the ability to identify the originating source of each master or transactional record.

SQL Server Analysis Services database

Unlike the data warehouse, which is a relational database, the Analysis Services database is actually a collection of Online Analytical Processing, or OLAP, as it is more commonly called, and data mining objects. These objects work together to aggregate data into predefined hierarchies and dimensions, giving us the ability to mine large sets of data quickly and easily. When browsing cubes in an Analysis Services database, users will find themselves beginning with a very high-level, aggregated look at the data. Then, when our user spots an anomaly or some other piece of data that looks interesting, he or she can quickly drill down to the underlying source data to learn more about it. This is made possible by the incredible OLAP and data mining functionality found in SQL Server Analysis Services databases!

 One common misconception for many who are beginning work with Analysis Cubes is that, in order to view data, we must connect to the data warehouse. This is not true! Instead, when we use an OLAP viewer such as Microsoft Excel, we are actually creating a data connection to an Analysis Services database. If the default database name is kept during the installation, we will be creating a connection to a database called **Dynamics GP Analysis Cubes**.

In the Analysis Cubes environment image that we included earlier in this chapter, we can see that the Analysis Services database sits on top of the data warehouse. Through a process known as processing the Analysis Services database, data stored in the data warehouse is pulled into the Analysis Services database and aggregated and stored in the various dimensions and measure groups that comprise the cubes. Without getting too much into the specifics of the various OLAP methodologies, this is accomplished through the use of the Multidimensional OLAP, or MOLAP. Rather than compute report values at the time an end user requests that data via a report (as is done with Relational OLAP, or ROLAP, environments), MOLAP environments compute these aggregated values ahead of time, making the cube browsing experience much faster for the end user.

By default, the Analysis Services database that we will create during our installation utilizes MOLAP. Although MOLAP environments provide us with quicker access to the data at run-time, some drawbacks do exist to this type of environment. In order to process and aggregate the data from the data warehouse into the Analysis Services database, we must utilize a substantial amount of server resources. Although most server environments are capable of handling the requirements of processing the SSAS database without adding additional resources, most companies will choose to process the database during off-peak hours to prevent performance issues for the rest of the server. This leads us to another potential drawback of MOLAP databases: datalag. If our server hardware only processes the data from the data warehouse once a day, then it stands to reason that the data in our cubes will always lag behind real-time data and be slightly out-of-date. Whether or not this lag is acceptable is a decision we will have to weigh against the perceived benefits of faster and easier data access that the cubes stand to offer.

SQL Server Integration Services packages

In our last section, we discussed how processing the Analysis Services database causes the data from the data warehouse to be aggregated and stored in the SSAS database objects. However, we didn't spend much time discussing how the data made it to the data warehouse in the first place! This is the job of SQL Server Integration Services, or SSIS. The installation of Analysis Cubes will create a series of SSIS packages that are responsible for collecting data from the various GP company databases included in our install and adding that data to the data warehouse.

The data load for Analysis Cubes is, by and large, an incremental data load. Rather than wipe the slate clean each time data is loaded, most of the SSIS packages attempt to identify records that have been inserted or modified in the GP company database since the last time a data load package was executed. Only this additional data is transferred over to the data warehouse and the existing data in the data warehouse remains unchanged. Because the Analysis Services database is processed against the data warehouse, we should make sure that the data load packages are executed just prior to the database processing. This will ensure that SSAS database will be processed with the most up-to-date information available from the GP company database(s).

Several different kinds of SSIS packages are created by the installation:

- **Individual Load Packages**: A series of approximately 25 generic load packages is created, and these packages are responsible for loading the master and transactional tables in the data warehouse. These packages, however, should not be run individually.

- **Company Master Packages**: Instead of executing the individual load packages, users should run the master packages that are created to correspond with each company database. Each master package is designed to pass down connection information for a specific GP company database to the individual load packages.

- **Budget Packages**: A series of packages are created to allow us to load budget data from each GP company database. Run these only in the event that GP budget data should be included with the cubes. Later on in this chapter, we will address some additional steps required to load budget data.

- **Cube Processing Package**: A single OLAP package is created that, when executed, processes the entire Analysis Services database.

That's a lot of packages to keep track of, but as we'll see in our next section, we can use another SQL Server related tool to keep track of them for us!

In versions of Analysis Cubes for GP 10.0 and earlier, the SSIS packages were encrypted. This meant that users who wanted to add additional fields or see more data on where a particular field originated were out of luck. Fortunately, several months after GP 2010 was released, Microsoft announced that the packages would no longer be encrypted. This is great news and greatly enhances our ability to customize the data that we are bringing into the data warehouse!

SQL Server Agent job

SQL Server Agent is a Windows service accessible from within SQL Server Management Studio that allows us to create and schedule jobs. In the case of Analysis Cubes, we can use SQL Server Agent to create a job containing the master and budget SSIS packages as well as the OLAP processing package that should be run after data has been loaded into the data warehouse. Once we've set up our job to execute the SSIS packages in the desired order, we can schedule the job to run at a certain time. For example, we could set the SQL Server Agent to execute a job that loads the data warehouse and then processes the SSAS database, beginning at 3:00 in the morning. This way, we can ensure that the cubes will be ready for access first thing in the morning as we are enjoying our first cup of coffee!

Multiple tier installations

Now that we've covered the various components of the Analysis Cubes, let's talk about the server environment to which these components will be installed. When we go through the installation in our next section, we'll see that we are given a choice as to which server each component should be installed to. Each choice offers several pros and cons.

Essentially, we have three options:

1. Single Server install: In this option, the data warehouse, the SSAS database, the SSIS packages, and the GP company databases will all reside on a single server. This configuration minimizes the amount of time required to load the data from GP company databases into the data warehouse. In order to process the Analysis Services database, however, we will take up valuable server resources that may have an adverse impact on users who are in the GP environment.

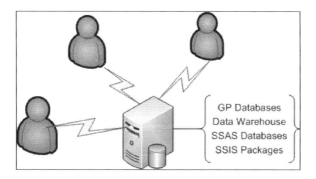

2. Two Server install: In this option, the data warehouse, the SSAS database, and SSIS packages are installed on a server separate than the server containing the GP company databases. Now, when we process the SSAS database, we can ensure we are minimizing the impact on GP performance. This option does, however, introduce the possibility of longer data load times as data must now be transferred across a linked server.

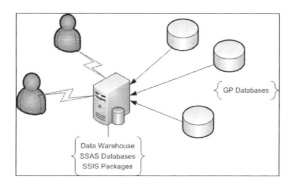

3. Three Server install: In this option, the data warehouse and SSIS packages are installed on one server, the SSAS database is installed on a second server, and the GP databases are hosted on a third server. With this configuration, the SSAS database is given the maximum amount of resources for data processing, but we are still faced with the issue of potentially long data load times as data is pulled into the data warehouse via a linked server.

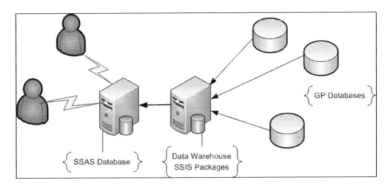

Before we begin installing the cubes in our environment, we should take some time to think of the pros and cons of the different tier-installation options available. For some of us, our decision may be easy: a lack of dedicated server resources may force us to utilize the single server install and schedule the SSAS database processing for off-peak hours to reduce performance issues. Other organizations may have a dedicated report server on which the SSAS database and data warehouse can be kept. We'll still want to limit the frequency with which we process the SSAS database, but at least we can feel more comfortable in doing this during business hours without impacting performance on our ERP database!

Installing Analysis Cubes

Now that we have a basic understanding of what Analysis Cubes for Excel is as well as the components that make up the Analysis Cubes environment, we will now walk through the installation process for the Analysis Cubes for Excel. The installation of Analysis Cubes for Excel is actually a quite simple product to install, but it is also very dependent on having the proper permissions to perform the installation as well as completing steps in a particular order. The installation process is made up of the following three steps:

- Pre-Installation Checklist
- Installing the Server Configuration Wizard
- Using the Server Configuration Wizard to Deploy the Cubes

Pre-installation checklist

Before proceeding with our installation of the Analysis Cubes, we need to review our Pre-installation checklist.

- Review system requirements for server components – This includes determining which of the deployment configurations discussed earlier in this chapter we will be using in our environment.

- Review security requirements for installing and configuring the server components:

  - ° To install and configure the server components, the Windows user account must be in the Windows groups in the following chart, as described in the latest Analysis Cubes for Excel manual:

Server Computer	Windows Groups
Microsoft Dynamics GP Server Computer	Administrators
SQL Server Computer for Microsoft Dynamics GP Company Databases	All versions of SQL Server: Administrators
	SQL Server 2005: SQLServer2005MSSQLUser
	SQL Server 2008: SQLServerMSSQLUser
Data Warehouse Database Server Computer (with Integration Services Installed)	All versions of SQL Server: Administrators
	SQL Server 2005: SqlServer2005MSSQLUser; SQLServer2005DTSUser
	SQL Server 2008: SQLServerMSSQLUser; SQLServerDTSUser
SQL Server Analysis Services Computer	All versions of SQL Server: Administrators
	SQL Server 2005: SQLServer2005MSOLAPUser
	SQL Server 2008: SQLServerMSOLAPUser

  - ° Dynamics GP server must be given access to read and write data on the data warehouse database server if it is a different physical machine.

- Gather information required for configuring the server components:

  - ° The Dynamics GP company databases that will be used to populate the data warehouse database

  - ° The name that will be used for the data warehouse database

- ° The SQL server name or instance name that the data warehouse database will reside on
- ° The locations of the data and log files for the SQL server instance
- ° The SQL Server Integration Services packages to install
- ° Whether to populate the warehouse database with detailed General Ledger transaction information for various modules or to use summary information
- ° Determine whether to populate each cube with all transactions or to enter an earliest date to import from the company databases
- ° Determine whether to include multicurrency information and if so, which reporting currency and exchange rate table to use for each company
- ° Define a password for the Dynamics User SQL Server login account that will be used by the company databases to access the data warehouse database using SQL Server Authentication

Installing the Server Configuration Wizard

Now that we have ensured we have met all system requirements and obtained the necessary security permissions to perform the installation, we can proceed with installing the Server Configuration Wizard. The installation can be started from the Dynamics GP 2010 Installation Media or by downloading the Analysis Cubes Installer package from either the PartnerSource or CustomerSource portals.

 Be sure that when downloading the package from these sites, you download the correct file whether you are on Dynamics GP 2010 RTM or Service Pack 1.

To install the Server Configuration Wizard, follow these steps:

1. Locate the `Microsoft_DynamicsGP11_AnalysisCubesServer_x86.msi` file you downloaded and double-click the file to open the Dynamics GP Server Setup Wizard.

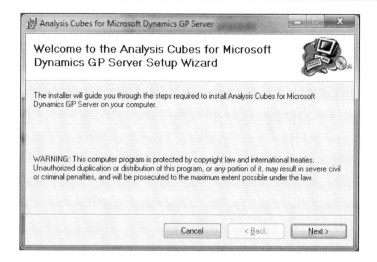

2. Click **Next** to proceed.

3. On the License Agreement window, select the **I Agree** radio button and click **Next**.

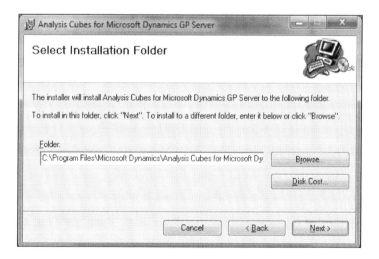

4. Enter the path for the destination folder to install the server configuration wizard program to. The default path is **C:\Program Files\Microsoft Dynamics \Analysis Cubes for Microsoft Dynamics GP Server**. Click **Next**.

5. Click **Next** to complete the installation.

6. Click **Close** to close the wizard.

Using the Server Configuration Wizard to deploy the cubes

Once we have installed the Server Configuration Wizard, we need to run the wizard to actually deploy the cubes. During the configuration wizard installation process, two files, named `Microsoft.Dynamics.GP.AnalysisCubes.ConfigurationWizard2005.exe` and `Microsoft.Dynamics.GP.AnalysisCubes.ConfigurationWizard2008.exe` are extracted to the destination folder. Shortcuts to these files, named **Analysis Cubes Configuration Wizard for SQL Server 2005** and **Analysis Cubes Configuration Wizard for SQL Server 2008** also are created on the desktop. Make sure you run the file for the version of SQL you are running. In our examples throughout this chapter and Chapter 7, we will be using Analysis Cubes for SQL 2008.

To use the Server Configuration Wizard to Deploy the Cubes, follow these steps:

1. Browse to the folder location where the Server Configuration Wizard was installed, or run the Analysis Cubes Configuration Wizard from the desktop.

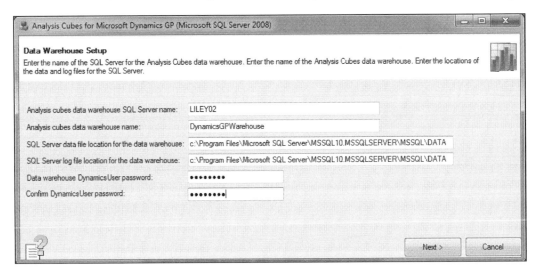

2. On the **Data Warehouse Setup** window, enter the values for the fields based on the information you gathered in the Pre-Installation checklist section.

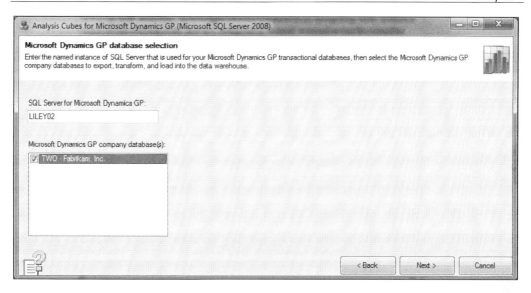

3. On the **Microsoft Dynamics GP database selection** window, enter your **Dynamics GP server name** and select each company database(s) that will be included in the Data Warehouse and click **Next**.

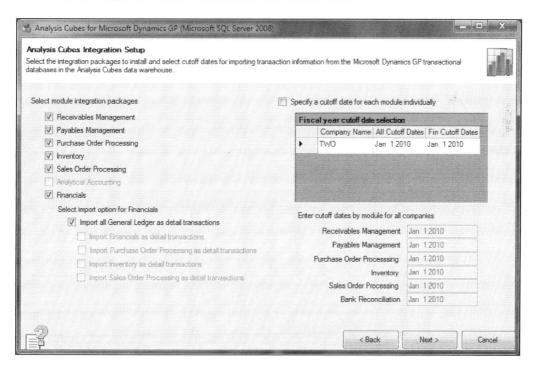

4. On the **Analysis Cubes Integration Setup** window, select the modules to include in the data warehouse and whether to import transactions in detail or in summary. A cutoff date can also be selected to limit transactions that are loaded. Click **Next**.

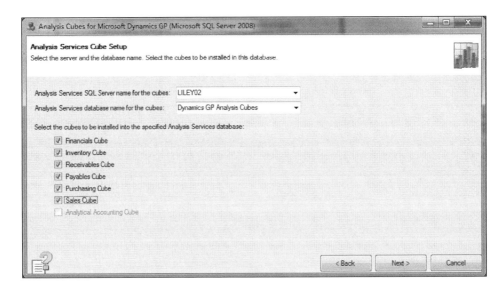

5. On the **Analysis Services Cube Setup** window, select the **Analysis Services SQL Server name** defined in the Pre-Installation checklist and choose which cubes to install. Click **Next**.

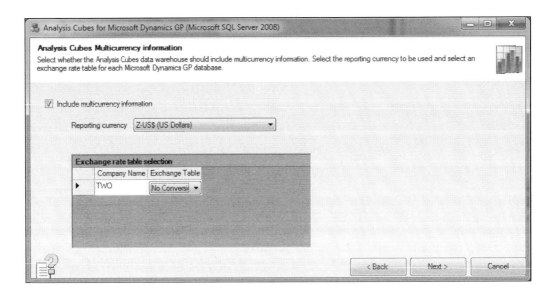

6. On the **Analysis Cubes Multicurrency Information** window, if there is a
   need to use a reporting currency for multicurrency, check the box **to include
   multicurrency information**. Choose the **Reporting currency** and then which
   Exchange table to use. Click **Next**.

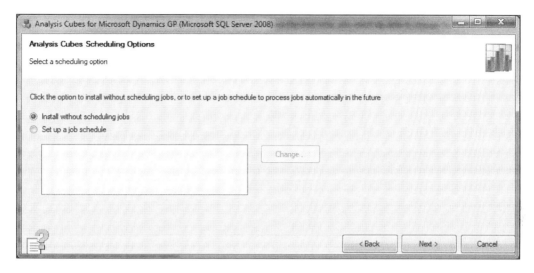

7. On the **Analysis Cubes Scheduling Options** window, choose whether to
   have the wizard create a job schedule or to install without a schedule. The job
   schedule can be set up at a later time.

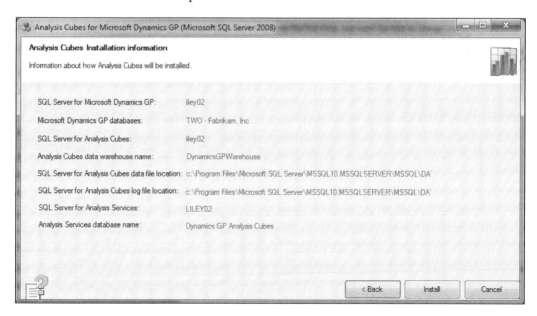

8. On the **Analysis Cubes Installation Information** window, review the information and click **Install**.

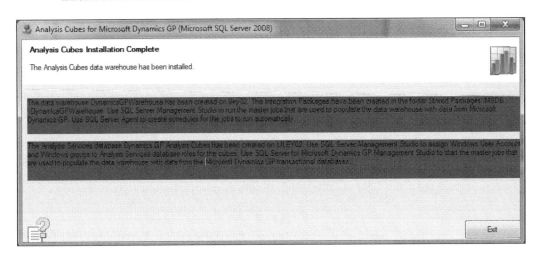

9. The **Analysis Cubes Installation Complete** window will provide information about the SQL Server configuration changes that were made. Click **Exit**.

Though these are fairly detailed installation instructions, it is always recommended to download the latest Analysis Cubes User Guide from the PartnerSource or CustomerSource portals and check for any updates or other important information for the installation process.

Populating the data warehouse and processing the cubes

Once the server configuration is completed and the data warehouse is installed, three master SQL Server Integration Services packages will be installed for each company. These packages are what actually populate the data warehouse database with data from the Microsoft Dynamics GP company databases. To run these packages, connect to Integration Services in SQL Server Management Studio, browse to **Stored Packages | MSDB | DynamicsGPWarehouse**, and right click them to run them. The names of the master packages are as follows:

```
DynamicsGP_<source_db>_to_<warehouse_db>_PackageMaster

DynamicsGP_<source_db>_to_<warehouse_db>_Run_GL_Budgets_Master

DynamicsGP_<source_db>_to_<warehouse_db>_Run_AA_Budgets_Master
```

Where `<source_db>` is the name of the Dynamics GP company (there will be these three packages for each company you selected to install) and `<warehouse_db>` is the name of the data warehouse database.

 The master package for Analytical Accounting should only be run if Analytical Accounting budget data should be included in the data warehouse.

If during the installation a scheduled job was not created to run the packages, this should be created now.

Once the master packages have been run and the schedule created, the OLAP processing package needs to be run in SQL Server Management Studio to process the cubes. The name of the OLAP processing package is `DynamicsGP_<warehouse_db>_ OLAP_DB_<server name>_<analysis services database>` where `<warehouse_ db>` is the name of the data warehouse database. To run this package, connect to Integration Services in SQL Server Management Studio, browse to **Stored Packages | MSDB | DynamicsGPWarehouse**, and right click the OLAP package and click run package and execute.

Granting security access to the cubes

Security to the cubes is controlled through the use of SQL Server Analysis Services security roles. Domain users or groups are assigned to one or more security roles, each of which allows a different level access to a single cube, multiple cubes, or specific objects within a cube. Although custom security roles can be set up in an Analysis Services database, the Analysis Cubes installation actually creates several default security roles for us. For us, then, allowing users to access the cubes is simply a matter of deciding which roles the users should be assigned to.

Accessing and modifying the security roles is fairly straightforward. In this example, we'll use a computer that has SQL Server Management Studio installed on it to accomplish this:

1. Open SQL Server Management Studio by selecting **Start | Programs | Microsoft SQL Server | SQL Server Management Studio**.

2. In the **Connect to Server** window, select **Analysis Services** as the **Server Type**.

3. In the **Server Name** field, enter the name of the server containing the Analysis Services database.

4. The **Authentication** method should be set to **Windows Authentication**. The Windows account with which we are logged should be a member of the Analysis Services server role to ensure that we can connect properly. For best results, use the account that was used to perform the Analysis Cubes installation.

5. Once the connection is made, expand the Databases node.

6. Find and expand the node for the Analysis Services database created by the installation. If the default name was kept, then expand the **Dynamics GP Analysis Cubes** node.

7. Expand the **Roles** node. This will show us a list of the available security roles in this SSAS database.

We can see that a single role exists for each cube that was installed. Essentially, assigning a Windows user or group to a specific security role will allow that user or members of that group read-only access to the cube identified by the role name.

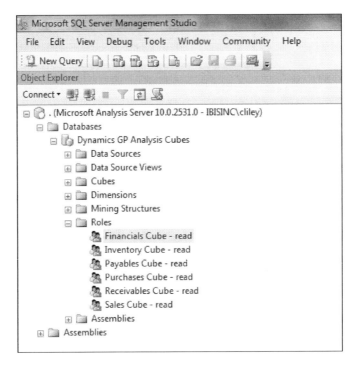

For example, to grant a user access to the Financials cube, we can double-click the role called **Financials Cube – read only**. Selecting the **Membership** tab brings us to a window from which we can select to add users and groups who should have read only access to the Financials cube. That's all it takes!

One recommendation that we can make for organizations that will have numerous users accessing the cubes is to utilize Windows groups. If we have ten users who will need access to six cubes, that will require us to add each user to each separate security role. Six assignments per user multiplied by ten users can quickly add up to a time-consuming chore that is difficult to maintain going forward!

Instead, we recommend setting up a Windows group called **AnalysisCubesReadOnly** or similar. By adding the ten users to this group via Active Directory, we can then just add this single group to each of the cube security roles. This greatly reduces the time required to maintain our cube security!

Exploring the Analysis Services database

Earlier, we discussed connecting to the Analysis Services database via SQL Server Management Studio. As we saw then, connecting to the SSAS database via SQL Server Management Studio is useful in some situations, such as when we need to add or remove users to security roles or when we need to process the entire database at once. By and large, however, most of our access to the Analysis Services database will occur through Business Intelligence Development Studio, or BIDS, for short. This product is installed as a component of the SQL Server installation, and is found under the same Program Files folder as SQL Server. Those of us who are familiar with Visual Studio will have no problem using BIDS, as it's nothing more than a spinoff of Visual Studio dedicated to designing and maintaining Business Intelligence projects and environments. This fits right in with our Analysis Cubes product!

When working with Analysis Services databases in BIDS, we must remember that we are working directly against the server. Any changes made to the database will immediately be saved back to the server with no option for undoing those changes. Be careful!

To connect to the default Analysis Services database created by our installation, we can follow these steps:

1. From our local computer, click **Start | Programs | Microsoft SQL Server | SQL Server Business Intelligence Development Studio**.

2. Once BIDS loads, select **File | Open | Analysis Services Database**.

3. In the **Connect to Database** window, enter the server that contains the Analysis Cubes database in the Server Name field.

4. Once a connection is made to the server, use the drop-down box for the **Database** field to select the Analysis Services database.

5. Click **OK** to connect to the database.

Now that we've made a connection to our Analysis Services database, we'll take a look at the various objects that exist in this database.

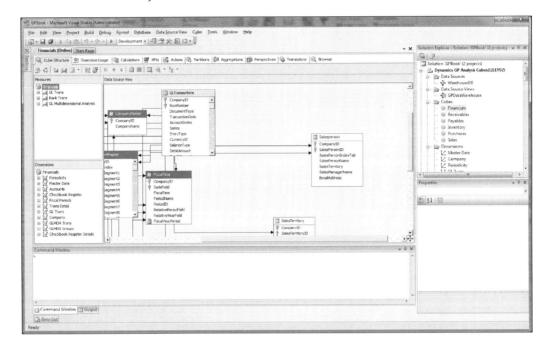

Objects in the Analysis Services database

By understanding what the various objects in our SQL Server Analysis Services database represent, we can begin understanding how we might customize them.

Data source view

The data source view represents the data model upon which the rest of the Analysis Services database is built. Objects such as dimensions and measure groups will be based on tables and structures found in the data source view. In the data source view, we can combine and add multiple data sources from multiple environments into one location!

Dimensions

The key building block of any report that accesses an OLAP database is the attribute. A dimension is a collection of similar attributes that can be grouped together. For example, our installation created a dimension called Customers that, within it, contains numerous attributes (such as Customer Class, Corporate Customer Number, Salesperson, and so on) that are associated with a customer in GP. Later, when we discuss reporting against the cubes, we'll use attributes to slice and divide our measures into more meaningful values. Additionally, we will see that attributes that share a common grouping can be grouped into a pre-defined hierarchy.

Measure groups

Just as dimensions contain attributes, measure groups are a collection of measures. Measures are the different numbers that we will expect to include in our cube reports. For example, in the Financials cube, we will see Debit Amount and Credit Amount as measures that we can include in our report. A measure is almost always useless unless it has been reported against attributes from a related dimension.

Cubes

Cubes are the objects responsible for bringing similar measures and dimensions together in the same location. It would not make sense for us to try to report measures from a payables invoice against a list of our customers, so it's highly unlikely that we'd ever see a Payables measure group in the same cube as a customer-related dimension!

Security roles

Security roles govern our access to the objects in the Analysis Services database. Without being included in a security role, we will be limited in what we can see when we try to create connections to the Analysis Services database!

Advanced objects (KPIs, Translations, Perspectives, Partitions, and so on)

Numerous other objects exist in Analysis Services database, but they are not heavily used by the Analysis Cubes for Excel product offering and will not be covered in much detail here. Nonetheless, these objects can enhance the value found in the product, so we encourage our interested readers to pursue information about these objects in other resources such as SQL Server Books Online!

Modifying our Analysis Cubes environment

One of the extraordinary benefits of Analysis Cubes for Excel is its endless possibility for customization. The Analysis Cubes product gives us a solid base from which we can then extend to include other customizations. Customizations to the cube environment run the gamut from adding new attributes and measures to an existing cube, adding a new cube for another GP module to the existing SSAS database, to even incorporating data from a completely separate application in the same data warehouse as our GP data! The possibilities are endless!

Although some customizations such as incorporating data from applications outside of GP require fairly extensive knowledge of the various SQL Server components involved, we have identified a few simple customizations that we can make to customize our environment. In this section, we'll explore the following customizations:

1. Renaming existing attributes in a dimension.
2. Adding attributes to a dimension.
3. Modifying the Account Category hierarchy.
4. Adding GP Budget and Forecast Data to the cubes.

For each of these examples that require modification to the Analysis Services database, we'll use Business Intelligence Development Studio to make the changes. Refer to the section earlier in this chapter for information on connecting to the SSAS database via BIDS.

Additionally, keep in mind that our next chapter will focus on connecting to Analysis Cubes and designing reports. With that in mind, we won't be able to see the real impact of our changes from this chapter until we start designing our cube reports in the next chapter!

Renaming existing attributes in a dimension

Perhaps one of the easiest changes to make that can customize our Analysis Cubes environment for our organization is to rename certain attributes. Perhaps the best example of this can be found in the Accounts dimension of the Financials cube. By default, this dimension happens to contain two attributes named similar to the following:

1. Account Segment 1
2. Account Segment 1 Desc

Now, imagine that we have several GP company databases in our data warehouse, each of which shares a similar chart of accounts with three segments in 3-4-2 format. The first segment represents divisions; the second segment represents natural accounts; and the third segment represents geographical territories. As we will see in the next chapter, Analysis Cubes provides a great way to create reports based on individual segments of our chart of accounts!

For example, if we were to include the **Account Segment 1** attribute in a cube report, we would expect to see individual numbers such as 100, 200, and 300 and so on with each representing a distinct numeric value that can be found in Segment 1 of the chart of accounts in our GP database. Similarly, if we were to include **Account Segment 1 Desc** in our report, we might expect to see values such as Administration, Accounting, and Sales and so on to reflect the names of various departments that correspond to the numerical values we just listed.

Now, let's go back to the attributes in our Accounts dimension. Wouldn't it be better if we could rename our attributes to reflect the fact that segment 1 actually represents divisions in our chart of accounts? Let's rename these to "1 Department Acct" and "1 Department Acct Desc" so that the attribute will be more easily understood by the average cube user.

With BIDS open and connected to our SSAS database, let's do the following to rename our attributes:

1. In the **Solution Explorer**, find and double-click the **Accounts** dimension to open it in the main viewer.

2. In the **Attributes** section of the main viewer, find and right-click the attribute named **Acct Segment 1**. Select **Rename**.

3. Rename the attribute to **1 Department Acct**.

4. Repeat this process for the attribute named **Acct Segment Description 1**, but instead name it **1 Department Acct Desc**.

5. Click **File | Save Selected Items** to save these changes to the server.

If desired, this process can be repeated for additional account segments used by our organization. Now, when users browse the Financials cube—or any other cube that uses the **Accounts** dimension for that matter—they will see a more intuitive description for the attributes that reflect the first segment of our organization's chart of accounts.

Adding new attributes to a dimension

By default, dimensions in our Analysis Cubes installation contain selected attributes that can be included in our reports. These attributes correspond to a field in the underlying source table of the data warehouse for the selected dimension. For example, the Customer Name attribute in the Customers dimension corresponds to the CustomerName field in the Customers table in the data warehouse. Not surprisingly, the Customers table is the underlying source table for the Customers dimension. If we want to add additional attributes to the Customers dimension, we should look at the Customers table in the data warehouse to see what fields are available for inclusion. We can also consider tables joined to the Customers table in the data source view, but for the sake of simplicity, we'll stick with the Customers table in our example!

Now, let's imagine that our organization is using the **User Defined Field 1** field on the Customer card in GP to store the old customer number from the ERP system our organization used before making the decision to migrate to GP. It would be helpful if we could include this information in the Customers dimension so that it can be used in our cube reports.

Fortunately for us, values from User Defined Field 1 are already stored in the Customers table of the data warehouse as UserDef1 field, so it will be easy for us to add this as an attribute to the Customers dimension via Business Intelligence Development Studio:

1. In the **Solution Explorer**, find and double-click the **Customers** dimension to open it in the main viewer.

2. Notice that the main viewer is now split into several sections, two of which are called **Attributes** and **Data Source View**. Find and select the **Customers** table in the **Data Source View** pane.

3. Scroll through the **Customers** table until we find the **UserDef1** field.

4. Click and drag the **UserDef1** field from the **Data Source View** pane and drop it into the **Attributes** pane.

5. Click **File | Save Selected Items**.

6. When prompted with a message that the following objects will also be saved, click **OK**. Note that doing this will render those SSAS objects inaccessible to cube users until they have been reprocessed.

7. We should then be asked if we want to reprocess the objects that have been affected by this change. Assuming we are able to devote server resources to this process, select **Yes**. Select **Run** when the **Process Objects** window appears. This will reprocess the objects with the new and add our new field to the Customers dimension.

Once our database has finished processing, we should be able to browse the Customers dimension in a cube report to see our newly added attribute. Adding a new attribute to a dimension is another good way to customize the cubes to fit the unique reporting needs of our organization.

Modifying the Account Category hierarchy by editing the GLAccountCategory table

Most Dynamics GP users are familiar with the Account Category. It is that nice little required field on the Account Maintenance window that many users even wonder why it is there and what purpose it even serves. For Dynamics GP purposes, it really does not provide much except for placement on out-of-the-box Dynamics GP financial reports, which most users don't use in the first place. However, in the data warehouse, the Account category takes on much more meaning and can let us really drill down and organize our data.

In cubes such as the Financials cube, we will see an Accounts dimension that contains a hierarchy called Accounts by Category. This hierarchy combines four related attributes that, together, provide an incredibly useful way of summarizing individual account balances with other similar accounts. These attributes include:

- Account Main Category
- Account Broad Category
- Account Category
- Account No

Only the data from the Account Category and Account Number attributes exists in GP. The other two attributes, Account Main Category and Account Broad Category, are set at the data warehouse level. We can assign different Broad and Main categories to the Account Categories from GP to create these natural hierarchies.

For example, suppose we have several Payables accounts, such as Accounts Payable, Taxes Payable, and Interest Payable. We can assign these Account Categories to a Broad Category called Current Liabilities. In turn, we can assign the Current Liabilities Broad Category to an Account Main Category called Debt. As we will see when we begin browsing the cube, this creates a hierarchy that looks like the following when browsing the cube from Excel:

Date	2017	⊤
Row Labels	⊤ **Amount - GL Trans**	
⊞ **Assets**	$291,625.86	
⊟ **Debt**	($962,787.05)	
⊟ **Current Liabilities**	($985,723.69)	
⊟ Accounts Payable	($658,282.30)	
000-2100-00	($658,282.30)	
000-2101-00	$0.00	
⊞ Dividends Payable	$0.00	
⊞ Interest Payable	$2,586.47	
⊞ Notes Payable	$0.00	
⊞ Other Current Liabilities	$0.00	
⊞ Taxes Payable	($330,027.86)	
⊞ **Long Term Debt**	$22,936.64	
⊞ **Equity**	$976,266.74	
Grand Total	**$305,105.55**	

Rather than view the accounts under Accounts Payable individually or the accounts assigned to Account Categories in the Current Liabilities Broad Category, we can summarize these related accounts into higher level attributes that make it easier for us to make sense of our data. Additionally, if we have a multi-company environment with different charts of accounts in each company, we can use this hierarchy to assist with multi-company reporting!

One suggestion for those using Analysis Cubes in multi-company environments: Prior to installing and loading Analysis Cubes data for the first time, consider standardizing the Account Categories across all companies. Each company database should use the same Account Categories, and these Account Categories should be listed in the same order in the Account Category Setup window inside of GP (for example if "Accounts Receivable" is number three in this window for one company database, every other company database should list "Accounts Receivable" as third in the list of Account Categories). Doing this will also standardize account categories in our data warehouse, allowing us to use this hierarchy for multi-company reporting.

So, how to do we modify this Accounts by Category hierarchy? This can be done after the first initial data warehouse data load has occurred. If we use SQL Management Studio to query the **GLAccountCategory** table in the data warehouse, we will see a list of account categories from GP. Additionally, we will see columns such as **AccountBroadCategory** and **AccountMainCategory**. By modifying these columns for each account category listed in the table (time to brush up on your SQL UPDATE skills!), we can control how the hierarchy will appear in our cube.

In the screenshot above, we demonstrated how the Accounts Payable Account Category from GP can be made to roll-up into the Current Liabilities and Debt Broad and Main categories. Assuming you also have an Account Category named Accounts Payable in your own environment; this is made possible by updating the Accounts Payable record in the **GLAccountCategory** table and setting the **AccountBroadCategory** field to Current Liabilities and the **AccountMainCategory** field to Debt.

Also in this table, be sure to take note of the **NativeSign** field. This handy little feature allows us to control how account balances will appear in our Financials cube. By default, the Financials cube comes with several measures that show us account balances, two of which are utilized more often than most:

- Amount

- Signed Amount

- The **Amount** measure is calculated as Debit – Credit. For accounts that typically carry a debit balance, these amounts will show as positive, and for accounts that carry a credit balance will usually display as a negative. But, for financial reporting purposes (and to keep our executive team from any unwanted panic attacks), we may prefer that some of our normal credit-balance accounts, such as Revenue, be displayed as a positive value in cube reports. This is where the **NativeSign** field and **Signed Amount** measure comes into play.

- By setting the **NativeSign** field for the Revenue account category record in the **GLAccountCategory** table to "Credit", the cube will display account balances for our Revenue accounts (assuming they are actually carrying a credit balance!) as a positive amount when the **Signed Amount** measure is used. In certain cases, this may be preferred over the **Amount** measure, which would be showing a negative balance for the same accounts.

Adding GP budgets and forecasts to the cubes

Another common modification is to include budget information from the budget IDs that have been loaded into our GP company databases. We can choose to have values from one budget ID populate a Budget Amount measure and to have values from another budget ID populate a Forecast Amount measure. This way, we can compare budget and forecast information with our actual transactions via the Financials cube. Of course, in order to do this, we must actually have budget information stored in our GP company databases in the form of budget IDs!

Earlier in this chapter, we discussed the various packages that must be run to populate our data warehouse. For each company database included in our installation, we can expect to see a corresponding SSIS package ending with **Run_ GL_Budgets_Master**. This package must be included in our SQL Server Agent job created to load and process the cubes if we want to see budget and forecast values populated in our data warehouse!

Modifying the GLBudgetSetup table

Once we've confirmed that our budget packages are in place, our next step is to identify the budget IDs that will be loaded in our data warehouse. This is done by editing the **GLBudgetSetup** table data warehouse database. After running the SQL Server Agent job at least one time, this table will include a list of budget ID's for each GP company that is included in our installation. Before we modify our table, we should note that only one budget ID can be used for budget numbers per company ID and fiscal year. Likewise, only one budget ID can be used for forecast numbers per company ID and fiscal year.

In order to make this change, first we need to update the **BudgetForecast** column in the **GLBudgetSetup** table with the string value of **Budget** for each budget ID that should contribute to the budget numbers for a particular company ID and fiscal year. Likewise, we need to update the Budget Forecast column in the same table with the string value of **Forecast** for each budget ID that should contribute to the budget numbers for a particular company ID and fiscal year.

Additionally, we need to update the **UseForReporting** column in the same table with the string value of **Yes.** This will tell the budget packages that data from this budget should be included in the data warehouse during the next data load.

Our next screenshot shows an example of what the **GLBudgetSetup** table might look like in a sample Fabrikam environment. We can see that four budgets have been identified and set to use for reporting. Additionally, we see that a budget ID called **FORECAST 2018** has also been added to GP, and it has been set to populate the forecast measure in the data warehouse.

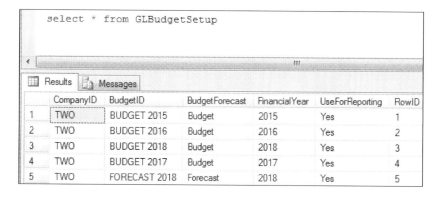

After making these changes, we have one final step to complete before re-running the cube load and processing job to populate our budget data in the data warehouse and the cubes.

Adding the Budget Measure to the Financials cube

Once we've set a budget and forecast to be used for each company-fiscal year combination, data from these budget IDs will be inserted into the GLTransactions table of the data warehouse as **Budget/Forecast** document types. The actual budget and forecast numbers are populated in the **Budget** and **Forecast** fields of this table, respectively. Surprisingly, these fields are not exposed as measures in the Financials cube. So, before we can view this data in the Financials cube, we must add these two fields as measures in the Financials cube.

Adding a measure to a cube is similar to adding an attribute to a dimension. We can accomplish this through Business Intelligence Development Studio:

1. In the **Solution Explorer**, find and double-click the **Financials** cube to open it in the main viewer.

2. Select the **Cube Structure** tab to open the Financials cube in a view that contains, among other panes, the **Measures** and **Data Source View** panes.

3. In the **Data Source View** pane, find the **GLTransactions** table. Scroll through this table and find the **Budget** field.

4. Click and drag the **Budget** field into the **Measures** pane and drop it. The Budget measure should now be added to the GL Trans measure group.

5. Right-click the newly added Budget measure and select **Properties**. In the **Properties** window that appears, find the **FormatString** value. In the drop-down box, select **Currency** as the format for this measure.

6. Repeat this process for the **Forecast** measure by selecting it from the **GLTransactions** table and dragging it to the **Measures** pane. Additionally, follow the step of assigning this newly added measure to the **Currency** format.

7. Click **File | Save Selected Items** to save these changes.

In order to see the effects of our changes, we must first run the SQL Server Agent job that loads the data warehouse and reprocesses the cubes. Our budget packages should load budget and forecast data from the selected budget IDs into their respective budget and forecast fields in the **GLTransactions** table. This, in turn, should be made visible to users in the Financials cube through the **GL Trans** measure group. We'll see how this looks in the next chapter as we discuss cube reporting!

Summary

Because Analysis Cubes for Excel is such a highly customizable product with several different components that must be maintained on the back-end, we have divided our chapter on Analysis Cubes into two. This chapter has covered the numerous aspects related to installing and setting up Analysis Cubes for first time use and then making some minor modifications to the Analysis Services database to make the cubes more useful for our organization. In doing so, we hope our readers have gained a measure of just how far we can expand the usefulness of this reporting tool. Although it takes time to learn the various inner workings of SQL to the point that we can make customizations to an Analysis Services database without reservation, the benefits of being able to do this are tremendous! As we move forward into a future of increased data consumption and storage, designing and maintaining Online Analytical Processing and data mining tools will be critical tools to have in our reporting toolset.

In the next chapter, we'll reap the benefits of the groundwork that we laid in this chapter. We'll see how our customizations look through the use one of the best OLAP viewers out there: Microsoft Excel 2010. We'll explore how to use Microsoft Excel 2010's robust PivotTable functionality to create a connection and browse the cubes that we installed in this chapter. Then, we'll take a look at what it takes to build an Excel-based dashboard using Excel cube formulas. These dashboards can offer a portal through which we can view refreshable data from multiple cubes in a single place. If we're looking to impress our organization's executive team, building colourful and engaging dashboards will go a long way!

7
Utilizing Analysis Cubes for Excel for Dynamic Reporting

We are in the home stretch with only two reporting tools left in our toolset and we have saved the best ones for last! Until now, we have covered reporting tools that allow us to extract data sets from Dynamics GP or write reports by accessing the Dynamics GP data directly. In all of these tools, any type of summation or grouping that needed to be done, we had to create ourselves and know what tables to join together and where to find this data. In the last chapter, we learned that Analysis Cubes for Excel is an out-of-the-box data warehouse that does all of this summation and grouping for us.

Now that we have learned the backbone of the Analysis Cubes for Excel product, we will explore connecting to this data and creating reports with every accountant's favorite tool, Microsoft Excel.

In this chapter, we'll discuss some of the following topics:

- Creating a connection to individual cubes via Microsoft Excel
- Exploring the Excel PivotTable and Analysis Cubes interface
- How to create ad-hoc reports using Analysis Cubes
- Using Excel's CUBE formulas to build static reports and dashboards
- New PivotTable functionality found in Excel 2007 and Excel 2010

Let's get started with this incredibly exciting reporting tool!

Using an OLAP viewer to connect to the SSAS database

Once we have deployed our Analysis Cubes, in order to actually start writing our reports, we need to make a connection to our Analysis cubes database. There are many OLAP (Online Analytical Processing) viewers on the market as well as on the Internet available for download. Anyone familiar with Microsoft SQL Server Management Studio can also connect directly to the Analysis Services database by connecting to the SQL Server Analysis Services engine. From here, SQL Management Studio can be used as the OLAP browser.

However, in our opinion Microsoft's Analysis Cubes product was clearly designed with Excel in mind, so let's get started with exploring the cubes through Microsoft Excel!

Creating a connection to the cubes

When creating a connection to the cubes, an individual connection must be created for each cube. For example, if we wanted to get information out of our Financials cube and our Sales cube, we would need to create two connections in order to accomplish this.

Dynamics GP 2010 does have a **Create PivotTable** window that can be used from within the Dynamics GP application to create Excel worksheets with PivotTable reports using data from our cubes. However, there are downsides to using the GP 2010 Create PivotTable window:

- Requires a Dynamics GP license, as a user must be logged into Dynamics GP in order to use the window
- Does not let us preview the resulting PivotTable

The preferred method is to simply use Microsoft Excel to make the necessary connection to the cubes, as this lets us preview the results as we are building our PivotTable.

Creating a new connection

In our examples, we will be using Microsoft Excel 2010. To create a connection to the cubes, we open Excel and browse to our Data tab. From the ribbon, click **From Other Sources** and select **From Analysis Services**. This opens the **Data Connection Wizard**. In the Server name field, enter the name of the Database server where the Data Warehouse database resides and enter the login information.

Once logged in, we will need to choose the database that contains our data; if we accepted our default data warehouse name during installation, this database is Dynamics GP Analysis Cubes. We are also provided with a list of the cubes that we can select from. Click **Financials** and click **Next**.

> Two main reasons exist for why the Financials cube—or any cube, for that matter—does not appear in our drop down: our login information has not been granted security permissions to the cube or the cube has not been fully processed. Both of these topics are covered in more detail in *Chapter 6, Designing Your Analysis Cubes for Excel Environment*.

The next step in the wizard is to name our connection. By default, the wizard will use `<ServerName><Data Warehouse Name><Cube Name>.odc` as the name of the connection. The key point to note in this step is the Friendly Name field. This will also default to the above nomenclature. It is a good idea to change this to something much simpler (such as "GP Financials Cube") as it will make it much easier to use in cube formulas. We can also set a location for where the ODC (Office Data Connection) file will be stored. We will discuss the differences in storing locally or on a shared network location later in this section.

Once the wizard is completed, we will be prompted with the **Import Data** window where we can decide whether to go ahead and create a **PivotTable Report**, **PivotChart**, and **PivotTable Report**, or **Only Create the Connection**.

Storing connection files on network share or locally

As with many other reporting tools we have discussed, we always have the decision as to whether to store our reports locally or on some network share where multiple users can access the report. Our PivotTable Reports and Dashboards with Analysis Cubes for Excel are no different. We can choose to store our Excel spread sheets in either method and we have provided some insight into each below.

Storing on a network share through the use of mapped drive letters or the UNC (Universal Naming Convention) allows for any user given the proper permissions to use the report, making it easily shareable. This method also makes backup much easier as the connections and the reports themselves can easily be centrally managed.

Storing locally on a user's machine can also be an acceptable method of storage; however, in order to share a report or connection, users will need to "repoint" their data connection to the data connection on their local workstation. This makes managing the connections and backing them up much more difficult. In the next section, we'll cover how to repoint PivotTables and workbooks to a different data source.

Repointing to a different data source

Depending on our situation, there are two methods for repointing to a new data source or new data source location:

- **Change the Data Source for a single PivotTable**
- **Change the Data Source for an entire Workbook**

Our choice of method will usually depend on the number and nature of PivotTables we have stored in our Excel workbook.

Changing data source for a single pivot table

If we find the need to change our data source for a single pivot table, first, select the PivotTable that needs to be changed. Selecting the PivotTable adds the **PivotTable Tools options to the ribbon bar.** Select **Options**, then **Change Data Source**. The **Change PivotTable Data Source** window will open. We will see our current connection name, which will be the Friendly name defined earlier. Click **Choose Connection**. This will bring up the **Existing Connections** window where we can choose any existing connection in the list or we can browse for more. Once we have selected our new connection, simply click **Open** and then click **OK**.

Changing data sources for an entire workbook

If the situation arises where we need to change our data source for an entire workbook, use the **Data** tab found on the Microsoft Excel ribbon. From there, select **Connections**. This will bring up the **Workbook Connections** window, which will allow us to either add a new connection or change the properties of our existing connection by allowing us to browse out to an ODC file located either on a local machine or a network share.

Using an existing connection to connect to a cube

Up until now, we have discussed using Microsoft Excel 2010 to create a data connection to our data warehouse at the time we are ready to start writing our PivotTable report. One of the many benefits of these data connections is that once they are made, they can be used over and over again. We typically won't see the need to create multiple connections to the Financials Cube for instance. To connect to an existing connection, open Microsoft Excel and choose the **Data** tab. Select **Existing Connections** and choose an existing data connection from the available list or browse for more. This will open the **Import Data** dialog where we can choose to create our report.

Another way to accomplish this is to click the **Insert** tab in Excel, choose PivotTable, and select either PivotTable or PivotChart. This will bring up the **Create PivotTable** or **Create PivotChart** window where we can select to **Use an External Data Source**, and click **Choose Connection** to browse the list of available connections or browse for more.

Excel Pivot Table-Analysis Cubes Interface

For those of us familiar with Excel PivotTables, this next section will be familiar; however, be sure to pay close attention because we'll point out some of the differences between PivotTables that use a standard dataset—such as a table in another Excel worksheet—versus PivotTables that use Analysis Services as a data source.

The next image shows us some of the features of Excel PivotTables that we will cover in this section:

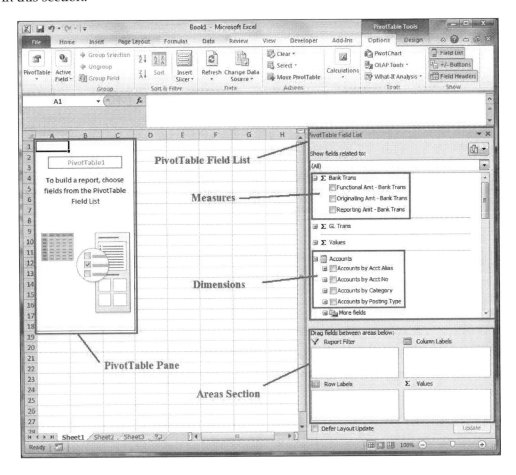

PivotTable pane

When we first create a connection to our cube, our Excel worksheet is transformed into an Excel PivotTable. The most immediate indication of this is the PivotTable pane that will appear in the upper left-hand corner of the spread sheet. This pane is where our report will be built. Right now, it is blank because we have not yet added any measures or attributes to our report.

As we begin to add measures and attributes to our report, the PivotTable pane will expand. Applying filters or refreshing the data over a period of time will cause this data to change, and the PivotTable pane will either expand or contract, depending on how much data is being presented. In short, PivotTables are dynamic, and we can't expect to control how much spreadsheet "real estate" our report will take up.

One thing to realize before we go much further: clicking outside of the pane will cause the PivotTable options on the toolbar and the Field List to disappear. Don't panic! Just click back into the pane to get it to reappear.

PivotTable Field List

Elsewhere in our Excel spreadsheet, we see a sidebar titled **PivotTable Field** list. Although our report will be built in the PivotTable pane, most of our interaction with the PivotTable will occur within the context of the Field List. This sidebar is split up into two main components: the Fields Section and the Areas Section.

A button at the upper-right hand corner of the Field List allows us to control the layout of the Field List. The default view, **Fields Section and Areas Section Stacked**, will be used throughout the rest of this chapter and is probably the best view for preserving extra room in our spread sheet. We definitely encourage those with a larger monitor to try the next view on the list—this view splits the Field List down the middle and places the Fields and Areas Sections side-by-side.

Fields Section

In the Fields Section, we see a list of groupings. Unlike a PivotTable connected to a standard dataset, the Field List for a PivotTable connected to an Analysis Services database is separated into Measure Groups and Dimensions. In our last chapter, we learned about these components and how they form part of the design of the cube. Now, let's consider them in light of how they are used in the reporting context.

Measure Groups

Measure Groups are always found at the top of the PivotTable Field List. They are easily identified by the sigma (Σ) symbol. Within each measure group, we can expect to see several related measures. We will use these measures to generate the numerical values in our report.

Nearly every cube will contain a special measure group titled **Values**. Measures in this grouping are generally calculated measures. In other words, these measures do not exist in a data warehouse table as a specific field, but they are instead created through the Analysis Services database. For the end user, however, these measures act and function as any other measure in one of the major measure groups.

Dimensions

Measures are pretty important, considering they will comprise the actual values in our reports, but a single number by itself is pretty useless. Instead, we will rely on attributes to slice and dice these numbers into more meaningful measures. Attributes are found on the Field List grouped together by corresponding dimension. Remember from our last chapter that a dimension is a collection of similar attributes. In the Field List, dimensions are identified by a rectangular symbol that looks like a list of attributes.

Depending on the dimension, we may see a plain list of attributes, or we may see a list of hierarchies, followed by a node called **More Fields**. The following image offers an example in the form of the **Master Date** dimension that is present in every cube:

The first three nodes—**Date**, **Date by Month**, and **Quarter by Year**—under the **Master Date** node are known as hierarchies. We can tell this by the presence of a plus (+) sign in front of each node. Hierarchies are groups of attributes that can be ordered in a natural manner. For example, in the **Master Date** dimension, if we expand the **Date** hierarchy node, we can see that it consists of four attributes: **Year**, **Quarter**, **Month**, and **Day**. Hierarchies are useful because they give us a way to easily expand our PivotTable nodes in order to drill down to more detailed data. If we were to add the **Date** hierarchy to our report, we'd have a high level look at all of the years in our data warehouse. If we wanted to drill down to a more detailed level for one of those years, then we could select the node for one of those years to drill down to the quarters of that year.

If we only want to see a single attribute, such as **Month**, in our report, we can expand the **More Fields** node to find a list of individual attributes. We can select from this list to ensure that only the selected attribute—and not additional attributes, as with a hierarchy—will be used in our report.

Incompatible dimensions and measures

Depending on how the underlying cube is designed, some measures may not be compatible with attributes from certain dimensions. When a measure is combined with an incompatible attribute in a PivotTable, the result is usually fairly obvious:

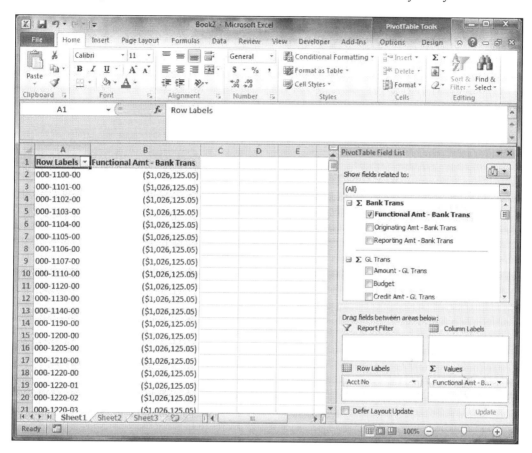

In the example above, the **Acct No** attribute from the **Accounts** dimension is paired with a measure from the **Bank Trans** measure group. Because this report is attempting to combine attributes from the General Ledger module with measures from the Bank Reconciliation module, the two measures are incompatible and the result is the same measure repeating itself over and over.

One way to ensure that only compatible dimensions and measures are used in a report is to take advantage of the drop-down box at the top of the PivotTable Field List. This drop-down box is found underneath the **Show Fields Related To** text as seen in the following image from the Financials cube:

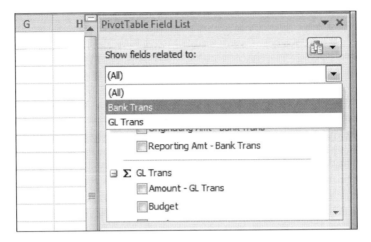

As we can see from the previous image, the selections in the drop-down box correspond to the two major measure groups available in the cube. Selecting **Bank Trans** will update the Field List so that only measures and dimensions that are compatible with this measure group will be displayed. In fact, with **Bank Trans** selected, the **GL Trans** measure group as well as the **Accounts** and **GL Trans** dimensions will be hidden from the Field List. Only the **Bank Trans** measure group will be available, and we can be assured that no matter what attribute we select for our slicing and dicing, it will be compatible with the **Bank Trans** measure group.

Areas Section

The Areas Section of the Field List is divided into four areas, each controlling a different aspect of our PivotTable report. In order to build our PivotTable, attributes and measures must be selected or dragged from the Fields Section into one of these four areas. As we add and remove these from the Areas Section, the PivotTable Pane will constantly adjust to reflect these new selections.

Before we get down to the business of creating a specific report in our PivotTable, let's take a look at the different units that comprise the Areas Section:

- **Values**: The **Values** section is where measures from the Field List should be placed. It's easy to make this connection considering the symbol for the **Values** section (that is, the sigma (Σ) symbol) is the same as the symbols for the measure groups found in the Field List. As we add measures to the Values section, numbers will begin to appear in our PivotTable. These numbers won't mean much until we've added attributes to the other three portions of the Areas Section.

- **Row Labels**: Adding attributes in the **Row Labels** section will cause the measures that we just added to the Values section to be sliced in a vertical direction. The distinct records that make up the attribute will become the row labels for our PivotTable report. For example, if we were attempting to create a refreshable Trial Balance report, we would add the **Account Number** attribute to the **Row Labels** section so that we can see a row of account numbers down the left-hand side of our report.

- **Column Labels**: Just like with the **Row Labels** section, we can add attributes to the **Column Labels** in order to slice our values. However, adding attributes to the Column Labels will cause the distinct records of this attribute to be arrayed across the top of the report. Add attributes to the **Column Labels** for effective side-by-side reporting. One popular attribute for the **Column Labels** section is the Company ID from the **Company** dimension. In a multi-company environment, this allows us to quickly and easily compare the same values across multiple company databases!

- **Report Filter**: The last area in which we can add an attribute from the Field List is the **Report Filter**. Adding an attribute here will cause that attribute to appear in the upper left-hand corner of our PivotTable report. We must then click on this filter in the actual report to select the values on which we want to filter the data in our report. This is incredibly useful for restricting the amount of data that actually appears in our report.

Now that we understand the basics of the PivotTable in Excel, let's try creating some reports of our own!

Creating ad-hoc reports

With our knowledge of the PivotTable basics, creating reports is actually quite simple and can be very fun once we get started. It's kind of like opening presents on Christmas morning, you don't really know how cool your report will be until you start playing with the different measures and matching them with different dimensions. An easy report to start with to get an idea of the power of Excel Analysis cubes for Excel is a simple one that uses the **Accounts by Category** dimension, **the Signed Amount – GL** Trans measure and the **Periodicity** dimension as the columns. To accomplish this, we will use what we have learned in earlier sections to create a new data connection or use an existing connection. Once we have made our data connection, we will drag our measures and dimensions into our area section. We can see from the following screenshot how each of these is placed in our areas section to create the report:

The **Periodicity** dimension is a rather interesting dimension in that it includes columns such as current amount, period to date amount, previous year period to date % changes, and more, all in one dimension. This is very useful in that it saves time having to try to write complicated formulas to calculate all of these amounts. The **Periodicity** dimension is pretty useless unless we define a date from which all calculations should originate. In fact, the underlying calculations require that whenever we use the **Periodicity** dimension, we also use the **Date** hierarchy from the **Master Date** dimension. Using other attributes or hierarchies from the **Date** dimension will not work with **Periodicity**!

In the following image, we can see our final product and the impressive thing is that it only took us a few minutes to build. Try building this report in FRx or SSRS that fast!

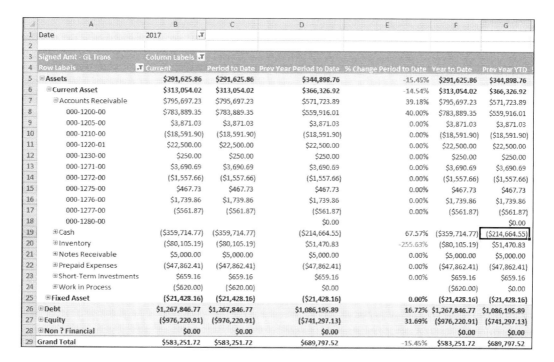

This is just the beginning. Wait until we see how we can combine multiple PivotTable reports and charts to create the beginning stages of a dashboard!

Using PivotTable design features to change report appearances

It's usually pretty obvious when a co-worker uses a default Microsoft Office template to produce a presentation. Don't be one of those people! Take the extra time to utilize the easy-to-use PivotTable design features to improve the look and feel of your report. All of these design features can be accessed from the **PivotTable Tools | Design** and **Options** tabs. Let's take a look at some of these features.

Changing the Report Layout

On the **PivotTable Tools | Design** tab, we can control different aspects of the Report Layout such as how to handle Subtotals, Grand Totals, our Report Layout, and how to handle placement of Blank Rows. The following options are available when working with the Layout section of the Ribbon:

- Subtotals: For some reports, we may not want to see subtotals for every grouping. We can use the following options to control when subtotals appear in our PivotTable:

  - Do Not Show Subtotals

  - Show All Subtotals at the Bottom of the Group

  - Show All Subtotals at the Top of the Group

  - Include Filtered Items in Totals

- Grand Totals: Grand Totals are the totals for all groups found at the very bottom of the PivotTable or at the far right of the PivotTable. Like subtotals, we can control whether or not these appear in our PivotTable:

  - Off For Rows and Columns

  - On For Rows and Columns

  - On For Rows Only

  - On For Columns Only

- Report Layout: As the name implies, we can use the options found here to control the way our PivotTable appears in our Excel spreadsheet:

  - Show in Compact Form: This is the default view for newly created PivotTables. It's best used for larger reports when lots of data needs to be consolidated into a smaller, more condensed report.

  - Show in Outline Form: Depending on the report, this report layout can appear a bit messy. Usually, turning off subtotals can help make this report layout a bit cleaner.

  - Show in Tabular Form: This layout is very similar to what many users are familiar with from SmartLists. As with the Outline form, it might help to turn off subtotals to make this a cleaner report.

  - Repeat All Item Labels: This is new to Excel 2010. By using this option in conjunction with the Tabular report layout, we can have Item Labels repeat down multiple rows, making this even more like a SmartList!

  - Do Not Repeat Item Labels: Use this option to turn off the Item Label functionality if it has been enabled.

- Blank Rows: For formatting and readability purposes, it may be helpful to insert a blank row at the end of each grouping. Use these options to control this functionality:
    - ○ Insert Blank Line after Each Item
    - ○ Remove Blank Line after Each Item

Applying styles to PivotTables

In addition to the Report Layout, we can also apply a wide range of styles to our PivotTable report. Like the Report Layout options, these options are found under **PivotTable Tools | Design** (remember, select the PivotTable pane to see these options on the ribbon bar). We can control such things as the colour scheme on the headers, groups and detail lines, whether or not we want banded Rows or Columns, and whether to include colouring on the Row and Column headers. By applying such styling to our PivotTables, we can create some really professional looking reports and add some flavour so that every report doesn't look like the same old default template.

Using slicers to filter PivotTable data

Slicers are an awesome addition to Microsoft Excel 2010. In earlier versions of Excel, we were forced to use Report Filters in order to filter our data in our PivotTables. Though this worked very well, it was not always easy to know what the current filtering state was, especially if it included multiple items. With the addition of slicers, we have been given a method of providing buttons that we can click to filter the data. So what is so awesome about these slicers? The buttons light up when we click them and stay lit so that at any time we can see the current filtering state, even if we are slicing on multiple fields. We can see from the following image how these slicers work:

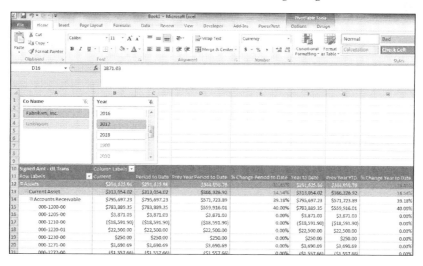

To add one or more slicers, from our **PivotTable Tools | Options** menu, we choose **Insert Slicer** from the Ribbon. Scroll through the list of available Dimensions and select the one to use for our slicer. From there we simply resize and position the slicer window to where we want it and click the button for the value we want to filter on and we are done. We can then add as many more slicers as we want.

Slicers are a great addition and are really great to use as replacements for filters on PivotTables. Though we have described creating a slicer for a single PivotTable, slicers can also be used to connect charts and other PivotTables when creating dashboards and we can use these slicers to control the filtering of the entire dashboard.

Utilizing the Excel cube formulas

In our last section, we explored creating Analysis Cubes reports by using the PivotTable functionality in Excel. For those of us who have used Excel's PivotTable functionality, it is a powerful tool that allows for effortless ad-hoc data analysis. When combined with Analysis Services, PivotTables can provide users with an unparalleled ability to peruse aggregated data and drill-down to the underlying data quickly and accurately.

But, for all of its usefulness, some drawbacks do exist for using Excel PivotTable functionality to access data in an Analysis Services database.

First, it's difficult to combine PivotTables in a worksheet containing other PivotTables or Excel objects such as charts and graphs. The dynamic nature of PivotTables also makes it extremely difficult to control the size of the generated report. Adding and subtracting measures and attributes or expanding and collapsing hierarchies in the PivotTable will cause the PivotTable pane to expand or contract within the spread sheet. If the PivotTable expands into an area of our spread sheet that already contains data, Excel will prompt us with a message that the PivotTable is about to replace the contents of the existing cell. Obviously, this is not ideal in most cases!

Aside from the potential of erasing sensitive data in the same spread sheet, another drawback with using PivotTables is that it's difficult to combine data from a PivotTable with data outside of the PivotTable. This data can exist in another cube, or even be a self-contained Excel spreadsheet that is used on a daily basis. Suppose we use an Excel PivotTable connected to the Financials cube to generate a report showing us up-to-date cash balances for each of our company databases. How do we use data from this PivotTable in conjunction with data that exists outside of this PivotTable? Although an Excel function (GETPIVOTDATA) exists for this purpose, it can be an unwieldy tool at times. We need a better way to combine data from the cubes with data from other sources.

Fortunately, since the release of Excel 2007, new formulas have been created to allow users to create connections to a cube in an Analysis Services database. By understanding and utilizing these new cube formulas, we can overcome some of the drawbacks presented by using PivotTables as an exclusive means for generating cube data. This is achieved, in part, by locking cube data into specific cells within a spreadsheet. Now, cube data is no longer free to roam about our spreadsheet. Additionally, because this data is no longer found within a PivotTable, our ability to combine this data with data from other sources is greatly improved.

In order to begin using the variety of cube formulas that exist in Excel, we must first understand the two most basic cube formulas. An understanding of these formulas serves as the building block for using the rest of the cube formulas in Excel. After we've used these basic formulas to calculate the year-to-date balance of our operating cash account, we'll go a step farther and use more advanced formulas to generate a refreshable top ten list of customers by current aging amount.

Basic cube formulas

Before we look at our basic formulas, keep in mind that each cube formula requires that we first identify a cube connection. To use a connection, it must be an active connection in the existing workbook. Refer to our earlier section for more information on cube connections within an Excel workbook. In the examples in this section, however, we will use a connection that we have named "GP Financials Cube". Additionally, our samples will utilize the sample TWO database that can be installed with Dynamics GP.

CUBEMEMBER

The CUBEMEMBER formula is used to introduce attributes into our report. These attributes can then be referenced by CUBEVALUE formulas. Recall from our previous discussion on PivotTables that we can drag-and-drop an attribute such as **Account Number** from the Fields Section into the **Row Labels** section of our report, and a list of unique account numbers would populate in our PivotTable. What we did not mention at that time, however, is that each individual account number is actually known as a unique member of the **Account Number** attribute in the **Accounts** dimension. With the CUBEMEMBER formula, it is not enough that we just reference an attribute; instead, we must actually specify the unique member that we want to see in the active cell.

Say, for example, we want to reference a specific account number in our cell. The CUBEMEMBER formula would look something like the following:

```
=CUBEMEMBER("GP Financials Cube","[Accounts].[Acct No].[All].[000-1100-
00]")
```

If we've entered our formula correctly, we should see **000-1100-00** in the cell containing this formula. Of course, this assumes we are using the TWO sample database; however, if the sample database is not being used, users simply need to substitute a valid account for the final section of the formula. By seeing an account number returned in our field, this indicates that the account number exists in our cube, and any CUBEVALUE formula that references this cell will be sliced by this account number.

Our second argument, the member expression, is a text string that requires us to identify the dimension, the attribute, and finally, the specific member that we wish to reference via this formula. Note that each argument is bracketed in quotation marks. These quotation marks are useful because they let Excel know that we're entering a new formula argument, and Excel responds by providing us with a drop-down box from which we can select from a list of available values for this argument. The following image shows an example of the screen tips that are available as we progress through our most recent CUBEMEMBER formula:

We can use our arrow keys and *TAB* to select one of these values for use in our formula. As we get into more complex cube formulas, this feature will make the process considerably easier for us!

CUBEVALUE

According to Microsoft Excel Help function, the CUBEVALUE formula "returns an aggregated value from the cube." In other words, we will use this formula when we want to return a specific measure in the current cell. For example, we can use the CUBEVALUE formula to return the **Amount – GL Trans** value for a specific account using our Financials cube:

```
=CUBEVALUE("GP Financials Cube","[Measures].[Amount - GL
Trans]","[Accounts].[Acct No].[All].[000-1100-00]")
```

Once it has calculated, the cell containing this formula will display the total sum of debits minus credits for the selected account for all dates and all transactions in our data warehouse. In other words, we will see the value at the intersection of the **Amount – GL Trans** measure and the 000-1100-00 account. Can you picture how this would look in a PivotTable?

Combining the CUBEVALUE and CUBEMEMBER formulas

Now that we've covered both the CUBEVALUE and CUBEMEMBER formulas, it's time to combine them. As we've said before, in order to be truly useful, our CUBEVALUE formula should reference one or more CUBEMEMBER formulas that are used to slice the value into a more meaningful one.

Before we get to combining the CUBEVALUE and CUBEMEMBER formulas, let's take a quick step back. In our last section, we actually inserted our two member references (remember, these were enclosed in square brackets) directly into the CUBEVALUE formula. While this is certainly allowed, it's not always best practice. Instead, it's more useful if we separately take these two strings out of our CUBEVALUE formula and insert them in our spreadsheet as CUBEMEMBER formulas like the following:

```
=CUBEMEMBER("GP Financials Cube","[Accounts].[Acct No].[All].[000-1100-
00]")
```

```
=CUBEMEMBER("GP Financials Cube","[Measures].[Amount - GL Trans]")
```

Again, we can use the helpful screen tips to make the process of typing formulas easier:

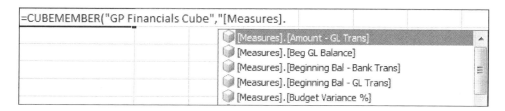

Now, let's consider an example whereby we display the year-to-date balance of our Operating cash account in a cell. To begin this example, our two CUBEMEMBER formula from the previous example are found in cells **A3** and **A4**, respectively. We've also taken the liberty to add two additional CUBEMEMBER formulas referencing a **Year-To-Date** calculation from the Periodicity dimension and specific date from the **Date** hierarchy of the Master Date dimension in cells **A1** and **A2**, respectively.

Our CUBEVALUE formula is being entered into cell A1:

```
=CUBEVALUE("GP Financials Cube","[Measures].[Amount - GL Trans]",$A$1)
```

The following image shows the final product with column **A** showing the calculated result of the formula found to its immediate right in column **B** (Note: The formulas in this and other images in this section have been added for emphasis. Your final report will likely not include these formulas!):

	A	B	C	D	E	F	G	H	I
1	Year to Date	=CUBEMEMBER("GP Financials Cube","[Periodicity].[Year to Date]")							
2	August	=CUBEMEMBER("GP Financials Cube","[Master Date].[Date].[All].[2017].[Q3].[August]")							
3	000-1100-00	=CUBEMEMBER("GP Financials Cube","[Accounts].[Acct No].[All].[000-1100-00]")							
4	Amount - GL Trans	=CUBEMEMBER("GP Financials Cube","[Measures].[Amount - GL Trans]")							
5	$778,709.82	=CUBEVALUE("GP Financials Cube",A1,A2,A3,A4)							

It's actually pretty simple. Once we've entered our CUBEMEMBER formula(s), all we need to do is add references to the cell containing the unique member in our CUBEVALUE formula. If we need to reference multiple members, we can add additional arguments that reference these formulas in their respective cells. This is the same thing as if we were to add additional attributes to the **Row Labels** and **Column Labels** section of our PivotTable, except now, we have greater control in determining where specific values and members should be placed in our spread sheet!

In the example we've just used, we now have greater flexibility in referencing the year-to-date cash balance as a value in a non-cube report elsewhere in this spread sheet. Rather than having to check the balance in GP and plug it into our report each time, we want to update the values; we can use the refresh button to refresh our year to date balance with the latest numbers from the data warehouse.

This is an extraordinarily simple example, but we're beginning to see some of the value that cube formulas can bring to our everyday reporting needs, especially when those reporting needs exist within an Excel workbook.

Building a "Top Ten" table

In our last section, we explored using the CUBEMEMBER and CUBEVALUE sections to access data stored in an Analysis Services database without using a PivotTable. This allowed us to lock data into specific cells, and gives us greater flexibility in formatting and controlling the appearance of our spread sheet.

Now, let's explore two slightly more advanced cube formulas that can help us build a refreshable report showing our top ten customers based on current aging amount. We'll use the CUBESET and CUBERANKEDMEMBER formulas to achieve this. Note that we'll use a connection to our Receivables cube called "GP Receivables Cube" in our example. Again, we will use our sample TWO databases for these examples.

CUBESET

The CUBESET formula is used to define a set or range of individual members in a single cell. We can then reference this cell with a CUBEVALUE member, just like we would with a CUBEMEMBER function. For example, suppose we had three customers that we like to group together for reporting purposes because they are actually child customers of a parent account that does not exist in GP. In our earlier examples, we would have to create three separate CUBEMEMBER formulas, each referencing one of the three individual members (or customers). Then, we would have to reference each of these formulas with three separate CUBEVALUE formulas and a final summation in order to find a single value for the parent entity. With a CUBESET, we only have to define our set one time, and then we can use a single formula to represent all three customers at once.

Let's use the CUBESET formula to create a set containing all of the customers in our data warehouse:

```
=CUBESET("GP Receivables Cube","[Customers].[Customer Name].[All].
Children","Top 10 Customers")
```

As usual, our first argument identifies the connection to the cube. Our second argument identifies the members that should make up the set. In this case, we are defining our set as all of the individual members, or children, of the **Customer Name** attribute in the **Customers** dimension. Finally, because the formula in this cell represents so many values, we are using the third argument, the caption, to return a value to our cell that is descriptive of what the cell actually contains.

The following image shows the calculation, plus the final result in an Excel spreadsheet:

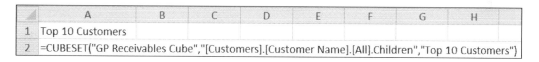

Now, instead of creating ten separate CUBEMEMBER formulas for ten separate customers, we have these ten customers represented by a single formula in a single cell. Additionally, even as our list of top ten customers changes over time, this cell will always continue to point to the most current group of top ten customers.

CUBERANKEDMEMBER

One of the problems with a CUBESET formula is that we can't always tell what individual members comprise the set. For example, suppose we have a CUBESET that represents all of our individual customers from GP. How do we know who those customers are? One of the ways we can extract these customers from the set is through the use of the CUBERANKEDMEMBER formula.

With the CUBERANKEDMEMBER formula, we can return a specific member from the list. Suppose we wanted to return the individual member with the third highest On Account balance from a cube set containing a list of customers ranked in order from highest balance to lowest balance? We could use a CUBERANKEDMEMBER to achieve this. It's important to realize that the ranking order is actually specified in the CUBESET formula; we are merely using the CUBERANKEDMEMBER formula to designate which individual member we want returned.

A sample CUBERANKEDMEMBER formula might look as follows:

```
=CUBERANKEDMEMBER("GP Receivables Cube",A1,3)
```

This formula will return the third value in the ranked cube set found in cell **A1**. We have to look in cell A1 to identify the cube set and the order in which it is ranked.

Let's use our newfound knowledge of CUBESET and CUBERANKEDMEMBER to create a refreshable table of our top ten customers by current receivables balance.

Creating the table

Before we begin, we need to modify the CUBESET formula that we created in our earlier example. In that example, we simply created a set containing all of our customers. We did not identify any particular order in which that set should be arranged, and so we will do that now:

```
=CUBESET("GP Receivables Cube","[Customers].[Customer Name].[All].
Children","Top 10 Customers",2,"[Measures].[Functional Amt - Receivables
Aging]")
```

This formula adds two additional arguments. The fourth argument tells us the order in which we'd like to sort our set. A value of **2** tells us that we'd like to sort it in descending order (hint: use the screen tips to help you populate this formula!). The fifth and final argument identifies the value that should be used to determine the sort order. In this case, we have selected the **Functional Amount – Receivables Aging** measure, as this reflects the total aging balance from the last time aging was run in GP.

So far, our report should look like this (with formulas added for emphasis):

	A	B	C	D	E	F	G
1	Top 10 Customers	=CUBESET("GP Receivables Cube","[Customers].[Customer					
2		Name].[All].Children","Top 10 Customers",2,"[Measures].[Functional					
3		Amt - Receivables Aging]")					

Next, we need to add some CUBERANKEDMEMBER formulas to our report so we can actually identify the top ten customers in the set. Our first formula will look like this:

```
=CUBERANKEDMEMBER("GP Receivables Cube",$A$1,1)
```

This formula references the CUBESET that we just entered in cell **A1** and tells Excel to return the first customer from that set. We can copy and paste this formula down one cell and change the rank argument to a 2 in order to return the second customer. Again, we can copy this, change the rank to a 3 to return the third customer, and so on. Eventually, our report should look like the following:

	A	B	C	D	E
1	Top 10 Customers				
2					
3					
4	Contoso, Ltd.	=CUBERANKEDMEMBER("GP Receivables Cube",A1,1)			
5	Office Design Systems Ltd	=CUBERANKEDMEMBER("GP Receivables Cube",A1,2)			
6	Alton Manufacturing	=CUBERANKEDMEMBER("GP Receivables Cube",A1,3)			
7	Vision Inc.	=CUBERANKEDMEMBER("GP Receivables Cube",A1,4)			
8	Vancouver Resort Hotels	=CUBERANKEDMEMBER("GP Receivables Cube",A1,5)			
9	Berry Medical Center	=CUBERANKEDMEMBER("GP Receivables Cube",A1,6)			
10	Johnson, Kimberly	=CUBERANKEDMEMBER("GP Receivables Cube",A1,7)			
11	Humongous Insurance	=CUBERANKEDMEMBER("GP Receivables Cube",A1,8)			
12	World Enterprises	=CUBERANKEDMEMBER("GP Receivables Cube",A1,9)			
13	Place One Suites	=CUBERANKEDMEMBER("GP Receivables Cube",A1,10)			

Notice how the rank number changes in each successive row.

It appears that our report is lacking only one thing: values. While we can already tell that **Contoso, Ltd** is our customer with the highest aging amount, wouldn't it be helpful if we could see the actual dollar value associated with this customer? Absolutely! To do this, we first need to enter a CUBEMEMBER formula in cell **B1** that identifies the measure we wish to display:

```
=CUBEMEMBER("GP Receivables Cube","[Measures].[Functional Amt -
Receivables Aging]","Aging Amount")
```

Finally, we need to add CUBEVALUE formulas that reference both the CUBERANKEDMEMBER formulas and the CUBEMEMBER formula that identifies the type of measure to be displayed. In the end, our spread sheet should look as follows:

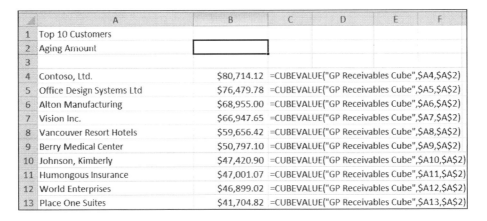

Congratulations! We now have a refreshable report that will always show us a list of our top ten customers based on current aging amount! If we save this spread sheet, open it at a later date, and select **Data | Refresh All**, our report will update to display data from the latest cube load and processing. If a new customer has supplanted **Contoso, Ltd.** as the customer with the highest balance, that customer would then be displayed in cell A4!

Adding a chart for visual effect

If we're really feeling creative, we can also add a chart to our report that will refresh and update based on the contents in the table we've just created. For example, here is what happens when we add a pie chart to the spreadsheet:

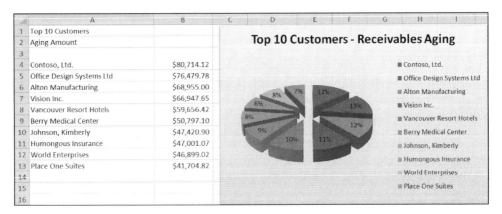

With Microsoft Excel 2010, we can easily insert a graph by selecting our data set, clicking the **Insert** button in the ribbon bar, and then clicking the chart of our choice. With just a few simple formatting changes, we can really enhance our spreadsheet with cool graphics that provide valuable, at-a-glance information!

Creating dashboards from Analysis Cubes data—a few thoughts

As we've seen from our previous examples, one of the great benefits of Analysis Cubes is that users can quickly and easily create their own reports from scratch. With the ad-hoc capabilities provided via PivotTable functionality, users can quickly move the building blocks of their report around in a manner that suits them best. If for some reason a report is lost, it's usually not too difficult to recreate that report from scratch.

Most users, however, will identify several key reports and/or metrics of information that they want to refer to on a regular basis. Rather than create these reports from scratch every time they open a new Excel workbook, these users will begin saving these reports in an Excel workbook. Then, anytime they want to refer to that information, they'll pull up that work book, hit Refresh All, and be on their way. Unbeknownst to some of these users, what they're doing is engaging in a primitive form of "dash boarding".

In short, a dashboard is nothing more than a single, one-stop place for users to quickly review, analyse, and interact with data that is relevant to them. A dashboard for a Purchasing agent, for example, may show several metrics and lists related things such as the value of items on pending purchase orders, orders expected to be received in the next week, items that will require purchase in the next week, and so on. All of this information can be consolidated into bite-sized pieces of information that can then be consolidated into a single spreadsheet. Each morning, when the Purchasing agent arrives in the office, he or she can pull up that spreadsheet, hit refresh, and have a quick, birds-eye view of the Purchasing landscape.

The topic of building effective dashboards is one that can take up several chapters, if not an entire book. Our hope is that this chapter has given you some thoughts on how you can create a dashboard using nothing more than a single Excel workbook and a connection to the various cubes provided by Analysis Cubes for Excel. Some dashboards are created by creating a workbook that consists of several useful PivotTables, with one PivotTable per spreadsheet. Other, more advanced dashboards may make use of the cube formulas to create static subsets of data that can be combined into a single spread sheet. In this manner, we can combine data from multiple cubes and even multiple data sources into a single, easy-to-access place!

Eventually, depending on our organization's environment, these cube reports and dashboards, using Analysis Cubes data as the underlying data source, can be published to an Office SharePoint Server website. This enables an entire team or organization to have access to the same reports and a single version of the truth. Truly, the possibilities become endless with business intelligence tools like Analysis Cubes and Excel.

The seven default cubes

Now that we've covered the basics of reporting against the cubes, let's make a few comments about each individual cube. When possible, we'll comment on the multiple measure groups that exist in a given cube. Refer to our previous discussion on incompatible measure groups and dimensions to ensure that mismatched measures and attributes do not cause havoc in your own report!

Financials cube

The Financials cube is probably the most useful and, not surprisingly, most popular cube. Data in this cube is pulled from the transaction tables of the General Ledger and Bank Reconciliation modules from GP. Additionally, Multidimensional Analysis information is included in this cube for those organizations that make use of this tool in GP.

Users should note the presence of an **Amount – GL Trans** measure and a **Signed Amount – GL Trans** measure in the GL Transactions measure group. The **Amount – GL Trans** measure is a measure calculated as debits minus credits. The **Signed Amount – GL Trans** measure group takes the Amount measure a step farther and adjusts the sign of the measure to a plus or minus depending on the native sign of the selected account. The native sign of each account is managed at the account category level via the GLAccountCategory table in the data warehouse. For example, under normal circumstances, we might expect an account assigned to the Sales Account Category to have a normal credit balance. If we used the **Amount – GL Trans** measure, this would show up as a negative in our report. In many circumstances, we would rather have this credit balance display as a positive, so we assign a Native Sign of Credit to the Sales Account Category and use the **Signed Amount – GL Trans** measure to display this value as a positive. In the chapter, we discussed how the Native Sign functionality can be utilized on the database end to change how these values appear in our reports.

The Financials cube is an incredible tool for building instantly refreshable trial balances, balance sheets, and other financial statements. Additionally, by building these reports in PivotTables, we can take advantage of the extra drill through and filtering tools that make these PivotTables so powerful. Although the ability to control formatting and the ordering of accounts is somewhat limited with PivotTables, we have seen some companies make use of the Excel cube formulas to overcome these obstacles and create instantly refreshable, professional-looking financial statements.

Accounts Receivable cube

Data in this cube is pulled from the Receivables Management module from Dynamics GP. Because this cube contains this information along with the aging period's aging details, it can be used to create reports such as cross company aging reports.

Two separate measure groups exist in this cube. One, the **Receivables Aging** measure group, pulls data from the aging related fields in the Customer Master Summary table (RM00103). These fields in GP are updated anytime aging is run against a particular customer, so users should note that the cube does not actually perform the aging routine. Instead, aging-related data in the cube is only up-to-date as of the last time aging was run in GP prior to the cube load and processing job run.

On the other hand, the **Receivables Revenue** measure group contains measures from Open and History transaction and distribution tables in the Receivables module. By including distribution information, we can use this measure group for account-level insights into our Receivables transactions. Apply information such as Credit Memos applied to an Invoice or payments from customers are not included in this cube.

Accounts Payable cube

Data in this cube is pulled from the Payables Management module from Dynamics GP. We can create such reports as Total Expenses by Vendor for a period using this cube.

Unlike the Receivables cube, the Payables cube does not include any aging information. Instead, only a single measure group, **Total Expense**, exists to provide us insight into values associated with our Payables transactions. These values are pulled from the transaction and distribution level tables in the Payables Management module, so we are able to gain an account-level perspective of these transactions.

Also, like the Receivables cube, we should not expect to see information related to payments or how they are applied to invoices. Unfortunately, this information is not included in the cube and separate customizations are required to include this sort of information.

Sales cube

Data in this cube is pulled from the Sales Order Processing module in Dynamics GP. Unlike the Accounts Receivable cube, this cube does not include distribution information, so we won't see dimensions such as **Accounts**. This cube does include an **Items** dimension, so we can use it to gain better insights into concepts such as the volume of inventory, items sold to a particular customer, or which items are generating the most revenue in a given period.

Two separate measure groups exist in this cube, and they relate to the stage at which a Sales Transaction exists in GP. The **Pending Sales** dimension pulls data from Open Sales Transaction tables, so, generally speaking, we can expect to see un-posted sales transactions reflected in this measure group. On the other hand, the **Sales Detail** measure group is comprised of data found in the History transaction tables. We can expect to find posted sales transactions, as well as voided transactions, here. Dimensions with similar names to the measure groups (that is, **Pending Sales** and **Sales Detail**) also exist in this cube, so we must be sure not to mix and match incompatible dimensions with the wrong measure group!

Purchases cube

Data in this cube is pulled from the Purchase Order Processing module in Dynamics GP. Although the Accounts Payable cube includes distribution information, this cube does not. Like the Sales cube, however, it does include an **Items** dimension, so we can use this cube to find things such as all orders for a particular item, statistics on purchasing volume by item, orders by vendor for a particular period, and more.

Also, like the Sales cube, two separate measure groups exist that reflect purchase order data depending on the stage a particular purchase order has reached. The **Pending Purchase Order** measure group reflects all purchase orders that are still open in GP. On the other hand, the **Purchase Order Detail** measure group reflects purchase orders that exist in a Received or Closed status as well as those that have been manually moved to history. Recall that in GP, purchase orders must be moved to history via the Completed Purchase Orders routine.

As with the Sales cube, dimensions with similar names to the measure groups (that is, **Pending Purchase Order** and **Purchase Order Detail**) also exist in this cube, so we must be sure not to mix and match incompatible dimensions with the wrong measure group!

Inventory cube

Data in this cube is pulled from the Inventory module in Dynamics GP. Two measures, **Inventory History** and **Inventory On Hand**, exist in this cube. The **Inventory History** measure group can be used along with the **Item Daily Quantity** dimension to provide cube users insight into the numerous inventory transactions that can exist in GP from modules such as Sales Order Processing, Purchase Order Processing, and Inventory. On the other hand, the **Inventory On Hand** measure group can be used in conjunction with the **Item Current Quantity** dimension to provide users with current inventory information. This sort of information is found in GP windows such as Item Inquiry and is only current as of the last time the cube job was run.

The Inventory cube can be a great way to keep a finger on inventory levels in an organization (or across multiple organizations).

Analytical Accounting cube

Shortly after the release of GP 2010, Microsoft announced that a new cube, one for Analytical Accounting, had been added to the line-up of cubes available as part of the standard Analysis Cubes for Excel package. As with other cubes, this cube provides users with the ability to crunch massive amounts of data generated by its respective module so that users can easily and quickly analyse their data. If your company utilizes Analytical Accounting, this cube is certainly worth having!

Summary

As we can see, Analysis Cubes for Excel is a very robust reporting tool. It can actually be quite fun to use and gives us the ability to create a wide array of reports that we may have found impossible or extremely difficult to create in some of the other reporting tools available to us. Hopefully, we can take what we have learned in this chapter and go beyond the examples we have provided and become a rock star in our organization by providing powerful dashboards for our executive and management teams to understand the health of our company.

If you thought that was cool, wait until you see Management Reporter! In the next chapter, we will be introduced to Management Reporter by exploring how to install, configure, and set up the product. We will then dive into topics such as understanding the range of building blocks and creating basic Report, Row, Column, and Reporting Tree definitions.

8

Designing Financial Reports in Management Reporter

In the next two chapters, we'll begin exploring the Management Reporter application. Management Reporter is a great tool to use when our goal is to enable multiple, non-IT users to create professional-looking financial statements based on source data from our ERP environment. Management Reporter is Microsoft's attempt to create a single performance management solution that can be used across the entire Microsoft Dynamics stack. The release of such a product represents a break from the old way of creating financial reports via Microsoft FRx, and Microsoft will more than likely continue to build upon and improve the technology and functionality present in the first versions of Management Reporter.

Because Management Reporter offers direct integration with our source databases, we can expect our reports to display information that is up-to-date as of the moment we generate a particular report. Additionally, as was the case with its predecessor, Microsoft FRx, Management Reporter continues the concept of self-service reporting. Creating reports with Management Reporter is made easier through the use of concepts like the building blocks and an easy-to-use user interface, making report-creation the domain of the actual users who need the report, and not that of a remote, possibly overwhelmed IT department. Although some initial training may be required to bring our key report designers up-to-speed on the many functions and concepts available in Management Reporter, the end-results are well worth it!

Because Management Reporter offers so much in the way of functionality, we can't possibly hope to cover it all in a single chapter. To this end, we've broken up our coverage of Management Reporter into two chapters:

- The first chapter (this one) will focus on a discussion of the underlying architecture of Management Reporter and then move to the use of the Report Designer interface and building blocks to create our reports

- The second chapter (the next one — *Chapter 9, Viewing Financial Reports in Management Reporter*) will then cover the process of generating our reports, using the Report Viewer to view these reports, and then offer some additional commentary on some of the changes between Management Reporter and FRx

Now that we have an idea of what the next two chapters will cover, let's take a look at what we will specifically cover in this first chapter on Management Reporter:

- Underlying architecture of Management Reporter
- Overview of installation of Management Reporter
- Management Reporter Security
- Navigating the Report Designer interface
- Working with the Building Blocks
- Taming Building Block sprawl

Before we start interacting with the tool, let's begin by taking a look at the architecture of Management Reporter.

Management Reporter architecture

With the release of Management Reporter, Microsoft has updated its code base from the one previously used for FRx Financial Reporting. Previous users of FRx will find the look and feel of Management Reporter very similar to FRx. An understanding of this new architecture is important for any user of Management Reporter, as this understanding can drive such things as system requirements.

Management Reporter was built with 64-bit environments in mind and does indeed fully support these environments. The code base has been updated to the powerful Microsoft .NET Platform and a new C# codebase that provides far superior application stability than its predecessors. In addition to the codebase, Management Reporter uses SQL Server for its data storage, which is a great leap from the days of Microsoft Access that FRx used, as well as the move to Internet Information Services (IIS) as the Report Processor. Due to these improvements, one can expect increases in performance, stability, and multi-user capabilities.

Installing and configuring Management Reporter

Before installing Management Reporter, we should first review the various installation options available to us. Before deciding on which option to use, we must first gain an understanding of our customer's environment. Is this a new installation, a server move, or something else? The answers to these questions will aid us in our decision. The following options are available for installing Management Reporter:

- Install Management Reporter application service and process service and create a new database
- Install Management Reporter application service and process service and connect to an existing database
- Create the Management Reporter database without installing the application service or the process service
- Install Management Reporter process service only and connect to an existing database
- Install Management Reporter application service only and create a new database

The following table summarizes the various installation options for Management Reporter and their impact:

Approach	Type of Service	Database
Full - New	Application & Process	New
Full – Existing	Application & Process	Existing
Database Only	N/A	New
Process service only	Process	Existing
Application service only	Application	New

After deciding on the install option to use, we will want to follow the step-by-step installation instructions for that option in the installation guide, which can be downloaded from PartnerSource or CustomerSource or found on the installation media. We must also be sure that we are logged in as a member of the local Administrators group to perform the installation.

During the installation, several server components will be installed. These components and their purpose are as follows:

- Application Service – Controls access to the data and provides connectivity to the client workstations
- Process Service – Used to generate the reports
- Management Reporter Database – Serves as the storage repository for all of the building blocks, available reports, and any historical reports

While we will defer the actual steps to installing the product to the Management Reporter installation guides found on PartnerSource and CustomerSource, we will offer a brief overview of the installation process as well as some detail on post-installation configurations required before using Management Reporter

Installation overview

Due to information changing as service packs and/or feature packs are released, we feel that using the latest installation guide (check PartnerSource/CustomerSource for updates) is always best practice when performing our installations. The main steps for installation are:

1. Install Management Reporter Server.
2. Install Data Provider.
3. Install Management Reporter Client.

Let's take a look at some of the additional configurations that need to be completed once the installation is completed.

Registering Management Reporter

Once installation is complete, we need to register Management Reporter before connecting to our Data Provider for Dynamics GP. This can be accomplished by doing the following:

1. Open Report Designer by browsing to **Start | Programs | Microsoft DynamicsERP | Management Reporter | Report Designer**.
2. Click **Tools | Registration**.
3. Enter the license key.
4. Click **Validate**.

Management Reporter should now be registered for use.

Configuring a data provider

After the registration is complete, we must add and configure a company in Management Reporter before it can be used as a data provider. To add and configure a company as a data provider, do the following:

1. Open Report Designer by browsing to **Start | Programs | Microsoft DynamicsERP | Management Reporter | Report Designer**.

2. Select **Create** a Company from the Welcome page. If the Welcome page doesn't display, click **Company | Companies**.

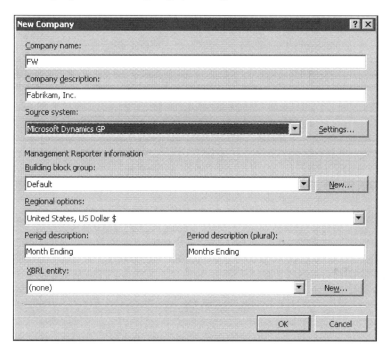

3. On the Companies dialog box, click **New**.

4. On the New Company dialog, enter the **Company Name** and **Company Description**.

5. Select the **Source system (Dynamics GP)**.

   If the source system is not listed, the Management Reporter application pool needs to be stopped and restarted within Internet Information Services (IIS).

6. Click **Settings** to open the Company Wizard page.

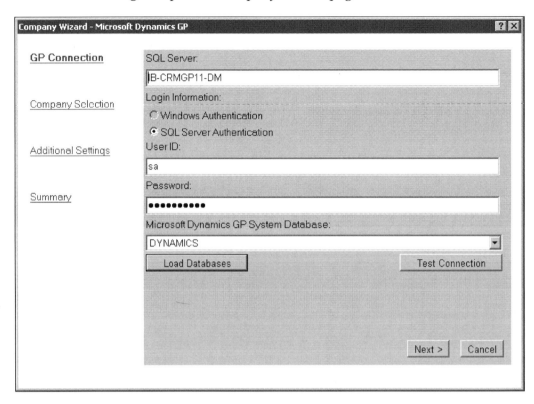

7. On the data provider connection page, do the following:

    ° Enter the name of the **SQL server** where the Dynamics databases are located.

    ° Select **SQL Server Authentication**.

    ° Enter the **User ID** and **Password**.

    ° Click **Load Databases**.

    ° Select the **Dynamics** database for the data provider.

 It is usually a good idea to click the **Test Connection** button to ensure there are no issues with the credentials provided.

° Click **Next** to open the Company selection page.

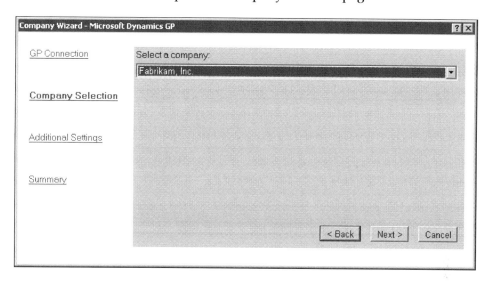

8. On the company selection page, select the company that will serve as the data provider.

9. Click **Next** to open the **Additional Settings** page.

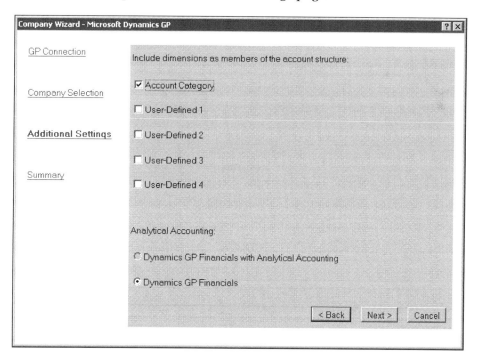

10. Select the checkbox next to any user defined segments that need to be appended to the end of the account structure.

11. Select **Dynamics GP Financials** and click **Next** to open the **Summary** page.

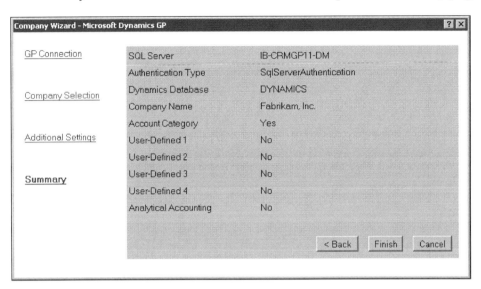

12. Review the selections and click **Finish**.

13. Click **OK** on the **New Company** window.

With Management Reporter installed and our data provider configured, we can now turn towards actually using the product!

Management Reporter security

Security in Management Reporter consists of Users, Groups, and Companies. Management Reporter works with Active Directory in that the user's domain login can be used to access Management Reporter. Don't forget, Dynamics GP still requires SQL authentication, so users will still be prompted to enter their SQL or GP login to access the Data Provider.

Users

Before users can access Management Reporter, we need to create their user in the application. When we are adding users to Management Reporter, we are actually adding the user's existing Active Directory account. To do this, we will select the **Security** button from the left-hand pane in Report Designer as seen in the following image:

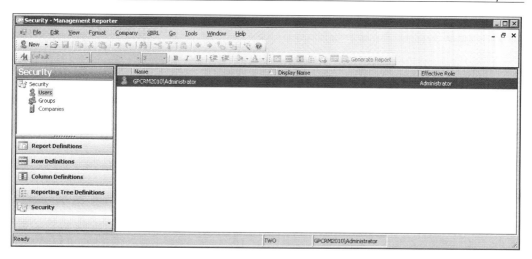

Once the security pane is open, we will highlight the **Users** node and click **New** from the menu bar. This will open the **New User** window. On the **New user** window, we will browse out to the user's account in Active Directory. Once we have located and selected the user's account, our New User window should look like the following image:

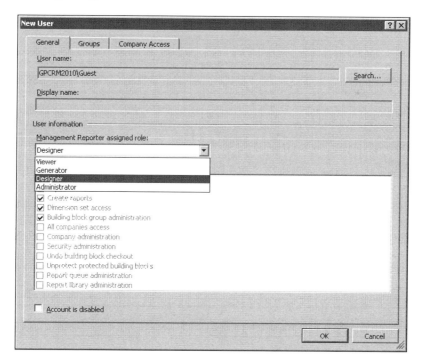

After selecting our user, we then assign the user to one of the four predefined roles, which are as follows:

- Viewer – Only allows access to view reports in the Report Viewer, which will be covered in the next chapter.

- Generator – Allows the user to generate and export Reports.

- Designer – The designer role allows the same access as Generator and adds the ability to create reports, manage dimension sets, and administer building block groups.

- Administrator – This role allows full access of Management Reporter including managing security. We want to limit this to maybe one or two users.

These predefined roles cannot be modified. After assigning the user role, we can also use this window to set a user's account as disabled. In addition, we can assign the user to a group if we wish and also assign company access.

Groups

Groups are optional, but are a great way to group users together to manage company access and application roles. To add a group, we select **New** from the **Menu** bar while in the **Security** pane and select **Group**. We can then give our group a name and description. We can see from the following image that we have created a **Designers** group and added **GPCRM2010\Administrator** to this group:

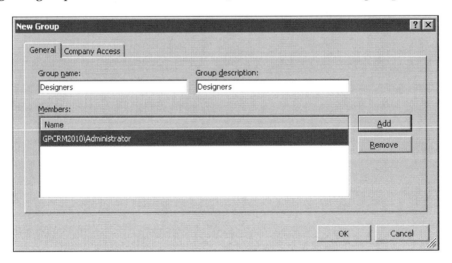

Once we've created our group, we can click over to the **Company Access** tab—as seen in the following image—and select one or more companies that this group will be able to access:

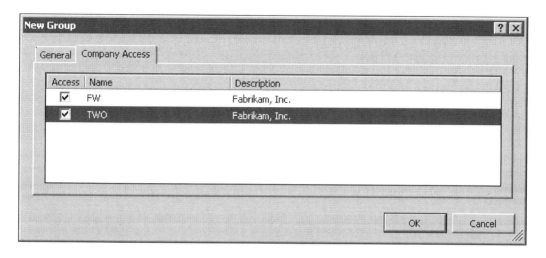

Companies

Management Reporter also allows us to add or modify security at the company level. To do this, we select the **Company** node from the Security pane. This will give us a list of the companies set up in Management Reporter. We can double click a company to view the users and/or groups that have access to that company. Users or groups can be added or removed from this window as seen in the following image:

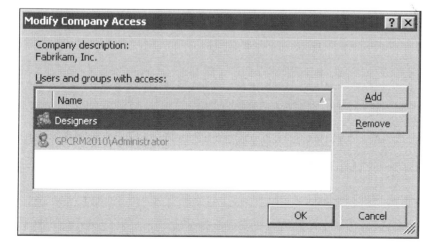

To add a new user or group, simply click **Add** and select a user or group from the list as seen in the following window and click **OK**:

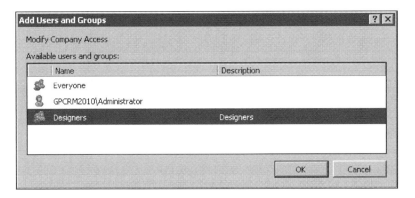

Navigating the Management Reporter report designer interface

Since the Report Designer is where we will spend the majority of our time working with the various building block definitions that will form our reports, it is worth our while to become more familiar with the general layout of the Report Designer. Fortunately, the latest version of Management Reporter includes a layout that is similar in both style and feel to other Microsoft products, including Dynamics GP. This makes the process of navigating the Report Designer and other Management Reporter components much more intuitive.

For example, after launching the Report Designer, a Management Reporter splash screen appears and calls to mind the splash screen that accompanies the launch of GP 2010:

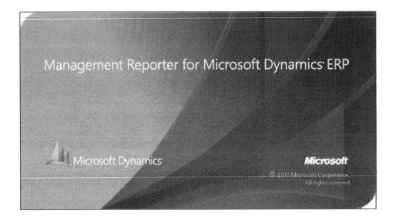

If we are opening Management Reporter for the first time, a Welcome screen appears as we can see from the following image; we can quickly launch other areas of the application to immediately begin working on new building blocks, creating new companies, or adding new users, depending on the option we have selected.

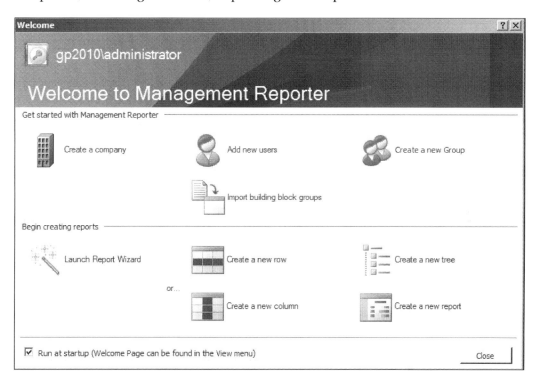

If you're one of those people who prefers to close this window immediately upon open, save yourself some time by unchecking the option to **Run at Startup** found at the bottom, left-hand corner of the Welcome screen. This will prevent the window from opening in the future. Users can reopen or re-enable the Welcome page by clicking **View | Welcome Page** from the menu bar after the Report Designer has fully launched.

Once the Report Designer is fully opened, we see a menu bar across the top of the window with the traditional File, Edit, and Help menus alongside menus specific to Management Reporter. Additionally, we see a navigation pane down the left-hand side of the page that calls to mind the navigation pane found in GP versions 10.0 and later.

Menu bar

Although later versions of the Microsoft Office suite replaced the menu bar with the ribbon bar, long-time Microsoft product users will recognize the appearance of the menu bar found at the top of the screen. As we can see in the following image, alongside traditional menus such as File, Edit, and Window, we see other menus such as XBRL, Company, and Tools that offer access to commands specific to Management Reporter. Let's take a look at some of the commands accessible from the menu bar that are specific to Management Reporter:

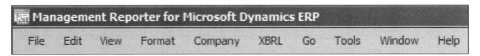

File

From this menu, we can easily start creating a new definition or select to open an existing definition in one of the building blocks. Near the bottom of the **File** menu, we find a section from which we can open definitions from building blocks on which we've recently worked. In environments where we have numerous definitions within a single building block (more on this later in the Grouping Building blocks section), this can help ensure that we are selecting the most recent definition.

Edit

From the **Edit** menu, we access our familiar Undo and Redo commands. This functionality was not available in FRx, but was added to Management Reporter after popular demand from users. We also have access to other traditional editing functionality such as **Cut**, **Copy**, **Paste**, and **Replace**.

Also, depending on what we have opened in the Management Reporter workspace, we may see additional commands on the **Edit** menu. For example, if we access the Edit menu while we have a Row Definition building block open, we will see additional commands such as **Insert Rows from Source System** or **Renumber Rows**. Options such as these can be extraordinary time-savers, especially when we are working with entities that contain a large number of accounts.

View

The View menu allows us to control what is visible in our Management Reporter workspace. For example, if we'd rather increase the amount of real estate in which we have to create new and modify existing building blocks, we can select **View | Navigation Pane** to remove the navigation pane from our view. Objects that are already visible in the Management Reporter workspace are designated with a checkmark in the **View** menu fly out.

Format

One of the great benefits of Management Reporter over other tools like FRx is the ability to format cells and modify how they will appear in a generated report. Some of the commands that we might use in order to modify a cell's formatting can be found under the **Format** menu.

We can create predefined styles and templates for use throughout the Management Reporter application by clicking **Format | Styles and Formatting**. This opens the Styles and Formatting window from which we can create font templates, each with predefined settings such as font size, font colour, and other font formatting options. Later, instead of selecting each individual cell and each individual setting to format that cell, we can select the cell and select the predefined template to apply to that cell. All of the individual settings assigned to that template are then applied to the selected cell.

Company

The **Company** menu may not be visible to all users, as access to this menu is restricted only to users who have been granted report designer or administrator access within Management Reporter.

From this menu, we can define new companies (or entities, as they are more commonly called in Management Reporter) for access in Management Reporter. In addition to creating new companies from here, we can also modify or remove existing entity connections from the **Entities** window.

Finally, we can use the Building Block Groups command to create new groupings of building blocks for a specific entity. This is a useful tool that can help us manage what we have termed "building block sprawl" and we'll cover this functionality in more detail later in this chapter.

XBRL

Another option available from the menu bar is the XBRL menu. The commands in this menu are designed to support the XBRL (short for extensible business reporting language) functionality found in Management Reporter. XBRL is becoming increasingly more common as the financial industry seeks to find ways to standardize and make consistent the process of reporting across multiple organizations and multiple industries. The process of utilizing XBRL involves "tagging" a financial report based on a taxonomy created by a regulating authority; in this way, all reports under the same taxonomy share common tags that make it easier for financial analysts to review and compare financial statements from multiple companies.

From the XBRL command menu on the menu bar, we can import and modify the taxonomy schema that we need for our reporting purposes. This requires administrator or report designer security access. This is accessed via **XBRL | Taxonomies**. This opens the **XBRL Taxonomies** window, from which we can enter the name of our taxonomy in the **Name** field and the path to the schema—either through a web URL or by browsing to a path on our local workstation if we've already downloaded the schema—so that it can be loaded into Management Reporter.

Additional commands on the XBRL menu allow us the necessary control we need in order to work with our imported taxonomy schema. Before we can create the XBRL instance document that contains the actual data with our tags, we properly set the entities and units by accessing them from the XBRL menu. Finally, once we've set these up, we must also make sure that we define an XBRL column in our column definition building block and links in our row definition to a specific XBRL taxonomy.

Go

If we have disabled the navigation pane from the **View** menu, we may find the commands found on this menu to be limited in their usefulness. By selecting one of the building blocks under the **Go** menu, we can choose which building block has primary focus in the navigation pane. This has the same effect as if we were to click a specific building block at the bottom of the navigation pane. Additionally, notice the keyboard commands that correspond to each building block. While knowing these keyboard shortcuts is not critical to using Management Reporter, it can save us the extra time required to shift from the keyboard to the mouse.

If we don't have the navigation pane open, the only real effect this menu has is to change the focus of the **New** button on the Standard toolbar. For example, if we select **Go | Row Definition**, clicking the **New** button on the Standard toolbar will cause Management Reporter to open a new Row Definition.

Tools

The **Tools** menu contains a wealth of commands that we can use to access important areas of Management Reporter. Many of these commands are only available to users with administrator or report designer access. Some of the useful commands in the Tools menu include the following:

- **Protect**: This option is only available when an administrator or report designer has a reporting definition open. Essentially, this option allows users to password protect certain building blocks in order to restrict access to only those users who know the password.

- **Report Queue Status**: From this command, we can access the report queue to see the status of recently generated reports.

- **Report Wizard**: This helpful tool can get us started down the road towards creating a new financial statement. From the Report Wizard, we can select from a list of report templates, then, depending on the report template we've selected, the Report Wizard asks us a series of questions that help determine the final format of our report. This is a great tool for beginners to use in order to see how Management Reporter creates the necessary definitions to support our selections.

- **Checked Out**: In order to see which users have building blocks open (and are thus "checked out"), we can access this command. It provides us a list of the building blocks that are currently checked out and the user who has checked it out.

- Other commands that are more administrative in nature, such as commands to open the Connection and Registration windows, are also available from the Tools menu for users with administrative access.

Window

Since new building blocks are opened in full-screen mode, it can often be a challenge managing the various windows we have open in Management Reporter. Several of the commands under the Window menu can help us manage our workspace more easily. For example, if we have two separate Row Definitions open, we can select **Tile Vertical** or **Tile Horizontally** to have Management Reporter to resize and rearrange our two definitions for vertical or horizontal comparisons, respectively. The following image shows what Management Reporter might look like with two Row Definitions rearranged side-by-side with the **Tile Vertically** command:

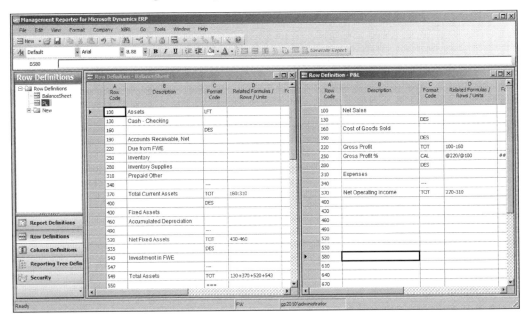

Additionally, from the **Window** menu, we can pinpoint specific building blocks to return to focus in our workspace. For example, if we have our P&L Row Definition open in the forefront, and we want to quickly switch to our Balance Sheet Row Definition, we can select **Window | Balance Sheet** to bring this Row Definition to the forefront of the window. This only works if we've already opened the Row Definition during this session with Management Reporter.

Help

For all the assistance it provides, the Help functionality in products such as Management Reporter and GP 2010 are often overlooked by users. Oftentimes, users question the relevance or use of a certain tool without ever thinking to look to the Help files associated with the product. We strongly encourage users, especially those who are just getting started with Management Reporter, to utilize the Help command whenever possible. Accessing **Help | Management Reporter Help** opens a searchable index of help topics related to Management Reporter. This index can be an invaluable tool in understanding the inner workings of Management Reporter.

Navigation Pane

At the far left hand of the Management Reporter workspace, users will note a sidebar that looks very similar to the sidebar that appears in Dynamics GP 2010. At the bottom of this sidebar are several buttons, and clicking these buttons dictates what appears in the uppermost portion of the sidebar.

If the Navigation Pane is not visible in the Management Reporter workspace, it may have been disabled. In order to re-enable the Navigation Pane, select **View | Navigation Pane** from the menu bar.

From the following image, we see that the buttons correspond to the four building blocks we can utilize in building our reports. A fifth tab, the Security, allows us to view more detail surrounding our Management Reporter security setup.

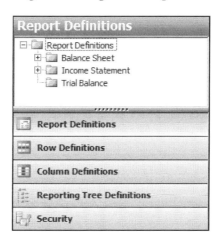

Selecting one of the building block buttons displays a list of existing definitions for that building block. From here, we can select one of the existing definitions to begin working with it. Additionally, the contents of each building block can be organized in folders, and this will be covered in more detail later in this chapter.

Working with the Management Reporter building blocks

Now that we have an understanding of the layout of Management Reporter, we can begin designing our reports starting with creating all of our building blocks. These building blocks consist of Row, Column, Reporting Tree, and Report Definitions. Due to the sheer amount of detail and options available in each of the definitions, we can't possibly cover them all in a single chapter. We will however be discussing the layouts and the more commonly used options in each definition type. For the complete listing of all the available options, we recommend reviewing the user documentation and the Management Reporter help. Let's begin!

Row definitions

Row definitions are a required component for any report. We can think of them as exactly as they sound; they are the rows of the report. Typically, these are account numbers, but we can also use departments, cost centers, and so on. as our rows. Let's look at the layout of the Report definition:

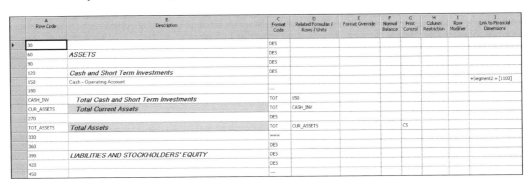

We can see from the screenshot above, that there are quite a few columns that can be populated in a Row definition.

- **Row Code**: We can think of this as a line number similar to Microsoft Excel. We will use this in our Related Formulas column to perform subtotals, totals, calculations, etc. Typically, this column is incremented in a way that allows for us to enter rows in between. This code can be a number or alphanumeric as we can see above for **CUR_ASSETS**. Row Codes can be renumbered at any time and will automatically update all occurrences in our Related Row column.

- **Description**: This is where we put our Account descriptions section headers such as Assets, section totals such as Total Current Assets, and so on. We can also control how these will look by applying font styles such as size, bolding, and shading.

- **Format Code**: This column is a code that basically tells the report what the line is doing. The most commonly used Format Codes are:

    ° DES: Description line.

    ° TOT: This means that it is a total row. This can be a range of row codes, 60:180 for instance, or it can be an addition or subtraction of row codes.

    ° CAL: This is a calculation. This allows for complex calculations. We can multiply and divide using calculations, as well as use If/Then/Else statements in a calculation.

    ° CBR: Change base row is used when creating reports that do some type of percentage allocation such as having each row be displayed as a percent of sales.

- **Related Formulas/Rows/Units**: This is the column where we will actually put our calculations for TOT and CAL format codes. We can also use this column to restrict a line to a particular reporting tree unit if we are using a Reporting Tree. Lastly, we can relate a row to another row. An example of this would be relating a header row or an underscore to a subtotal so that when the subtotal is zero and suppressed, the header row and/or underscore will also be suppressed.

- **Format Override**: This column allows us to change the formatting of currencies, decimals, and percentages.

- **Normal Balance**: This column lets us control whether an account is typically a credit in Dynamics GP and will reverse the sign. An example of this would be Revenue accounts. By setting this to C, revenue numbers would show as positive numbers on our report.

- **Print Control**: This allows us to set options such as Non printing, use currency symbol, suppress if all zeros, and so on. for our rows. This is on a row-by-row basis. We can also specify whether the row prints debit or credit balances only if we wish.

- **Column Restrictions**: This column has multiple uses depending on the type of row. One of the common uses is to limit the printing of the row's amounts to specific columns.

- **Row Modifier**: This allows for overriding the period data or overriding the book code. We can override a row to pull the beginning balance for that row if we wish. As for overriding the book code, this would allow for us to use say an amount from a budget for a particular row instead of the actuals.

- **Link to Financial Dimensions**: This is probably the most important column in the Row definition. This is where we actually link to our GL data. We can either type in the segment we are building the row off of and the segment value(s), or we can double click to get a lookup window that will format the syntax for us. Keep in mind, this can be accounts, departments, cost centers, and so on. The important thing to note is that whatever value we are using for our link, MUST be of consistent lengths.

As we mentioned, more detail on additional options exists in the user documentation.

Column definitions

As with Row definitions, Column definitions are also required to generate a report. Column definitions are used to create the columns of the report. This is typically the periods or months, but can also be companies, departments, cost centers, and so on. in consolidate reports, as well as actual, budget, or forecast data. Let's take a look at the Column definition layout:

	A	B	C	D	E	F	G	H	I	J
Header 1		@CalMonthLong	YTD							
Header 2										
Header 3										
Column Type	DESC	FD	FD							
Book Code / Attribute Category		ACTUAL	ACTUAL							
Fiscal Year		BASE	BASE							
Period		BASE	BASE							
Periods Covered		PERIODIC	YTD							
Formula										
Column Width	30	14	14							
Extra Spaces Before Column										
Format / Currency Override										
Print Control										
Column Restrictions										
Reporting Unit										
Currency Source										
Currency Filter										
XBRL Currency										
XBRL Dimension										
Dimension Filter										
Attribute Filter										
Start Date										
End Date										
Justification										

As we can see in the example above, the Column definitions are broken into two sections, a header section and the detail section. In the header, we can either type in headings or we can use auto text that will let the column headers be dynamically set based on the report. An example of this would be using the @CalMonthShort text to display the abbreviated month name for the month we generate the report for.

The detail section is where we actually specify what type of column we need as well as where to get the data and for which period. The more common selections are the following:

- **Column Type**: This specifies what type of data will be in the column. The most common are:
    - ° **DESC**: Descriptions from the Description column in the Row definition.
    - ° **FD**: Amounts from the Financial Dimension (that is Dynamics GP data).
    - ° **CALC**: A calculated column. An example of this would be if we needed to add three columns together to calculate a Quarter to Date column.
- **Book Code**: This lets the system know what book to get the data from. This can be actuals, budget, or forecasts.
- **Fiscal Year**: This is the year for the column. This can be hardcoded, set to BASE (the year the report is generated for) or any combination of BASE+# or BASE-#.
- **Period**: Similar to fiscal year, it is the period the column will have. This can also be set to BASE, BASE+#, BASE-#, or hardcoded.
- **Period Covered**: This tells the system whether the column should have current activity, YTD activity, or force in beginning balances.

These are the required lines, but there are quite a few other options that can be set. Some of the more commonly used are:

- **Formula**: This is used in conjunction with a CALC column type. This is where the actual formula resides, for instance B+C+D or B:D.
- **Print Control**: This can be used to set conditional column printing. This is typically used in twelve month rolling columns. As each month becomes current, that month will show up on our report so we don't have empty columns for future periods.
- **Reporting Unit**: Typically used in side-by-side reporting where we need to restrict a column to a particular unit of a reporting tree, company, or department for example.

- **Dimension Filter**: This is used when we want to filter a column of data to a particular dimension.

As with our Row Definitions, we did not cover every column option in detail. For information on some of the other less used options, see the user guide or help.

Reporting Tree definitions

Reporting Trees are optional components of reports, however, they do provide a very powerful method of performing company consolidated reporting based on any type of tree hierarchy you can design. Typically, this is company, department, or cost center based.

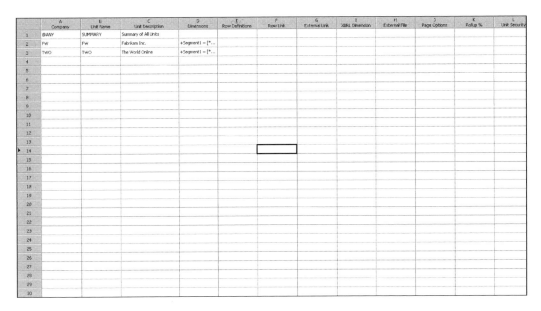

	A Company	B Unit Name	C Unit Description	D Dimensions	E Row Definitions	F Row Link	G External Link	I XBRL Dimension	H External File	J Page Options	K Rollup %	L Unit Security
1	@ANY	SUMMARY	Summary of All Units									
2	FW	FW	Fabrikam Inc.	+Segment1 = [*...								
3	TWO	TWO	The World Online	+Segment1 = [*...								
4												
5												
6												
7												
8												
9												
10												
11												
12												
13												
14												
15												
16												
17												
18												
19												
20												
21												
22												
23												
24												
25												
26												
27												
28												
29												
30												

As we can see from the screenshot above, there are a few columns that seem pretty straightforward, and it is no coincidence that these are the most used when creating a Reporting Tree definition.

- Company: This tells the system which Dynamics GP company to read the data for that unit from. A value of @ANY means to use any company and is typically reserved for summary units.

- Unit Name: This is a short name for the unit.

- Unit Description: This is a longer description for the unit and can be used in the Report definition as part of the page headers.

- Dimensions: This is where we enter the dimensions that our tree is going to be built from. Again, typically, this is the department numbers or cost centers that we are creating a reporting hierarchy for.

Other columns that are sometimes used are:

- **Row Definitions**: This can be used in a circumstance where we are consolidating two companies that have two different charts of accounts. We can use this to link each unit to a different Row definition to account for this.

- **Row Link and External File**: These are used when linking to an Excel spreadsheet.

- **Security**: This can be used to set access to individual units of the reporting hierarchy.

Although Reporting Trees can give us highly segmented reports, they are also usually the building block that causes the most problems when generating reports. Reporting Trees can be as small or large as we want to make them. It all depends on what our end product needs to be. Our advice is to always start small. Build a small rollup to try out the design. If it works, we can continue building the entire hierarchy.

If we run into a problem generating a report with a tree, we can simply turn off the tree and see if the report generates without it. If this is the case, we know our tree is the culprit and we can begin to search the tree for errors.

Report Definitions

The final building block is the Report Definition. This is where we actually combine our Row, Column, and if necessary, Reporting Tree definitions to form our report. When creating a Report definition, we can also set up the output and distribution, headers and footers information and any additional settings.

Report

As we define our Report Definition, we notice several tabs across the top of the window. The first of these, as seen below, is the **Report** tab:

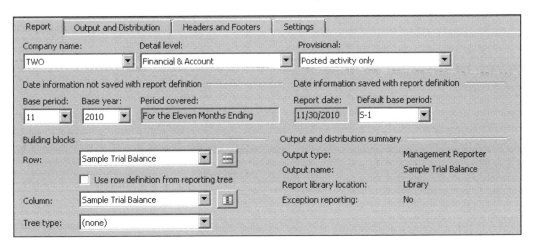

On the **Report** tab, we set up the following fields:

- **Company Name**: Select the Dynamics GP company from the dropdown or select the @ANY.

- **Detail level**: Selections here range from Financial all the way down to Financial, Account, and Transaction detail.

- **Provisional**: Allows for running on posted activity only, unposted activity, or both.

- **Base Period**: The period that will be set as our base period. Typically, the current month.

- **Base Year**: The year that will be set as our base year. Typically, the current year.

- **Building blocks**
    - ○ **Row**: Select the Row definition from the dropdown. If using a Reporting Tree with Rows assigned to individual tree units, check the box to Use row definition from reporting tree.
    - ○ **Column**: Select the Column definition from the dropdown.
    - ○ **Tree**: If using a tree, select Reporting tree as the Tree type and select the tree to use in the report.

Output and Distribution

Beyond the **Report** tab, we see the **Output and Distribution** tab, which contains options for modifying the appearance of our final report.

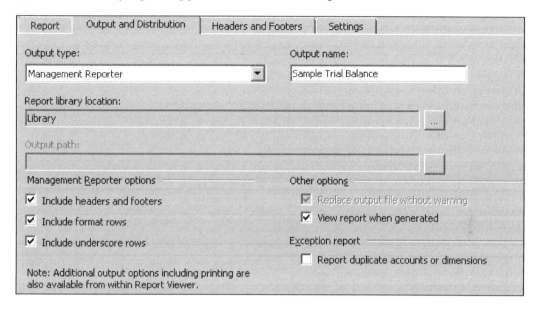

On the **Output and Distribution** tab, we assign the following fields:

- **Output Type**: Select Management Reporter, Microsoft Excel, or XBRL Instance Document.

- **Output Name**: This is the name of the report.

- **Report library location**: Only used for Management Reporter type. This is the location in the Report library where the report will be stored. The library will be covered in more detail in the next chapter.

- **Output path**: This is used for both Microsoft Excel and XBRL Instance document types. This is the location on the local machine or network file share where the file is to be stored.

- Management Reporter Options

- Include headers and footers

- Include format rows

- Include underscore rows

- Other Options

- Replace output file without warning
- View report when generated
- Exception reporting

Headers and Footers

Our third tab is the **Headers and Footers** tab, which can be seen in the following image:

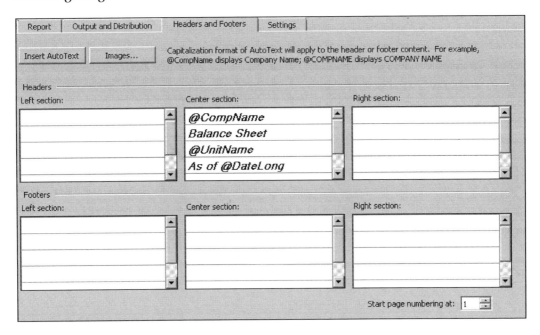

In the headers and footers tab, we have many different AutoText selections to choose from for report names, dates and times, page numbering, and so on. We can also quickly and easily add images to any of the sections by clicking the **Images** button and adding the image.

Settings

The last tab is the **Settings** tab.

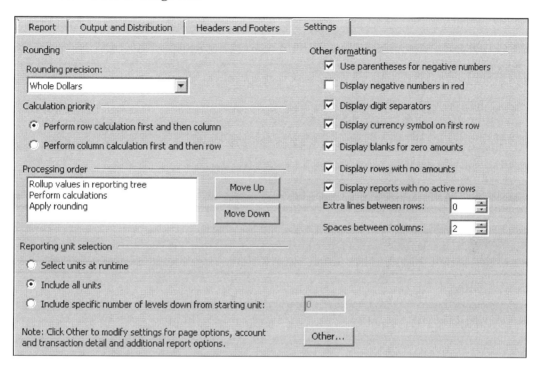

This is where we will find options such as rounding preferences, calculation priorities, and processing order as well as how to handle blank rows, negative numbers, rows with no amounts, and so on.

Tools for reducing building block sprawl

One of the challenges of using an enterprise-wide reporting tool such as Management Reporter is that multiple users can access the application and each user can create his or her own building blocks. As we've seen, building blocks are extremely portable and can be used in multiple **Report Definitions**. Hopefully, through good training and careful report design, our users will first seek to utilize existing building blocks to assist in the creation of new reports before creating a brand new set of building blocks.

Inevitably, however, we encounter building block sprawl. This is especially common in multi-company and multi-user environments. The symptoms of building block sprawl usually make this a pretty easy disease to diagnose:

- Selecting **Row** or **Column Definition** in the Navigation Pane reveals a seemingly unorganized collection of building blocks that, in some cases, may extend past the bottom of the screen.

- Multiple building blocks exist that share similar names such as "P and L", "Profit and Loss", "PL", or "Income Statement" in the **Row Definitions** pane or "Actual_YTD" or "Cur_YTD" in the **Column Definitions** pane.

- When queried on the purpose of specific building blocks, users can only point to the ones they've used most recently with little to no knowledge of how other building blocks are used or why they even exist.

- Building block sprawl is a nuisance and it is completely capable of creating confusion and worse, causing users to build incorrect or incomplete financial statements! We should do our best to proactively manage the creation of too many building blocks in our Management Reporter environment. Fortunately, Management Reporter provides us several tools that can be used to get a handle on an exploding list of building blocks.

Group building blocks in the Navigation Pane with the use of folders

One of the great new features of Management Reporter is the ability to group building blocks in folders in the Navigation Pane. Folders can be added to each of the four building blocks and the contents of each building block can be grouped within these folders. By judiciously creating folders in each building block area, we can encourage our users to insert newly created building blocks in the appropriate folder.

For example, we might have several **Column Definitions** that can be used depending on whether or not we only want to see posted amounts or if we want to see budget amounts compared to actual amounts for a given time period. We can use folder groupings to group all column definitions that contain budget amount columns together and all column definitions that don't contain budget amount columns in another folder. Such a scenario might look as follows:

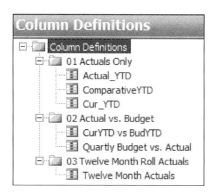

Several other concepts are worth noting about using folders to group building blocks:

- First, we can see in the previous image that numbers can be used to sort folders in a particular order in the navigation pane. Due to the nature of the sorting engine, if we plan to have more than ten folders in a certain building block, it is helpful to begin numbering with 01, 02, and 03 and so on. Otherwise, if we used only a single digit for the first nine folders, we would see the tenth folder appear as second in the list (that is, the sort order would appear as 1, 10, 2, 3, 4, 5, and so on).

- Second, only single level folder groupings can be created. While it would be nice if folder within folder groupings were allowed, this is currently not possible in Management Reporter. Hopefully, we'll see this in a future version!

- By setting up folders ahead of time, we can be proactive in taming building block sprawl before it really ever gets out of control!

Creating building block groups in environments with multiple entities

Another handy feature offered in Management Reporter to tame our building block sprawl is the Building Block Groups feature. This feature is especially useful in environments where we have multiple entities (or companies) set up for reporting purposes. By assigning a building block group to an entity, we can control what building blocks appear in Management Reporter when that entity is selected for reporting.

Creating a new building block group and assigning it an entity requires a fairly easy set of steps:

1. From the menu bar, select **Company | Building Block Groups**.

2. Click the **New** button to open the **Building Block Groups** window.

3. Enter a **Name** and **Definition** for the new building block group and click **OK**.

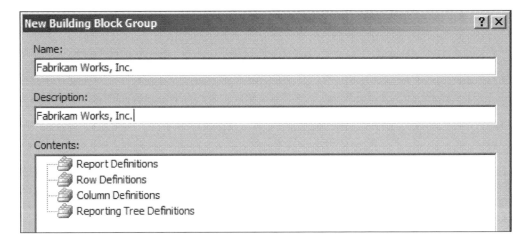

4. After the new building block group has been created, close the **Building Block Groups** window.

5. To assign the building block group to the current entity, select **Company | Companies** from the menu bar.

6. Select the company to assign to the new building block group and click **Modify**.

7. In the **Modify Company** window, change the value in the **Building Block Group** drop-down to the newly created building block group.

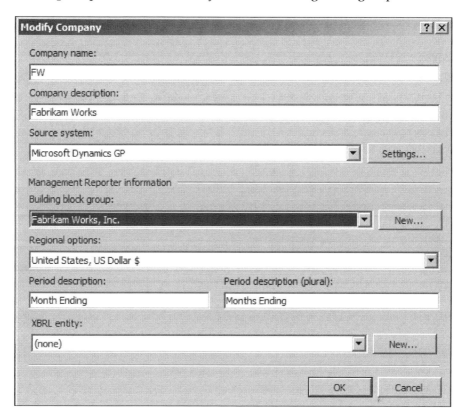

8. Click **OK** to close the window.

Management Reporter will refresh and the navigation pane will no longer show the building blocks associated with the building block group prior to making this change. Now, any new building blocks that we create in this entity will be assigned to the building block group we just created.

In order to see the same building block in other entities, we can use the building block import and export functionality to duplicate the building blocks. The following set of instructions demonstrate how we can export two report definitions and their associated row and column definitions from our **Default** building block group into our newly created **Fabrikam Works, Inc.** building block group:

1. From the menu bar, select **Company | Building Block Groups**.

2. Select the building block group from which building blocks are to be exported.

3. Click the **Export** button to open the **Export** window.

4. Select the report definitions to be exported. Use the *CTRL* key to select multiple report definitions at once. As new building blocks are included in the selection, notice how the **Current selection:** field updates to let us know how many building blocks of each type will be included in our export.

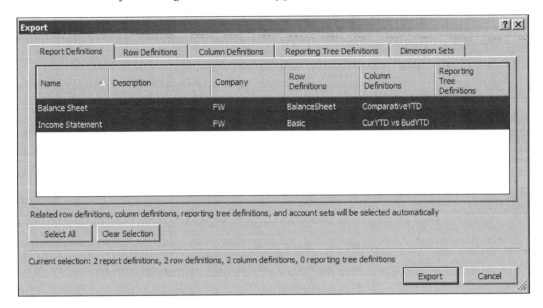

5. Additionally, we can select the other tabs at the top of the Export window to identify and select individual building blocks for export that may not be included by association with any of the selected definitions.

6. Once we've found and selected all of our definitions for export, we can click the **Export** button.

7. We are prompted to save an export file (of file format .tdbx). Save this file to an accessible location.

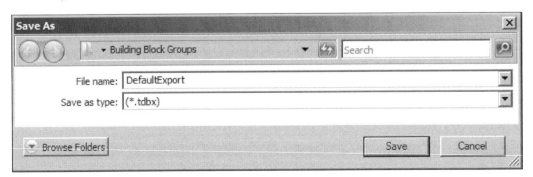

8. Once the file has been saved and we are returned to the **Building Block Groups** window (**Company | Building Block Groups**) we should then select the building block group into which we wish to import our newly created file.

9. Once we've selected the target building block group, we can select the **Import** button to open the file explorer window.

10. Find and select the .tdbx file saved in our earlier step. Click **Open**.

11. In the **Import** window, select the definitions that should be imported into the new building block group. Be sure to check the various tabs at the top of the screen to make sure all relevant definitions are included in the import!

12. Once our Import is complete, we can select the target building block group in the Building Block Groups window and click the View button to open the View Building Block Group window. We can then see the various definitions that have been imported into this building block group:

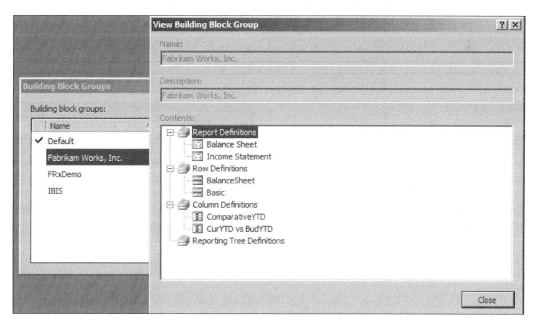

Now that we've learned how to use building block groups, we may want to consider creating a building block group for each separate entity as we set up Management Reporter for the first time. This will allow us to maintain a separate set of building blocks for each company from the very beginning. After creating these building block groups, we may also want to consider creating a generic set of building blocks and using the import/export functionality to copy this generic set from one building block group to the next. In this manner, each company will have a clean set of basic building blocks from which to begin.

Finding and eliminating unused building blocks by using building block associations

Often, as the number of building blocks in our system increases, it can be a challenge to tell which building block is used with a particular report definition. Additionally, over a period of time, certain building blocks may no longer even be used in Management Reporter. In these cases, the best course of action might be to find and identify these building blocks so that a decision can be made on whether or not they should remain in the system.

Fortunately, Management Reporter provides us with a handy little tool in the form of the Associations feature that can help us make this determination. If we have a particular building block open in the Navigation Pane, we can right-click a specific building and select **Associations** to see the report definitions associated with the selected building block. The following image shows us that the **ComparitiveYTD** Column Definition is associated with a Report Definition called **Balance Sheet**:

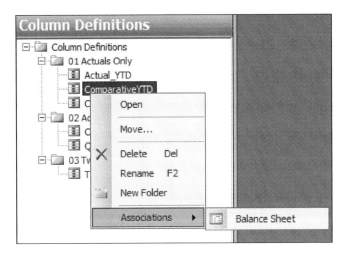

By using the Associations feature in Management Reporter, we can quickly identify building blocks that are not associated with any report definitions. While this does not necessarily mean the building block should be removed, it does give us some insight into whether or not this is a duplicate building block or one that can possibly be removed to make room for more utilized building blocks.

Management Reporter Feature Pack 1

Microsoft released Management Reporter Feature Pack 1 in Mid December 2010. This feature pack added the following features:

- Integration to Microsoft Dynamics AX 2009
- Currency translation in Microsoft Dynamics GP

To find out more about these features, see the FP1 installation guide that can be downloaded from Microsoft.

Feature Pack 1 requires Management Reporter 2.0 with Service Pack 1 already be installed.

Summary

Before we can actually generate professional looking financial statements based on the latest data in our source system, we need to have the tools to build those reports! In this chapter, we covered the basic tools and building blocks that we need in order to design our financial statements. To begin with, we discussed the underlying architecture of Management Reporter, how to navigate throughout the Report Designer interface, and how to use the building blocks to create our row, column, reporting tree, and report definitions. With this information in hand, we also covered some tips and techniques for taming the inevitable building block sprawl in a multi-company, multi-user environment.

In our next chapter, we'll see the end-result of our work with the reporting tools we used in this chapter. Specifically, we'll look at the various options related to generating a report from the Report Designer. Then, we'll cover the separate Report Viewer interface from which we can view and manage the reports we've generated. Finally, we'll discuss some of the differences between Management Reporter and FRx.

9
Viewing Financial Reports in Management Reporter

Continuing from where we left of in our last chapter on Report Design, this chapter will take us further into Management Report and utilizing the Report Viewer to organize and view our generated reports. Not only is the Report Viewer for Management Reporter the tool we will use to view our generated reports, we can also use its library functionality to organize our reports in a number of ways including by company, report type, time frame, and so on. Additionally, we can add external supporting documents such as Microsoft Excel or Word documents to our library. The topics we will discuss with regards to the Report Viewer for Management Reporter are:

- Overview of Report Viewer for Management Reporter
- Report Library Permissions
- Generating Reports to the Report Library via Report Designer
- Navigating the Report Viewer for Management Reporter Interface
- Differences between Management Reporter and FRx

After reading this chapter, we should be able to not only generate board quality financial reports, but also distribute those across our organization in a meaningful and easy-to-understand structure.

Overview of Report Viewer for Management Reporter

Report Viewer for Management Reporter is the component of Management Reporter that is used to display our generated reports and organize them into a meaningful structure, thus making it easier for our users to find the reports they are looking for. It is important to note that we will discuss the Report Library often in this chapter and this is not to be confused with Report Viewer. The Report Library is simply the repository that stores and organizes our objects. The Report Viewer is the tool itself.

Before we proceed to generating our reports, it is important to discuss how security permissions work in Report Viewer for Management Reporter so that we don't run into an issue where either one of our users or ourselves generate a report to the library but then don't have the proper permissions to view the report.

Report Library permissions

Security in the Report Library works a little different than it does in the Designer, but also builds upon what we've already seen. As we learned in the last chapter, security is broken out by roles. The roles function differently in the Report Viewer than they do in the Report Designer. Let's take a quick look at what permissions the roles provide in the Report Viewer:

- **Administrator**: Administrative users have full access to all viewing tasks.
- **Designer**: Users assigned this role are able to delete, edit, create folders, rename reports, and folders and view any report they have been granted access to.
- **Generator**: This role provides the same abilities provided by the Designer role within Report Viewer.
- **Viewer**: Members of this role only have access to view reports that they have been granted access too.

In addition to the access provided by the Report Designer roles, the Report Viewer can have permissions to view, create, edit, and delete objects in the Report Library such as folders, reports, reports, report versions, and any external supporting documents can be granted to Management Reporter users or groups by a user with administrative privileges. We also have the ability to restrict access to certain versions of a report such as the final version that is to be published to our executive board. Let's look at the four permissions for the Report Library:

- **View**: Users with this permission can view contents of any folder, report, report version, and external supporting documents they or their user group is assigned too

- **Create**: Users with this permission can create new sub folders and add supporting documents to the Report library or folder they have access too

- **Edit**: Users with this permission can edit folder names, report names, and supporting documentation that they have access too

- **Delete**: Users with this permission can delete folders, reports, report versions, and supporting documents that they have access too

By default, all new users are added to the "Everyone" group. This is a system group and cannot be edited or deleted. There is also a Public folder that the Everyone group has access to. This is a good place to have users generate reports if they are having trouble generating to a location that they may not have access too. This folder can be renamed or deleted if it is not going to be used, but it is highly recommended to keep it and just create a new structure to use.

To assign or change library permissions, we browse to the Report Library Permissions window by doing the following:

1. Launch Report Viewer for Management Reporter by browsing to **Start | Programs | Microsoft Dynamics ERP | Report Viewer.**

2. Click **Tools** to open the **Report Library Permissions** window.

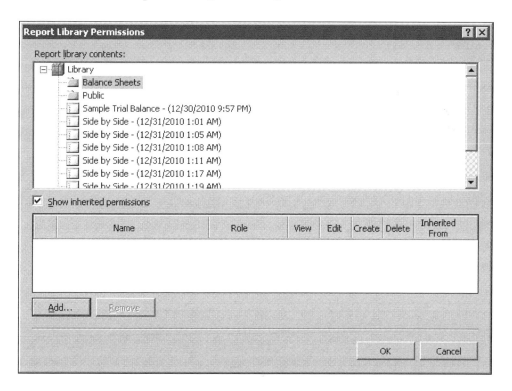

3. On the **Report Library Permissions** window, we can browse through the objects in the Library including folders, reports, and external documents.

4. Locate the object we wish to grant permissions to, highlight it, and click **Add** to open the **Add Users and Groups** window. In this case, we have the Balance Sheet folder selected.

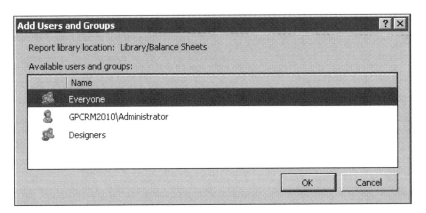

5. On the **Add Users and Groups** window, select the user or group that we wish to add to the object and click **OK**. Note that the object location is listed at the top of the window. In the following image, we've selected the **Balance Sheets** folder:

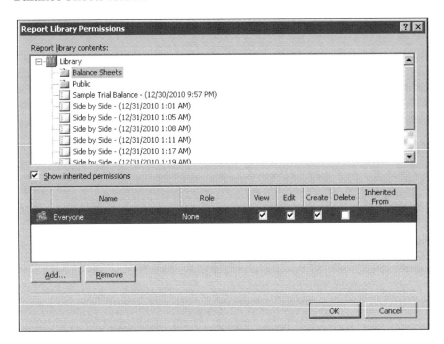

6. Back on the **Report Library Permissions** window, we will now see our user or group that we selected. If that user or group is assigned a Management Reporter Role, that will be displayed in the Role column. We can also select or deselect the Show inherited permissions option to show us which permissions have been inherited from parent objects.

7. Select any combination of **View**, **Edit**, **Create**, and **Delete** that we wish this user or group to have permission to perform.

8. Click **OK**.

Report Library permissions can be as simple or as complex as we need for our organization. We want to take this into account when designing our final solution and what type of library structure we need to build.

Generating reports to the Report Library via Report Designer

In our last chapter, we covered the process of creating row definitions, column definitions, and reporting trees. These building blocks are then combined together to create our final report through the use of the Report Definition, which we also covered in the last chapter. We did not, however, go through the final step of actually generating our report.

To generate a report, we need to have a report definition to which, at the very least, a row and column definition have been assigned. Depending on our reporting needs, we may also assign a reporting tree definition to our report definition. Once we've designated the specific building blocks to use with our report definition, we can then work our way through the various tabs on the report definition to control the final output of our report. For more information on these various tabs and the settings that can be controlled by them, refer to our section on Report Definitions in Chapter 8.

If you recall, on the **Output& Distribution** tab of a Report definition building block, we can designate the **Output Type** for our report. We can generate our report to Excel or create an XBRL instance document. A third option, **Management Reporter**, allows us to generate our report to the Report Viewer. As we change our selections in the Output Type drop-down, additional settings specific to the selected output type will appear on this tab.

The Report Viewer and reports generated with an output type of **Management Reporter** will be the focus of the remainder of this chapter. With this output type selected, our view will look like the following image:

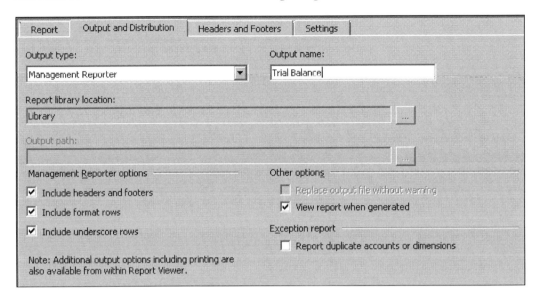

Notice the ellipses button next to the **Report library location:** field. Prior to generating our Trial Balance report, we can click the ellipses button to open the **Select a Library Location** window seen in the following image:

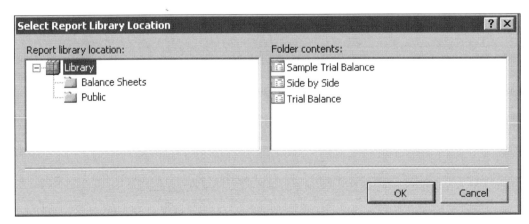

Although we'll cover the folder structure of the Report Viewer in a later section, it should be fairly easy to understand that we can use this window to control where in the Report Viewer our newly generated report will appear. If, for example, we have several folders set up in our Report Viewer, each of which correspond to each different company database in our multi-company environment, we can select the folder corresponding to the company for which we are generating this report. If we aren't ready to assign the report to a folder just yet, we can select to generate our report to the Public folder under the Library node. As we'll see later, users assigned to the Everyone role in Report Viewer will have access to reports or other objects under the **Public** folder. Later, if we want to change the location of our report, we can move it to another folder.

Assuming that we've reviewed and made changes to the settings on this tab and the other tabs under our report definition, we are now ready to generate our report to the Report Viewer. To do this, select the **Generate Report** from the Management Reporter toolbar. This button is highlighted in the following image:

The **Report Queue Status** window will appear, and users will see their report listed in the queue. Depending on how far along the report is in the report generation process, we will see various status such as **Queued**, **Processing**, and **Complete**. An example of this can be seen in the following image.

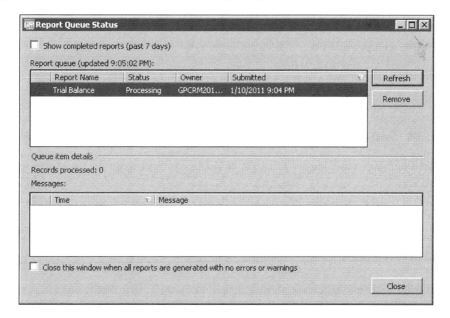

Once the report has finished processing, the **Report Queue Status** window will close and our newly generated report will open in the Report Viewer, assuming we also have permission to view this report.

Navigating the Report Viewer for Management Reporter interface

Although the Report Viewer is completely separate from the Report Designer component of Management Reporter, the look and feel of the two components are very similar. Because we are not creating reports in the Report Viewer, it's the simpler of the two to understand in terms of navigation and the commands and options that are available to us. In this section, we'll explore some of the key menus and concepts such as report packages and version control that are only available to us in the Report Viewer.

Overview of Report Viewer interface

Just like we saw in the Report Designer component, the Report Viewer component has the look and feel of Microsoft Dynamics GP and other Windows applications. Across the top of the interface, we find our familiar menu bar, with menus and commands that extend our Report Viewer experience. Down the left-hand side of the interface, assuming it's enabled for viewing, we find the Navigation Pane.

Menu bar

Although menu names such as File, Edit, and Tools may be familiar to many of us, some of the commands within these windows are specific to Report Viewer. These commands are found at the top of the interface in a view similar to the following:

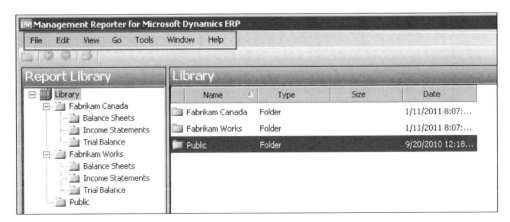

File

Because we can open multiple reports for viewing in the Report Viewer, we can use the **File** menu to quickly close the current report. Or, if we want to start over from scratch, we can select **File | Close All** to close all reports that we have open in the Library.

The **File | Insert External File** command is extraordinarily useful in the event that we need to add supporting documentation in the form of non-Management Reporter reports to the Report Viewer. As we'll see shortly, these external files which can come in PDF or Excel format, among others, can then be combined with Management Reporter reports to create report packages that our management team can use to access all financial statements and supporting documentation in one location.

Also useful from the **File** menu are the **Print** and **Export** commands. Depending on the setup of printers on our environment, we can print the selected report to a printer or even to a PDF file if we have a PDF printer set up. In a similar fashion, the Export command allows us to convert our existing report into another output type. This saves us the trouble from having to return to the Report Designer, pull up the report definition, and change the output type of our report. If we select to create an Excel report, the Export to Microsoft Excel window appears (as seen in the following screenshot), and we are presented with a list of the same options that we would have received on the **Output & Distribution** tab in Report Designer if we had selected an **Output Type** of **Excel**.

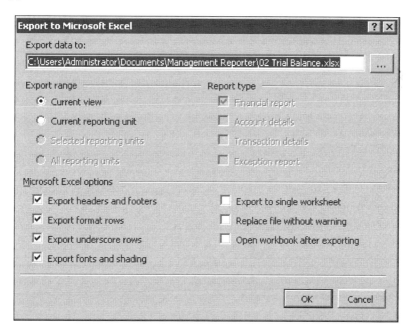

Once we've identified our settings and selected to Export to Excel, our new Excel file will be deposited in the location found in the **Export Data To** field.

Before we continue, make sure to note that the Export to Excel functionality only works for Excel 2007 and higher environments.

Edit

The **Edit** menu provides us with a limited set of commands that may behave differently depending on the kind of object we have selected in the Report Viewer interface. The three main commands in the **Edit** menu: **Delete**, **Move**, and **Rename**, are typically available on the command menu that appears upon right-clicking the selected object in the interface.

The **Move** command is particularly useful when we want to rearrange the location of our generated reports in the various folders we've created in the navigation pane. The **Rename** command is also useful when we need to modify the name of our selected object.

View

From the View menu, we can control which toolbars and windows will appear in our report. For example, if we want to remove the Navigation Pane to provide more space for the selected report, we can select **View | Navigation Pane** to clear the checkbox and the Navigation Pane from the interface.

Additionally, from the View menu, we can select **Show Versions** to see additional versions associated with the selected report.

Go

If we have several reports open, the **Go** menu allows us to quickly switch back and forth between the Report Library and the Report Data sections of the interface. Alternatively, we can click the buttons in the Navigation Pane.

Tools

From the Tools menu, we can modify our connection to the Management Reporter database, open the Report Library Permissions window, or select **Options** to open a window from which we can modify a few settings related to Management Reporter. In the **Options** window, we can control the default file location to which exported files will be sent when using the **File | Export** commands.

Window

If we have multiple reports open in the Report Viewer interface, the **Window** menu can help us easily switch back and forth between these reports. Commands on this window are only available if more than one report is open in the Report Viewer.

Help

As one might expect, the **Help** menu offers us the ability open the Management Reporter help functionality. From here, we have a searchable index of topics related to Management Reporter, and this should be one of the first stops for anyone seeking to learn more about Management Reporter related topics.

Also from the **Help** menu, we can access the About Management Reporter command to see more information about the version of Management Reporter we are currently using.

Navigation Pane

When compared to the Navigation Pane in the Report Designer, the one in the Report Viewer is much simpler. Here, we only see two buttons: **Report Library** and **Report Data**. While viewing the contents of a report, we will have the **Report Data** button selected. All other times, we can expect to see the **Report Library** button enabled.

With Report Library selected, we will see a list of the folders we have created underneath the Library node. By clicking on a folder or node, we will see a list of reports available in the Library section of the Report Viewer interface. Reports not assigned to any of our folders will appear when we have the Library node selected.

When compared to that in Report Designer, one of the most unique aspects of the Navigation Pane in Report Viewer is that we can create subfolder groupings. This allows us to create multi-layer folder structures and grants us a greater degree of organizational control over our reports. The following image shows an example of what a Navigation Pane would look like if we arranged our reports in a company-report type structure:

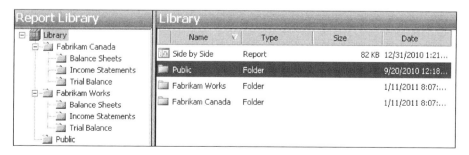

As we've said, the ability to organize reports in folders and subfolders introduces to us new possibilities for storing and organizing our reports. Some of the more common ways in which we can group our reports include:

- By Company: In multi-company environments, this can be extraordinarily useful to us in the event that we want to store our report versions on a company-by-company basis.

- By Report Type: Others may choose to store generated reports based on the type of report that has been generated. For example, variations of a balance sheet financial statement can be stored in a Balance Sheet folder.

- By Time Frame: In an effort to organize reports over a length of time, others still may choose to organize reports by time frame. For example, at the end of each year, all report versions can be moved into a folder with a name corresponding to the recent year.

- In addition to creating single level folder structures as described above, the subfolder functionality allows us to mix and match these groupings for even more control over our reports. In the last image, we saw an example of an organization that has grouped reports in a folder structure arranged by Company and Report Type. Next year, this organization could archive prior year versions of these reports by adding an additional Time Frame layer so that we have a Time Frame – Company Name – Report Type hierarchy.

- Folders and their contents can be moved by right-clicking the object and selecting Move or by dragging and dropping the object to its new location in the Navigation Pane.

Inserting external files to create report packages

Now, let's take a look at one of the interesting ways we can leverage Management Reporter to impress the executive team members in our organization! By using a combination of folder groupings and the ability to insert external files into the Report Viewer, accounting teams can create report packages to present a full package of financial statements and supporting documentation in one easy-to-access location. Our executive team members will love the ease with which they can locate, view, and browse the contents of this report package that has been prepared by the accounting team. Depending on how our reports are designed, they may even be able to use additional functionality, such as report drillthroughs, to answer their own questions about the source of a particular roll-up balance.

So, how do we accomplish this?

First, we need to set up a folder (or folders) that will contain the contents of our report package. There's no right or wrong way to do this. As we mentioned earlier, we can mix-and-match a combination of groupings including By Company, By Report Type, or By Report Time Frame. In this example, we've created a folder structure with a Company – Time Frame format with the time format broken down by the Quarter. The following image shows what this might look like in the Report Library:

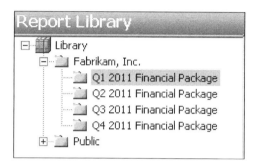

Next, we need to add our supporting documentation to the Report Viewer. Let's say we've created the following supporting documents to be included in our report package:

- A Table of Contents detailing the contents of the report package.

- A Summary of Performance for the quarter.

- An Excel spread sheet containing supporting information for our Income Statement.

- These supporting documents must be added to the Report Viewer with the **Insert External Files** command:

    1. In the navigation pane, select the folder to which these external files should be added.

    2. From the Report Viewer, click **File | Insert External Files**.

    3. In the **Insert External File** window, find the first internal file to be added to the Report Viewer.

    4. Select **OK** to add it to the selected folder in Report Viewer.

    5. Repeat this process for additional supporting documentation.

Once these files have been added to the Report Viewer, they can be treated in similar fashion to the reports that also exist in the Viewer. For example, if we need to move these files to another folder, we can drag and drop them in the Navigation Pane or we can right-click them and select **Move**. Additionally, we may wish to rename these files, and this can be done by right-clicking the file and selecting **Rename**.

When documentation is added to the Report Viewer, these documents are stored as a snapshot of the original document stored outside of the Viewer. In other words, if we make changes to the original document (outside of Report Viewer), then we need to reinsert the file again to ensure that we have the most up-to-date file in Report Viewer!

Now that we've added our supporting documentation, we need to add our reports to the same folder. If we've already generated the reports from the Report Designer with a Management Reporter output type, we simply need to find these reports in the Viewer and make sure they are added to the appropriate folder(s) containing our report package. Otherwise, we may need to generate up-to-date versions of these reports from the Report Designer. While in the Report Designer, don't forget that we can control the destination folder for our newly generated report by selecting the ellipses button next to the **Report Library Location** field in the **Output & Distribution** tab of our Report Definition, as can be seen in the following image:

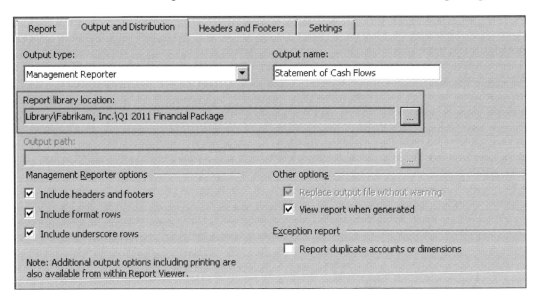

Now that we've added both our supporting documentation and the appropriate reports to our folder(s), we only need to complete a few more steps before we can turn our management team loose on this report package!

Since we've likely pulled our documentation from a number of different sources, and because the Library pane of the Report Viewer interface typically sorts documents in a given folder by name, it's likely we have a jumbled mess of documents in our folder. To fix this and present a more ordered appearance to our report package, we can add a numerical prefix to each report that corresponds to the order in which we want it to appear in our folder. For example, if we want our Table of Contents to appear first in the order, we can use the Rename functionality to insert the prefix **1** at the beginning of the object name.

If we have fewer than ten documents in our package, then it's ok if we use single digit prefixes to order our documents. If we plan to include ten or more documents within the same folder, then it's recommended to use a two digit prefix, even for the first nine documents. If we don't do this, then the tenth document will appear in the sort order between the first and second documents. By adding a zero to the beginning of the first nine documents, we ensure that they will remain sorted properly when the tenth and additional documents are added.

The following image shows our folder with all of our 2011 Q1 documents sorted in their appropriate order and ready for viewing by the management team:

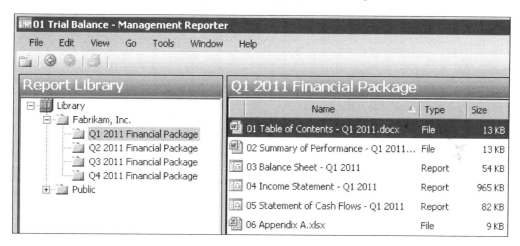

Our last step is to grant the appropriate permissions to this folder to our management team. At a minimum, we need to grant Viewer access to our management group for this folder.

Once these steps have been completed, we will have a fully functioning, professional-looking report package that our management team can access at their next executive team meeting. They can, at their leisure, browse through each of the reports and supporting documents to gain a clearer picture of the organization's financial health.

Understanding Version Control

One thing we should be aware of when using the Report Viewer is that we are viewing a specific version of a particular report. Anytime we select to Generate Report from the Report Designer, we are creating a new version of that report specific to the data in our company database at the point in time.

If we continue to generate a report to the same output location, then the existing report at that location will be updated to reflect the newer version. Management Reporter will, however, save the older version of the report as part of the version history of the new report. This continues to occur for successive regenerations of the report.

To see the version history for a particular report, we simply need to right-click the report in the Report Viewer Library and select **Show Versions**. We can then select and open previous versions to see what has changed since that version.

When we attempt to move a report that contains version history, we are prompted with the following image on whether or not we'd like to move just the most recent version of the report or if we'd like to move all versions of the report.

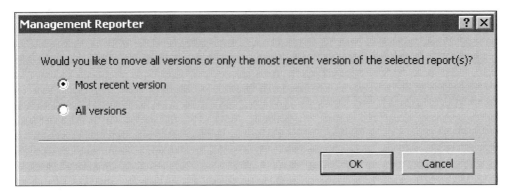

Moving the most recent version of the report creates an orphaned report at the new destination. Successive regenerations of the same report will no longer update the version history of the report we've just moved. Instead, it will create a new report at the designated location and successive regenerations there will create a new string of report versions.

Differences between Management Reporter and FRx

Though this section is trying to show some of the differences between Management Reporter and Microsoft FRx, it is important to note that Management Reporter uses the same approach to report design as Microsoft FRx. Management Reporter has made many improvements over its predecessor. Let's take a look at some of these enhancements.

64-bit compatibility

Management Reporter was built using 64-bit environments. In an ever expanding landscape of companies moving to 64-bit environments, this is a major advantage Management Reporter has over FRx, in that companies no longer need to maintain a 32-bit machine in order to house their financial reporting tool, as FRx was not supported on 64-bit environments.

Enhanced stability and performance

Management Reporter takes advantage of the Microsoft .NET platform and a new C# codebase that provides superior application stability over FRx. In addition to the codebase, all processing with Management Reporter takes place on the server utilizing IIS (Internet Information Services) instead of running locally on the client machine. This allows our users to continue working while their reports are generating.

SQL Server

With the move to SQL Server with Management Reporter, gone are the days of corrupted Microsoft Access databases that were used as the data storage medium for FRx. In addition to the increase in performance, we can expect more stability and a much improved multi-user experience.

User experience

In addition to the technical enhancements made with Management Reporter, there are quite a few other enhancements that were made more on enhancing the user experience. Some of these are as follows:

- **Report Library**: As we have discussed earlier in this chapter, the library allows us to organize our reports instead of just having a massive list of reports in our catalog like we used to have in FRx.

- **Undo**: All we can say is YAY to this one, been a long time coming!

- **Dimension Flexibility**: Gone are the days of the structured rules regarding segments in FRx. We can now use larger and variable-length account masks to better scale to larger customers.

- **Logo Support**: We can now add company logos to our reports with a few clicks of the mouse.

Summary

In this chapter, we expanded on the knowledge we learned in the previous chapter of designing our reports and explored generating our reports and storing them in a meaningful manner in the Report Library. We then moved on to navigating the Report Viewer for Management Reporter tool, describing how to use it to organize and store our reports as well as attach those many supporting documents we all have for our financial reports such as Microsoft Word tables of contents and Microsoft Excel spreadsheets detailing out certain allocation calculations. Finally, we wrapped up with some commentary on some of the major improvements that Management Reporter has over its predecessor Microsoft FRx.

In our final chapter, we will bring all of these tools in our reporting toolkit together and show how they can address the challenges and theoretical issues described in our first chapter, by linking them to the practical application of the tools that we have explored throughout this book.

In addition, the final chapter will strive to provide a side-by-side comparison of the pros and cons of each reporting tool in the context of the reporting challenge it may or may not fulfill, with an emphasis on when to use each tool under the correct circumstance.

10
Bringing it all Together

As more and more reporting tools are made available for Enterprise Resource Planning tools such as Dynamics GP, it becomes more of a challenge for us to select the right tool for a given circumstance. Every organization has a unique set of requirements when it comes to analyzing its data, and our goal should be to ensure that we select the right tool to meet those requirements. Additionally, each tool has its trade-offs, and we must always be aware of these trade-offs while we are selecting a reporting tool to meet our needs. In the end, we don't want to try and fit the proverbial square peg in a round hole as by forcing a reporting tool to meet challenges that simply don't align well with the strengths of that tool.

In this chapter, we'll answer some of these questions about selecting the right tool to meet our challenges by:

- Recapping what we've discussed in each of the last nine chapters
- Discussing each of the reporting challenges we covered in Chapter 1 in light of what we've learned about each reporting tool
- Taking a look at the future of reporting with Dynamics GP

By the end of this chapter, we should be well-versed in the art of selecting the right reporting tool(s) to meet the reporting needs of our organization!

Looking back at what we've covered

How often do we try to force a reporting tool to meet a challenge for which it is not well suited? For example, it's not uncommon to witness a user who exports a Sales Transaction SmartList containing thousands of rows into Excel, then uses Excel formulas to summarize the values from that record-set, plugs the end-result into a single cell into yet another spreadsheet, only to have to repeat this process for several other values. All of this for a single Summary Sales Report by Division that's out of date the minute the data is exported to Excel! Rather than continue to waste productive hours watching a SmartList export to Excel on a regular basis, it may be time to consider other reporting tools such as Excel Reports—which refresh SmartList data directly to Excel or Analysis Cubes, which provides support for Excel based dashboards—to meet the needs of our report user.

In the end, our goal with this book has been to reduce potential frustrations that are caused by using the wrong reporting tool for the reporting challenge at hand. We want our readers to be aware of each of the capabilities of each reporting tool. Then, with these capabilities in mind, we want to be able to apply the right reporting tool to the unique challenge (or challenges) faced by those in our organization who require some level of reporting.

Chapter 1: Reporting trends and challenges

Too often, an end user approaches us with a request for a report, and before he or she has even finished telling us about the requirements, we've selected the reporting tool that we're going to use. While most of us are experienced enough to make such a quick judgment, we should remain careful to jump to hasty conclusions. This can lead to us selecting a reporting tool that does a poor job of meeting the end user's requirements, and can lead to more difficult problems down the road when a report consumer finally gives in and says "Enough! This is not working for me!"

So what do we need to think about when a user approaches us about a new set of reporting requirements? The process of selecting, creating, and maintaining new reports and reporting tools has numerous challenges, and we designed Chapter 1 to present some of the more important challenges in this process. While some of the challenges may not be relevant to a particular scenario, chances are that atleast one or more challenges will manifest themselves. As successful report developers and consultants, we must be prepared to consider the myriad of challenges associated with report development so that we can design the most effective report possible.

Chapters 2-9: Reporting tools for Dynamics GP

Before we can cover any specific reporting tools, we needed to discuss some basic concepts for reporting in Dynamics GP. We covered these in Chapter 2 as we took a look at techniques that can be used on the database and SQL server level, as well as those that can be used from within the GP application.

With a basic understanding of these reporting concepts under our belt, we then moved on to covering the following reporting tools:

- SmartLists and SmartList Builder
- Excel Reports and Excel Reports Builder
- Report Writer
- Pre-defined SSRS reports
- Analysis Cubes for Excel
- Management Reporter

While a host of other reporting tools can be used with Dynamics GP, we selected these tools for our discussion because they are among the most well-known and widely-used reporting tools. For the most part, each tool is representative of several other third-party reporting tools in terms of capability and usefulness. As long as we focus on understanding how the pros and cons of each of the tools we've discussed in this book can be used to meet our reporting challenges, we can extend the same concepts to other, similar reporting tools.

Viewing our reporting tools in light of reporting challenges

Now that we have given a brief overview of what has been covered this far, we now turn our attention to reviewing our reporting tools in light of the challenges that we covered in the first chapter. Hopefully, you noticed in Chapter 1 that each challenge contains diametrically opposing conditions. For example, as we consider the intended audience of our report, we must decide if our report should meet the needs of day-to-day operations personnel, or if we are trying to satisfy external stakeholders. In comparing two reporting tools side-by-side, we may discover that one reporting tool perfectly meets the set of requirements imposed by our day-to-day operations personnel, whereas the other tool is more suited for external stakeholders. Other tools, we might find, fit somewhere more towards the middle of these two extreme conditions.

Our goal, then, is to select the reporting tool that has the best capability to meet our required condition. Of course, in the perfect world of this chapter, we will consider all of our reporting tools against each individual challenge. In reality, however, we will have to consider the varying conditions we need to meet with each challenge, and accept some trade-offs in our reporting tool's ability to meet all of our conditions.

Intended audience

A report almost always turns out useless when it hasn't been designed and created with the eventual end user in mind. Not only is it likely that the report will not provide the critical data our end user requires, but in many cases, the reporting tool we've selected to design the report may not even contain the functionality we require to meet the requirements of the end user. This can lead to ballooning investments in time and money and is often has the feel of trying to fit a square peg in a round hole!

For the most part, our reporting audiences can be classified as either external or internal consumers of our organization's data. External consumers include auditors who require insight into the financial health of our organization, potential investors, and current stakeholders. On the other hand, internal consumers can range from operations personnel such as a warehouse manager, members of the accounting team, as well as members of the executive team.

For external auditors who require insight into our organization's transaction journals, the default reports that come with tools such as Report Writer and SmartList Builder can easily be modified to provide auditors with the exact information they need. Although these reports are internal to GP, we can convert them to printouts or, in the case of SmartLists, export them to Excel and send the finished document over to the auditor. Other external consumers, such as potential investors and current stakeholders are primarily interested in seeing a summary of our organization's financial statement. This can be provided via numerous types of financial statements, and fortunately, Management Reporter can be used to create a wide variety of professional-looking financial statements that can then be distributed externally.

One thing to keep in mind about most of our internal users is that they are more likely to operate within GP on a daily basis. We can assume that most of these users already have a GP login and are familiar with navigating through the GP environment. By creating reports with a reporting tool that is built-in to GP, we can add a new dimension to the user's GP experience without having to introduce the user to another application and another environment. Tools such as SmartList Builder and Report Writer allow us to develop such reports, and users will more than likely appreciate the ease of access that comes with their new reports.

But, this is not to say that all internal users want to see their new reports in GP. It's entirely likely that members of our executive team will not have access to GP, much less the time or desire to navigate through the raw output that comes from SmartLists or posting journals designed in Report Writer. Instead, our executive team members want to see summarized information in a single, easy-to-reach location. Reporting tools such as the pre-defined SSRS Reports Library, Analysis Cubes for Excel, and Management Reporter are all alike in that they can provide these team members with a central repository of summary reports that do not require a GP user login to view.

For a better, more visual understanding of the relationship between internal and external report consumers and the tools that they would most likely benefit from, take a look at the following image:

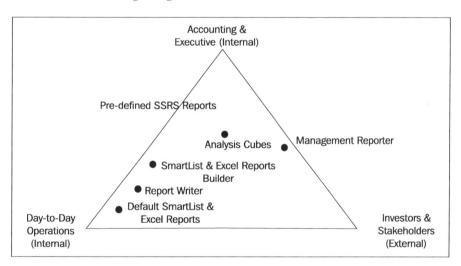

Data sources

Since the end result of the kind of reports we've discussed in this book is to present our end user with data from our ERP solution, we should be concerned with the source of that data. At first glance, the answer seems obvious: if we're trying to provide data from our ERP environment, shouldn't we pull it straight from the underlying company database itself? Unfortunately, the answer is not always that simple. We must be aware of potential performance impacts against our company databases that might result from our reporting processes. Additionally, even though our focus is primarily on GP 2010, we must keep in mind that data can reside in other, non-GP related data marts, as well. These separate data sources may exist due to other proprietary applications. If our end user wants to include information from separate data sources in his or her report, we need to be sure that we have a reporting tool that can access this data and use it in conjunction with what we are pulling from our GP database.

By their very nature, some of the reporting tools we've discussed in this book can easily be used to combine data from multiple data sources. One tool that lends itself to this kind of reporting is the Analysis Cubes for Excel product. Because this product is built on a data warehouse, we have a ready-made location in which data extracted from multiple data sources can be transformed for consistency purposes and then loaded into the data warehouse. The transformation piece of this is critical, as one of the biggest challenges of using disparate data sources is finding a way to join the data together through some common key value(s). For example, one data source may refer to customers via a unique eight digit numeric customer code, whereas the other data source may refer to the same customer with a ten digit alpha-numeric code. In order to combine these two sets of data, we need to find a way to relate the eight digit codes to their corresponding ten digit codes from the other data source!

Although Analysis Cubes for Excel offers a unique environment in which data from multiple data sources can be staged, other reporting tools we've discussed can also pull data from multiple data sources. This is largely due to the flexibility they offer in the form of using SQL queries to extract data for reports. For example, in SSRS, we can use SQL queries to create the data set from which our report is built. These SQL queries offer us flexibility to pull data from multiple tables, multiple databases, and even multiple servers. Unlike Analysis Cubes, however, the transformation required to create commonality between these different data sources must be done entirely within the SQL query. While this can be achieved, it is usually the domain of those with more advanced technical skills, and it can also cause an unnecessary drain on system resources each time the report is generated. SQL queries can also be used to generate data for SmartList Builder and Excel Report Builder reports, although this does create some limitations that may or may not be an issue for our end users.

The image below shows where each reporting tool falls in the spectrum of reporting against a single data source or multiple data sources:

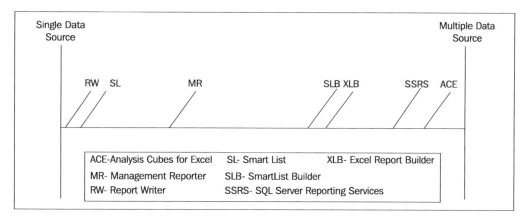

Latency

As we discussed back in Chapter 1, latency deals with the idea that, depending on the reporting tool we select, the data in our report may lag a bit behind the actual data that exists in our ERP environment. Although it is likely that our users will profess a need for real-time data in all of our reports, in reality, this is not always easy to achieve. While it may be relatively easy to display up-to-the minute transactional data with certain reporting tools, this is usually only half the battle in reporting. To provide reports capable of analyzing large data sets and offering insight into trends in our data, we cannot rely on simple reporting tools that spit nothing but raw transactional data back at us. Instead, we must use reporting tools that can analyse large amounts of data and return to us a summarized look at the trends and movements within our organization. To do this requires a blend of time, money, and resources.

So, while ERP applications like GP 2010 have long since been able to provide us with reporting tools that can spit raw data back at us, the effort to provide reporting tools that can truly help us aggregate and make sense of our large data sets are increasingly gaining in importance. For example, reporting tools like Management Reporter allow us to create a structure in which bits of data can be summarized into meaningful financial statements that provide both inside and outside stakeholders a look at the health of our organization. With such an analytical tool, we can see the big picture, or the trends, in our organization's data, even though this data originally came to us in the form of individual journal entries. As we saw in our discussions in Chapters 8 and 9, the process of creating a financial statement in Management Reporter is two-fold:

- Creating the structure, or the building blocks of our report
- Generating the content of our report

Although this is usually a fairly quick process, made even faster by the fact that we are using only standardized information from our general ledger, it still requires some time and resources to ensure that our reports are up to date. Here, then, we see an example of a great reporting tool that provides up-to-date data without too much of a drain on resources; however, we are limited to viewing this data in the rigid structure of a financial statement.

But what happens when our users tell us that they want the same analytical capabilities provided by Management Reporter, but for other modules in GP, and with the flexibility to quickly and easily modify their reports? This sounds like a job for Analysis Cubes for Excel! The trade-off, however, comes in the form of extraordinarily large time delay (or latency) between the data found in the cubes and what actually exists in our production databases. Because Analysis Cubes stages data in a data warehouse and then processes the data into cubes for faster querying by the end user. The end-result means users will spend less time sorting through copious amounts of transactional data and more time analysing organizational trends that can be used to provide organizational advantage. While this data may not be up-to-the minute (more than likely, it won't even be up-to-the-hour), this should not scare our report-users away from this tool. Instead, we need to remind them that trends found in our data are often the result of a length of time far greater than the latency of our data; in fact, the cost and impact of reacting to every minute shift in a trend analysis caused by the addition of last minute data to our data set can often have far-reaching and devastating consequences on our overall business plan!

And finally, let's not overstate the importance of tools such as SmartList and Excel Reports Builder in the face of far more sophisticated reporting tools like Management Reporter and Analysis Cubes. Tools such as SmartList and Excel Reports Builder do a great job of providing transactional data quickly and accurately. Because these tools don't offer much in the way of analysis, they do the best job of any reporting tool of providing up-to-the minute data without a major drain on costs or performance. These tools also provide search mechanisms that make it easier to navigate to a specific transaction among hundreds and thousands of others. Tools such as these, while probably not much use to an executive team member, can be incredibly valuable to day-to-day operations personnel such as the Customer Service representative who must quickly navigate to a customer's transactions within GP. Using SmartList, for example, our representative can quickly find the right transaction and use the drilldown functionality to actually open the transaction directly in GP. So, while presenting real-time data can be achieved, we must determine from our end user whether the goal is to see purely transactional data that can be retrieved quickly and easily, or if there is a larger goal of using a report for trend analysis or to provide a summary of a large set of data.

As we've seen, the opposing concepts of this reporting challenge consist of real time reporting versus potential data lag. While most of the tools we've discussed tend to lean towards real-time reporting, we can see from the following image that some tools do a better job of providing real-time data. Even though some tools do provide real-time data, some of these tools, like Management Reporter, require the user to go through a more defined report-generation process that can take some extra time to access the data.

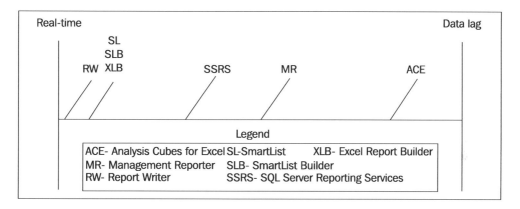

Formatting and presentation

Many times, we don't really put formatting and presentation very high on the priority list when first beginning to develop our reports. In fact, it is usually the last thing we need to consider. With this being said, it actually is a critical piece to consider when developing our reports.

In most cases, our formatting and presentation needs fit in with our intended audience. For example, if this is a financial statement being presented to auditors or our board of directors, it should be professional looking and easy to follow. Functionality such as company logos, graphs, proper page numbering, and reports laid out in sections can all add to the presentation of our reports. Reporting tools such as Management Reporter, Analysis Cubes for Excel, and SSRS are all very good tools to accomplish this type of formatting.

As we have seen in the previous chapters covering these tools, we can easily add logos and graphs, as well as add groupings so that the report has a logic flow and is easy for our audience to follow. For instance, we can use SSRS to send professional looking invoices to our customers with our company logo included. Management Reporter and Analysis Cubes for Excel allow us to lay out our data in a meaningful manner. We can use Management Reporter for creating properly formatted financial statements while in Analysis Cubes for Excel, we can create company dashboards for our executive team.

Tools such as Report Writer, SmartList Builder, and Excel Report Builder, while great at pulling raw data, have very limited formatting options available. These tools are best used when presentation is not necessary and the report will be primarily used by a user who needs to crunch through raw data and analyse things, such as an auditor needing a list of all journal entries posted in a given year.

The challenge of selecting a reporting tool that provides support for graphics, multiple fonts, and the ability to easily modify the appearance of the report can be broken down diametrically into rigid reporting tools versus flexible reporting tools. Flexible reporting tools provide us the ability to easily modify the appearance of a report and can support the inclusion of graphics and logos. On the other hand, rigid reports are difficult to change, and we should not expect them to provide us much in the way of formatting and clean presentation. As the following image shows, the reporting tools we've discussed cross the gamut of rigidity versus flexibility:

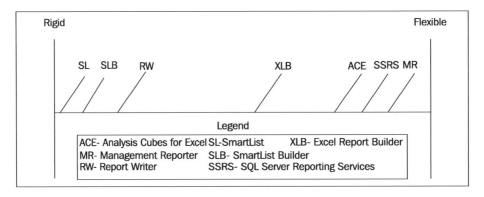

Ad hoc queries versus traditional reports

In report design, one of the major challenges is deciding on using an adhoc report or some type of Traditional report. As we mentioned in Chapter 1, this decision can be made more easily when we learn from our users what the output of the report needs to be and how often that report needs to be generated. We can use the example of an auditor requesting journal entries for the year as something we would consider ad hoc. We are not going to save that report and run it on an on-going basis. However, if our Sales Department needs a list of all open sales orders, that would lend itself more towards some type of Traditional report in that it could be run every day, every week, and so on and give our Sales Department a method of analysing what type of backlog they have or how they are doing with regards demand for certain products.

Most of the reporting tools we have discussed can be used for both of these types of reports and the challenge is figuring out when to use which tool in the right circumstance. While tools such as SmartList Builder and Excel Report Builder can be created and saved and used over and over again, they are typically best used for ad hoc reporting. The same thing can be said for SSRS and Analysis Cubes for Excel. Though they can be used to do some level of ad hoc reporting, typically, they are better fashioned for creating traditional reports that will be used over and over again on some interval.

In addition to this, another thing to consider is the output. Do we need to email our report? Does the reporting tool allow us to export to PDF? Is there an ability for us to subscribe to a report and have it delivered automatically? These are all questions we should answer before deciding on whether to use an ad hoc report or a traditional report.

As the following image shows, we see that some reporting tools such as SmartList and Excel Reports Builder are reporting tools through which temporary reports can quickly and easily be generated. If we want more traditional reports, such as financial statements or sales invoices, we can use tools such as Management Reporter or Report Writer to accomplish this objective.

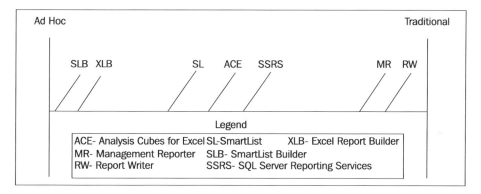

Security

Throughout this book, many of the reporting tools we have discussed have some type of security model. In deciding on the most effective tool to use for a particular report, we need to be aware and take care to thoroughly think through what type of security model we will need. As we mentioned in Chapter 1, depending on the end user of our report, certain security will need to be set.

Reporting tools such as Report Writer, SmartList Builder, and Excel Report Builder can easily be controlled from within the Dynamics GP application and can therefore be managed by a GP Administrator. SSRS, Analysis Cubes for Excel and Management Reporter have a different security model in that they use the user's network logins or SQL server accounts. This can lend itself to needing the support of an organization's IT department or some other Power user who has the appropriate permissions.

In addition to being able to have the proper user access for the eventual end users of our reports, we also need to think about what permissions are needed for us as report developers utilizing each of these reporting tools so that we can access the necessary data to develop the reports. All of these considerations must be made while keeping in mind the proprietary and sensitive nature of the data.

In general, we can break down security as that which is controlled through the Dynamics GP application and that which is maintained via some separate application. In the case of Report Writer and SmartLists, security is maintained entirely within the GP application. But, as we see in the following image, security for reporting tools such as Analysis Cubes and SSRS is maintained outside of the GP application, even though the data found within each tool is based on Dynamics GP data:

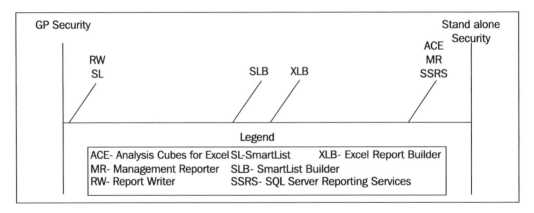

Network access and general IT infrastructure

As we have covered each of these reporting tools throughout this book, we have only briefly discussed the IT infrastructure necessary for each tool's installation and use. While determining which tool is best to use, we must ensure that the IT infrastructure can support it. The last thing we want to do as a report developer is design reports that bring an organization's infrastructure to a crawl or even worse bring down a server completely.

Some tools such as SSRS and Analysis Cubes for Excel, although they can work on the same server as the Dynamics GP application or SQL server, usually work much more efficiently when they are on a dedicated reporting server.

Because of the nature of the SmartList Builder and Excel Report Builder, in that they are used from within the Dynamics GP application, if we design reports using these tools that are again mainly used to extract large amounts of raw data, we may find the need to increase resources such as RAM, Disk Space, and/or processors to our servers.

Although the general IT infrastructure may vary from company to company, we can generally break this challenge down between reporting tools that can fit within the existing infrastructure required for Dynamics GP and reporting tools that, by their very nature, may lend themselves to additional resources such as new servers or additional SQL Server components. For example, while the traditional GP environment utilizing only the Financial modules may not have SSAS and SSRS installed, larger organizations that want to take advantage of SSRS and SSAS can expect to need more in terms of additional infrastructure and resources. As the following image shows, some reporting tools fit well within the general GP infrastructure while others will require a greater investment in resources:

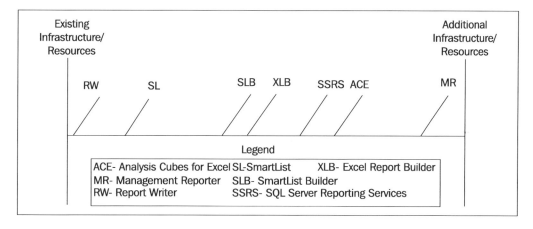

Developer resources

The final important challenge we must consider in the selection of a reporting tool to use is what sort of drain it will provide on developers. More than likely, as report developers and consultants, we can consider ourselves under the umbrella of "developer resources." Ideally, we should select a fool-proof tool that anyone can use, thus freeing us up from having to do any work! Actually, this may be a bit unrealistic, but we still do need to consider whether or not our end users will have the technical know-how to work with reports. Additionally, if our IT department is small or underfunded (we bet if you ask everyone in your IT department will probably already agree with you on both of these points!), we don't want to select a reporting tool that adds even more in the way of developer interaction for creating and managing reports. While some developer interaction is still recommended to ensure corporate control over sensitive data and to ensure that new silos of data are being created, we do want to free our developers from devoting extra time to troubleshoot minor problems each time an end user encounters something he or she doesn't understand.

One of the ways that we can minimize the drain on our development staff is to find and train a power user on the use of our selected reporting tool. A power user is someone who possesses a bit of technical knowledge (our tip for finding this person—look for the person in your company who is an Excel guru) and can be a champion for our reporting tool. This power user is someone who has a better grasp of our organization's business processes and, thus, can relate more easily to the end users who will be utilizing our reporting tool. This power user can stand as the gateway to the development team and ensure that only the most pressing questions and concerns are brought to the staff.

As we look back over our reporting toolbox, we see a few tools that require minimum interaction from our development team. For example, with a little training up-front, the basic SmartLists, pre-deployed Excel Reports, and pre-deployed SSRS reports can be used by just about anyone who has been trained on GP. Depending on the strength of our GP power user, our development resource(s) may even be comfortable ceding control of report development via SmartList Builder and Report Writer to the power user. Because these tools are contained within GP, our development staff can be rest assured that new silos of data are not being created and maintained elsewhere.

Finally, we have some tools that will require extra attention from the development resources. Some, like creating custom SSRS reports and Analysis Cubes for Excel require developers who are experienced with all aspects of SQL including T-SQL, relational databases, SSAS, SSIS, and SSRS. Without some kind of experience in some of these areas, it will be very hard to deploy, much less maintain, the environments required to support custom SSRS reports and the cubes. While it may be possible to deploy the pre-defined SSRS reports and Analysis Cubes with a modicum of SQL Server knowledge, extending the usefulness of the product will require the kind of knowledge we've just discussed. These two tools, in particular, can also lead us down the slippery slope of creating new silos of information outside of GP. Without attention, our organization may become a bit more lax in ensuring that this external data is safeguarded properly and that it does not give rise to a new silo of information.

Some reporting tools do not require users to possess a great degree of technical skills, while others may require knowledge of technical concepts such as query-writing against relational databases and effective table joining. As the following image shows, some tools are well-suited to the average GP users, while others require the support of a more technical resource such as a developer.

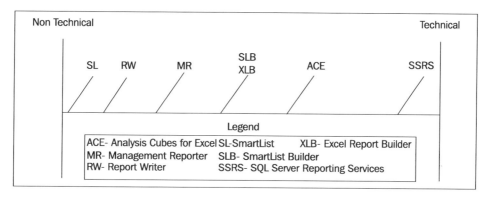

The future of reporting for Dynamics GP

Before we bring this book to a close, let's pause and consider the future of reporting for Dynamics GP. In our very first chapter, we covered three major trends in reporting:

- Increased Flexibility
- Reporting Through All Levels of an Organization
- Increased Access to the Report Generation Process

We expect (and hope) that future reporting in Dynamics GP will be geared towards these trends. GP continues to enable users to work smarter, and in a more productive fashion. New releases of GP bring with them enhancements to reporting, and GP users from top-to-bottom continue to expect increasing flexibility and availability of reports that they can generate themselves. Users must also find ways to cope with increasing amounts of data in their ERP systems, and we expect reporting tools that can easily handle large and varied data sets (like SQL Server Reporting Services and Analysis Cubes for Excel) will continue to grow in relevance and importance in the Dynamics GP space.

As we move forward in this ultra-competitive environment, we look to Microsoft Dynamics GP to continue to provide cutting edge reporting that empower users with the necessary information to stay ahead of the curve and find a true competitive advantage for their organization. Although it is not expected until shortly after this book goes to press, Microsoft has just announced a new release called Dynamics GP 2010 R2. Not surprisingly, this release is full of enhancements and additions to reporting tools already present in GP 2010! Although we have yet to interact with these new tools ourselves, we can identify some of them here:

- Additional SQL Reporting Services reports (including charts, maps, and Tablix reports) that offer improved user interaction and additional drilldown functionality from the Dynamics GP Home Page, among other places.

- Enhancements to the Word template functionality introduced with GP 2010, including a Partners-only Word Template Generator tool that enables users to create their own Word templates.

- Improved report export capabilities from within the Dynamics GP client.

- Introduction of Business Analyzer, a contextual BI application that will offer users an improved look at their data from within Dynamics GP.

- Improved features with each successive release of GP, along with updates to stand-alone reporting tools (such as Management Reporter and additional cubes for Analysis Cubes for Excel), continue to indicate that Microsoft is aware how critical the reporting space is for continued success in the ERP market. As users, we are happy to reap the benefits!

Summary

In the end, we can consider ourselves fortunate that we can choose from such a wide variety of reporting tools for Microsoft Dynamics GP. Each reporting tool meets a unique set of needs, and, if we are willing to be open and honest about the challenges we face with our organization's reporting requirements, we can select the most appropriate tool for the challenge at hand. While some tools may appear to work in the short term, we must consider the long term during this process, as well. As users begin to develop reports and grow more comfortable with using a particular reporting tool, it becomes more and more difficult to instigate a change in tools. If we do opt for the quick-fix, the quick-term solution, we may find ourselves devoting even more time and energy in the near future implementing a new set of reporting tools that are more appropriate than our first choice.

Additionally, as we have seen in this chapter, the challenges we face with report development are interrelated. We cannot expect to consider each reporting challenge on its own, as the answer to one challenge may dictate the answer to another challenge. For example, as we consider our intended audience, we may realize that we are developing a report for an executive team or external stakeholders. More than likely, these report consumers will not have access to GP, so we know we do not have to concern ourselves with a reporting tool for which security can be controlled via the GP application. Additionally, these report consumers are likely to have strict requirements to how a report is formatted, and we find ourselves needing a reporting tool that offers excellent graphics and formatting tools, as well as a more traditional reporting structure that can provide consistent financial statements.

We hope that this book served as an invaluable tool that serves as a part-reference manual and part-user guide. Rather than hope to learn everything about the reporting tools we've covered, we hope we've increased your desire to learn more about the reporting tools we've covered. As we've said quite a few times already, each reporting tool has its place, and we hope this book helps our readers understand what each tool is capable of achieving for our organization. By using this book as a starting point, our readers should be capable of understanding where to begin, and be able to draw upon the resources found in this book as well as the other countless Dynamics GP resources found throughout the Dynamics community to provide reporters with every bit of information required to build accurate and useful reports for our organization.

As the mountain of data in our organization continues to grow, we can be well assured that we have the tools at our disposal to help our organization make sense of that data. We now have the means at our disposal to help everyone from the Accounts Payable Coordinator to the Chief Financial Officer access the data they need to make effective and practical decisions that will help our organization gain a competitive advantage.

Happy reporting!

Comparing the Dynamics GP Reporting Tools Against Different Reporting Challenges

As we've seen, one of the most critical aspects of report design and development is selecting the appropriate reporting tool for a given set of challenges. But, with so many reporting tools available to us, and with so many challenges that we are likely to face, it can be difficult to know which reporting tool is the best one for the job. The following table summarizes this information in a helpful, quick-reference format that can help us answer the question: Which reporting tool is best for the current situation?

Comparing SmartList Builder, Excel Report Builder, and Report Writer

	SmartList Builder (SLB)	Excel Report Builder (ERB)	Report Writer (RW)
Intended Audience	Day-to-day operations personnel; GP Power Users	Day-to-day operations personnel; GP Power Users	Day-to-day operations personnel; GP Power Users
Data Sources	Production Database; Add'l customizations may include add'l databases	Production Database; Add'l customizations may include add'l databases	Production Database
Latency	Real-Time; Report must be regenerated to include up-to-date data	Real-Time; Report must be regenerated to include up-to-date data	Real-Time; Report must be regenerated to include up-to-date data
Formatting/ Presentation	Very few formatting options; Record-by-record view; Best used for internal reporting	Slightly improved formatting options (over SLB) with Excel; Record-by-record view; Best used for internal reporting	Limited graphics options; Reports can be developed for internal use (Trial Balance) or external use (Sales Invoice)
Ad-Hoc/ Traditional	Ad-hoc; Internal to GP; Larger datasets may be slow in regenerating (when compared to Excel Reports)	Ad-hoc; Reporting in Excel workbook; Instantly refreshable (when compared to SmartList)	Traditional; GP reporting engine (internal); Used for many reports; Reports are not easily modified "on-the-fly"
Security	Integrated with standard GP security	Not integrated with standard GP security; Folder level and data source considerations required	Integrated with standard GP security
Network Access/ IT Infrastructure	Fits within existing GP application	Requires Microsoft Excel & access to production server/databases	Fits within existing GP application
Developer Resources	New SL can be created by GP Power Users; Advanced SmartLists can use SQL or Extender, which may require more technical skills	Excel Reports are based on SQL views; Modifications to existing Excel Reports require technical knowledge	RW can be challenging to learn, but is possible for GP Power Users; Otherwise, add'l developers may be required

Comparing SSRS Reports Library, Analysis Cubes, and Management Reporter

	SSRS Reports Library (SSRS)	Analysis Cubes (AC)	Management Reporter (MR)
Intended Audience	Day-to-day operations personnel; GP Power Users; External users with no GP access	Day-to-day operations personnel; GP Power Users; External users with no GP access	Accounting team; GP Power Users; Executive team members (Report Viewer only)
Data Sources	Production Database; Add'l customizations may include add'l databases	Refreshable Data Warehouse	Production Database
Latency	Real-Time; Report must be regenerated to include up-to-date data	Dependent on no. of times cube load & refresh job is run; Typically run once a day	Real-Time; Report must be regenerated to include up-to-date data
Formatting/ Presentation	Capable of producing colorful & professional-looking reports; Multiple font options; External & internal reports	Excel PivotTables provide numerous formatting opportunities; PivotTables structure can limit how data appears in spreadsheet	Capable of producing financial reports worthy of a board-room presentation; Supports logos, multiple fonts and other formatting options
Ad-Hoc/ Traditional	Traditional; Reports viewed via web browser; Rigid report structure (requires Visual Studio to modify)	Ad-hoc; Easy to create new reports "on-the-fly"; Existing reports can be refreshed & manipulated quickly	Traditional; Reports viewed in MR Report Viewer; Board-room style reports; Often saved and re-used at the end of each financial period
Security	Folder-level security within SSRS; Data source security controls access to database(s)	Managed through SSAS; Access can be restricted by cube, dimension or cell	Security is controlled by role for each MR user in the application; Different levels of security such as Content Manager or Viewer
Network Access/ IT Infrastructure	SSRS requires add'l memory; May require a separate reporting server	Data warehouse requires add'l space; SSAS requires add'l memory; May require a separate reporting server	Requires Internet Information Services (IIS) and a domain; Add'l database requires some extra space
Developer Resources	Accessing pre-deployed reports requires little technical experience; Modifying or adding custom reports requires knowledge of SSRS	Use of "out-of-the-box" cubes requires minimal developer resources; Customizing cubes requires knowledge of SQL (DB Engine, SSAS, SSIS)	Based on chart of accounts; Easy to use, even for non-technical users; Knowledge of SQL not required

Index

temp 32
transaction 31
groups, Management Reporter 254

H

headers and footers tab, Management Reporter 272
help menu, Management Reporter 263

I

IIS configuration, SSRS
  for Windows Server 2003 142, 143
  for Windows Server 2008 143
individual load packages 189
Insert External Files command 295
installation overview, Management Reporter 248
installation prerequisites, SSRS 142
installing
  SSRS 144, 145
installation, Analysis Cubes
  about 192
  cubes, processing 200, 201
  data warehouse, populating 200, 201
  pre-installation checklist 193
  security access, granting 201, 202
  server configuration wizard, installing 194, 195
  server configuration wizard, using to deploy cubes 196-200
Inventory Cube 243

M

Management Reporter
  64-bit Compatibility 299
  about 245
  Ad-Hoc/ Traditional 321
  architecture 246
  building block sprawl, reducing 274
  building blocks, working with 264
  comparing 321
  data provider, configuring 249-252
  Data Sources 321
  Developer Resources 321
  features 245

Formatting/ Presentation 321
installation options 247
installation overview 248
installing 247
Intended Audience 321
latency 321
Microsoft FRx, differentiating 299, 300
Network Access/IT Infrastructure 321
registering 248
Report Designer interface, navigating 256
Report Viewer 284
security 252
Security 321
server components 248
SQL Server 299
user experience 299
Management Reporter Feature Pack 1
  about 281
  features 281
Master Date dimension
  nodes 222
master tables 187
measure groups 205
menu bar, Management Reporter
  about 258
  company 259
  edit 258
  file 258
  format 259
  go 260
  help 263
  tools 261
  view 259
  window 262
  XBRL 260
menu bar, Report Viewer interface
  commands 290
  Edit 292
  File 291, 292
  Go 292
  Help 293
  Tools 292
  View 292
  Window 293
Microsoft Dynamics GP
  company database 27
  DYNAMICS database 26

R

W

Window Descriptions
  accessing 38-40
window menu, Management Reporter 262
Windows Explorer
  Excel reports, accessing 67, 69
Word template modification process 125
Word templates
  enabling 122, 123
  fields, adding 131

  fields, adding to Check Remittance template 132-137
  formating changes, applying 126-129
  modifying 126
  setting, for company database 129, 130

X

XBRL menu, Management Reporter 260
XBRL Taxonomies window 260

Thank you for buying
Microsoft Dynamics GP 2010 Reporting

About Packt Publishing

Packt, pronounced 'packed', published its first book "Mastering phpMyAdmin for Effective MySQL Management" in April 2004 and subsequently continued to specialize in publishing highly focused books on specific technologies and solutions.

Our books and publications share the experiences of your fellow IT professionals in adapting and customizing today's systems, applications, and frameworks. Our solution based books give you the knowledge and power to customize the software and technologies you're using to get the job done. Packt books are more specific and less general than the IT books you have seen in the past. Our unique business model allows us to bring you more focused information, giving you more of what you need to know, and less of what you don't.

Packt is a modern, yet unique publishing company, which focuses on producing quality, cutting-edge books for communities of developers, administrators, and newbies alike. For more information, please visit our website: www.packtpub.com.

About Packt Enterprise

In 2010, Packt launched two new brands, Packt Enterprise and Packt Open Source, in order to continue its focus on specialization. This book is part of the Packt Enterprise brand, home to books published on enterprise software – software created by major vendors, including (but not limited to) IBM, Microsoft and Oracle, often for use in other corporations. Its titles will offer information relevant to a range of users of this software, including administrators, developers, architects, and end users.

Writing for Packt

We welcome all inquiries from people who are interested in authoring. Book proposals should be sent to author@packtpub.com. If your book idea is still at an early stage and you would like to discuss it first before writing a formal book proposal, contact us; one of our commissioning editors will get in touch with you.

We're not just looking for published authors; if you have strong technical skills but no writing experience, our experienced editors can help you develop a writing career, or simply get some additional reward for your expertise.

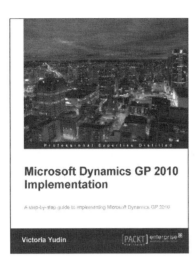

Microsoft Dynamics GP 2010 Implementation

ISBN: 978-1-849680-32-5   Paperback: 376 pages

A step-by-step guide to implementing Microsoft Dynamics GP 2010

1. Master how to implement Microsoft Dynamics GP 2010 with real world examples and guidance from a Microsoft Dynamics GP MVP

2. Understand how to install Microsoft Dynamics GP 2010 and related applications, following detailed, step-by-step instructions

3. Learn how to set-up the core Microsoft Dynamics GP modules effectively

Microsoft Dynamics GP 2010 Cookbook

ISBN: 978-1-849680-42-4   Paperback: 324 pages

Solve real-world Dynamics GP problems with over 100 immediately usable and incredibly effective recipes

1. Discover how to solve real-world Dynamics GP problems with immediately useable recipes

2. Follow carefully organized sequences of instructions along with screenshots

3. Understand the various tips and tricks to master Dynamics GP, improve your system's stability, and enable you to get work done faster

Please check **www.PacktPub.com** for information on our titles

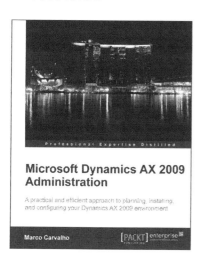

Microsoft Dynamics AX 2009 Administration

ISBN: 978-1-847197-84-9   Paperback: 396 pages

A practical and efficient approach to planning, installing and configuring your Dynamics AX 2009 environment

1. Effectively consolidate and standardize processes across your organization with a centralized source for a variety of business needs

2. Discover how to effectively plan and implement Dynamics AX 2009 in your business and fully grasp the necessary hardware, network, and software requirements to do so

Implementing Microsoft Dynamics NAV 2009

ISBN: 978-1-847195-82-1   Paperback: 552 pages

Explore the new features of Microsoft Dynamics NAV 2009, and implement the solution your business needs

1. First book to show you how to implement Microsoft Dynamics NAV 2009 in your business

2. Meet the new features in Dynamics NAV 2009 that give your business the flexibility to adapt to new opportunities and growth

3. Easy-to-read style, packed with hard-won practical advice

Please check **www.PacktPub.com** for information on our titles

17482563R00192

Made in the USA
Lexington, KY
13 September 2012